MICHAEL PACHER

Nicolò Rasmo

Michael Pacher

Phaidon

Translated by Philip Waley

Phaidon Press Limited, 5 Cromwell Place, London SW7

Published in the United States of America by Phaidon Publishers, Inc.
and distributed by Praeger Publishers, Inc.
111 Fourth Avenue, New York, N.Y. 10003

First published 1971
Originally published as *Michele Pacher*
© 1969 by Electa Editrice® - Industrie Grafiche Editoriali S.p.A., Venice
Translation © 1971 by Phaidon Press Limited

ISBN 0 7148 1417 2
Library of Congress Catalog Card Number: 70–111063
All rights reserved

Printed in Italy

CONTENTS

PREFACE

In 1750 a Tyrolean scholar, Anton Roschmann, visited the treasury of the convent of Novacella (Neustift); he paid particular attention to the altar of the Fathers of the Church, one of Michael Pacher's masterpieces, which in the course of alterations to the church made in the Baroque period had been removed from the place where it had originally stood. He noted the incomparable skill shown by the artist in the foreshortening of the Infant in his cradle at the feet of St. Ambrose, and of St. Jerome's lion. His inquiries as to the identity of the artist, however, met with such vague replies, there being evidently some confusion as to whether the work should be attributed to Pacher or to Perger, that he came to the conclusion that it was by the well-known German painter Christoph Amberger. All record of the great artist who had left the imprint of his personality on a whole period of history had by this time been lost.

This episode is significant and also serves to explain why, in the course of the eighteenth century, Pacher's works were removed from their altars, dismantled and for the most part destroyed, without a word of protest. The Gries altar was removed in 1738, and it was only by good fortune that the shrine remained intact and it was subsequently possible to recover it and to replace it in the church on a side altar. Much worse was the fate of the imposing altar at Salzburg, which was taken to pieces in about 1710 and burnt so that the precious metal from the gilding could be extracted. The altar in the church of S. Lorenzo di Sebato was also dismantled and almost entirely destroyed, probably, as was common practice, in order to recover the gold. There can be no doubt that other works by the artist disappeared in the same way, leaving no trace or record.

Even in 1830 Pacher's name was practically unknown; it does not appear in the Dictionary of Tyrolese Art published in that year by Lemmen, although by 1822 Primisser had discovered and called attention to the inscription with Pacher's name on the St. Wolfang altar. Only in 1844 did Staffler acquire this information and make it generally known, thus marking the beginning of the revival of interest in Pacher which coincided with the Romantic enthusiasm for all things medieval.

Then followed, over a period of more than half a century, the discovery and publication of documents from archives and of actual works: in 1846 the contracts for the Gries altar and the altar of St. Michael at Bolzano (Koch); in 1853 the documents concerning the artist at Brunico (Förster); in 1869 the documents on the Salzburg altar (Spatzenegger); in 1886 the collection and publication of all the known documents relating to Pacher (Vischer); in 1907 the documents concerning the lost Aschhof altar (Fischer); and finally in 1912 the contract for the St. Wolfgang altar. Additions were soon made to the catalogue of Pacher's works. The St. Wolfgang altar was followed in 1846 by the Gries altar (Koch); in 1853 by the Monguelfo Tabernacle (Förster); in 1862 came the Castel Novale altar, which subsequently disappeared (Atz); in 1869 the Salzburg altar (Spatzenegger); in 1885 the St. Candidus fresco (Dahlke); in 1887 the altar of the Fathers of the Church in Munich (Semper); in 1892 the Virgin of S. Lorenzo di Sebato (Atz); in 1894 the fresco in the Welsberg Chapel at Tesido (Semper); in 1895 the Graz panels and the statue of St. Michael in Matzen Castle, now in Munich (Stiassny); in 1912 the panels of the S. Lorenzo altar, attributed by some to Pacher's workshop (Hammer). Thus in little more than half a century, the fundamental data for a biography of Michael Pacher and a preliminary catalogue of his works were assembled.

It was only natural that such enthusiastic research should have resulted initially in the appearance of some monographs. In 1910 Mannowsky attempted a reconstruction of Pacher's artistic personality. This sensitive and valuable study was followed in 1913 by Doering's incoherent and on the whole negative work. Finally in 1919 Stiassny set out to examine the validity of some attributions. His conclusions led him to adhere to Mannowsky's thesis, assigning both the painting and the carvings to the same artist.

In the meantime, acceptable conclusions had been reached as to the formative influences on Pacher. Already in 1853 Förster had recognized Flemish and Paduan influences, and the latter were specified in detail by Schnaase (1862) and later by Mannowsky, who distinguished and defined the part played by Mantegna as compared with Flemish painters (Dirk Bouts and Rogier van der Weyden), and finally suggested links with Konrad Witz and Lucas Moser, wich I find untenable. After Stiassny's work came a period of reassessment and of minor contributions. In 1931 two monographs appeared, one by Von Allesch and the other the monumental work by Hempel. Hempel was later entrusted with the task of writing the biography of Pacher for Thieme and Becker's Dictionary, and since this Dictionary was very widely used, he won further acceptance for his account of the artist's character and stature. In the twenty years which followed, at least five abridged editions of his book appeared.

Hempel's work was for a long time regarded as definitive, and as such it was made known in Italy by Salvini (1937), who adopted as his own the conclusions reached by the earlier scholar. But this served neither to make Pacher's art understood in Italy nor to place it in the context of Italian art, even as a marginal factor. Longhi's unfortunate attempt in 1945 to discuss this artist is typical of the kind of treatment Pacher received.

The Exhibition of Medieval Art of the Upper Adige at Bolzano in 1948–9 and that of the Gothic Art of the Tyrol at Innsbruck in 1950 offered opportunities for a full examination of the Pacher problem from a new angle. Further information came to light as the result of a more precise and detailed knowledge of conditions at Padua during the Renaissance, due principally to the studies by Fiocco and Salmi, in addition to Rigoni's discovery of new documents. The revised chronology of Pacher's work (proposed by Rasmo) was adopted by Hempel in the sixth edition of his monograph (1952). Subsequently, doubts were expressed about the relationship between the Master of Uttenheim and Pacher. Some scholars, taking up an old theory (Pächt, 1929) already dismissed by Hempel, inclined towards regarding

Pacher as the pupil and imitator rather than the teacher of the Master of Uttenheim—a misleading view of Pacher's position which implicitly showed a failure to recognize his importance (D. Frey, 1957; Stange, 1960).

The time therefore seems opportune for a full review of all that has so far been written about Pacher, and for a careful examination of the various theories concerning the chronology of his work; and also for a new assessment of his stature as an artist based on a strict discrimination between works by his own hand and those of this workshop.

No less pressing is the need for a fresh presentation of illustrative material, brought up to date by means of modern techniques and providing the reader with the basis for an unbiased examination and an independent evaluation of each theory. Finally, there is one other reason which induced the present author to turn his attention to this artist: Pacher was born in the Upper Adige region—which now seems to divide rather than unite Germans and Italians—and few, if any, in the history of the representational arts have been capable, to the extent that Pacher was, of blending and harmonizing the German capacity for detailed analysis and inward dramatization with the calm and balanced vision of the Italians. In his work Pacher has demonstrated that genius can overcome conflicts and translate them into concord and harmony, and also, perhaps, that Europe was at its greatest when the races which constitute its mainspring could give their best in collaboration.

INTRODUCTION

The name of Michael Pacher is as yet practically unknown in Italy, as the few and inadequate lines devoted to him by Roberto Longhi prove. In Germany, on the other hand, Pacher is known to all students of medieval art and he cannot be said to be underrated. Pinder, to whom we owe perhaps the most perceptive description of the St. Wolfgang altar, said that if we possessed only this single work it would be enough to ensure the immortality of the artist responsible for it. But apart from these admiring comments and observations, which are frequently both penetrating and pertinent, concerning the artist's masterpieces, it is noticeable that German scholars are subject to a significant confusion when confronted with his artistic personality. This confusion (Hempel's fundamental study being an exception) is particularly evident in their interpretation of those works, whether earlier or later than the imposing altar of St. Wolfgang, which are most relevant to an understanding of the origins, development and maturity of Pacher's thought. For some time the interpretation of Hempel, who hadcarri ed out a great deal of research in the area, prevailed to silence the differences of opinion. At the present time, however, misunderstandings such as the tendency to place Pacher later than the Master of Uttenheim, making the latter the mentor of Pacher and crediting him with having brought about the renaissance of art in Padua, are continually gaining ground. They result in inconclusive or contradictory theories, all of them untenable. An understanding of Pacher demands something more than a knowledge of German art, to which he does not really belong, but rather constitutes a chapter apart. Pinder, the greatest expert on German art, realized this and pinpointed the problem in an illuminating observation. Discussing the connection between Mantegna and Pacher, he notes "a profound inner affinity, which provides the true explanation of the effect which the older man had upon the younger"; and he concludes: "It is the Alpine spirit of the two men which, looking beyond the different languages of visible and sensible form which make one an Italian and the other a German, unites them in the expression of a lapidary style."

Although the conclusions drawn by Pinder from this perceptive comment are closely bound up with the climate of thought of his time and limited by his insufficient knowledge of North Italian art and the art of a German border region such as the Upper Adige, the point he made proves that had it been possible for him to examine this particular problem deeply he would certainly have found the correct solution in that direction. For between Mantegna and Pacher there is a close similarity, just as between Pacher and the Kefermarkt Master or

Rueland Frueauf the Elder, who are often compared with him, there is a sharp and profound difference. It is now a question of seeking the causes of these similarities and differences, which arise, as Pinder rightly says, not from the external considerations of language and culture, but from an inner world. I believe therefore that it will be useful to describe and define the geographical and personal background from which Pacher's art emerged. This approach may at first be confusing because many of the ideas are unfamiliar and will conflict with current theories, although they support Pinder's observation. The environment which must be discussed in order to understand the phenomenon of Pacher is a specific geographical and ethnic zone within the region of the Alto Adige. Only if we bear this in mind can we hope to arrive at original conclusions and also, perhaps, at a better appreciation not only of Pacher's art but also of other artistic styles which are closely related or parallel to it.

In the first place, it must be emphasized that the part of the southern Alps through which the Adige and its tributaries flow, even if it constitutes a single geographical entity and may also at some periods of its history, perhaps under the Romans, have been united culturally and linguistically, has never been an ethnical entity. The primitive peoples who climbed up the valleys from the Po basin, or from the Veneto spread over the Alpine zone, met on either side of the well-defined cleavage formed by the valley of the Adige and, to the north of Bolzano, the valley of the Isarco. The two valleys were not fully populated as they were marshy and frequently blocked by the torrential waters of the river, so that crossing and communication between the opposite sides was possible only at a few points, notably in the depressions around Trent and Bolzano. So it was that the peoples known by the Romans as the Ligurii gathered to the west of the Adige. Their presence is attested by the series of menhirs ranging along the top of the valley, from Termeno to Lagundo, S. Verena and Villandro. To the east the land was occupied by the Venetii and their kinsmen the Illyrii. The Ligurii were belligerent by nature, but their expansion was restricted by their restlessness and by internal strife; the Venetii were peaceful, although well able to defend themselves, and had a strong communal organization. Romanization gave to both a common language and culture very different from their primitive ones, without, however, disturbing their fundamental ethnic characteristics. This was particularly true in the Alpine valleys, which only interested the Romans as transit routes and were sparsely populated and of little strategic importance. The advent of Germanic peoples who penetrated into the Adige Valley via the Brenner Pass, and the Latin or ancient Italian peoples who made their way up into the same valley, renewed the division of the two areas, which had temporarily been united under the influence of Roman culture. The Romanized inhabitants to the west, the Romanci, and to the east, the Ladini, were parallel but not interdependent groups, and the fact that they retained a neo-Latin language differentiated them only superficially from the peoples who were dominated by the German cultural world to the north, the Italian to the south, and the Slav to the east. The argument that the Romanci and the Ladini share common ethnic origins seems to me without foundation, and the various attempts which have been made to attribute common characteristics to a supposed "art of the Ladini" are rightly unsuccessful. In fact, the ethnical background of this population can only be studied by examining the individual areas, consisting of Lombardy together with all its mountainous hinterland to the west of the Adige, and of the Veneto and the valleys of its tributaries to the east. This distinction is not of course absolute, but it is a guide which helps to explain some basic tendencies which recur in the individual areas and differentiate one from another. In the Lombard region the belligerent character of its early inhabitants was replaced by an activism inclining towards practical and useful achievement, which in the sphere of art has given us perhaps some of the greatest European architects, certainly the most able and skilful in adapting architectural forms to the most varied environmental and cultural requirements. In the Veneto region emerged a tendency towards lyrical speculation, towards a refinement of visual sensitivity and the expression of feelings through the exaltation of form in colour and tone. On the right bank of the Adige and the Isarco we meet only isolated artistic outcrops, which in both the Italian (Anaunia) and the German (Venosta) linguistic groups lack unity and cohesion. Artists, and particularly painters, often came to this area from the other side of the Alps, from German territory, or the region to the east where a fundamental and important feature was the setting up of artistic communities both in the Italian-speaking part (the Fiemme valley) and in the German (Pusteria) and Ladin parts (Gardena and Badia); these artistic communities were the expression in the cultural field of the old communal spirit.

Let us now view Pacher against the background of Pusteria and, by extension, the ancient community of the Veneto which, through the ages, has preserved a basic ethnic unity, and whose art of the "situlae" has been documented from Magdalenska Gora to Matrei and from Bolzano to Este. Only if we keep this setting in mind can we make a distinction between what is the fruit of Pacher's cultural heritage, which is German, and what is the fruit of his ethnical background, which is the region of the ancient Veneto. Titian emerged from this area, and Mantegna, Ricci, Piazzetta, Giorgione, the Bellini and Tiepolo are all products of the same cultural environment. Their work in the representational arts differs only in loftiness of tone from the art of Morlaiter, Troger, Unterperger or Lampi, who all belong to the school of Pusteria although similar observations could be made about the artists of Styria and Carinthia.

If we set Pacher in the vast Illyrio–Veneto area—today divided among Austria, Italy and Yugoslavia—and consider this as an ethnical rather than as a geographical zone, we shall be better able to understand the artist and in time perhaps to determine the basic characteristics of the figurative arts of the region. It will then be possible to differentiate these characteristics—which are not formal but personal and result from individual choice rather than cultural forces—from those of the ethnical sphere of the Slavs, Bavarians and Germans.

CHAPTER ONE

Art in Pusteria in the first half of the Fifteenth Century

We do not know either the date or the place of Pacher's birth. He is first heard of in 1467 as the master of a workshop and a citizen of Brunico (Bruneck), so that if he was not born there he must at least have been living and settled there for some years. This is implicitly confirmed by a later document which shows that around 1462 he was working on the main altar for the parish church of S. Lorenzo in Pusteria (St. Lorenzen im Pustertal), near Brunico, a work of considerable importance which would only have been entrusted to an artist well established in the area whose work was already appreciated. Further confirmation is provided by the fact that his son Hans is first heard of in 1484–5 as a master, and therefore already an adult; Hans must have been born before 1463 and probably not later than 1460.

If we compare the remnants of the St. Thomas altar with the St. Lawrence panels we may deduce that Pacher executed the former before the erection of Hans Multscher's altar at Vipiteno (Sterzing) had overturned the theories the young artist had learned in Padua—in other words, before 1458. It follows that Pacher must have started working in his native country in about 1455 at the latest, that he was therefore in Padua probably between 1450 and 1455, and that he received his early training, which lasted four to five years, in his own country between 1445 and 1450. Since the choice of profession was generally made at about the age of 12, it seems likely that Michael Pacher was born between 1430 and 1435, and that the artistic manifestations on which he first formed his taste belong to the period between 1430 and, at the very latest, 1450.

As far as the problem of his birthplace is concerned, it seems certain that Pacher's family was not from Brunico, for the name is not found there before him. It is probable that he came to the town from one of the neighbouring valleys, such as the German valley of Vila (Wielenbach), from where a Pacher family of jewellers came in the seventeenth century to settle at Brunico; or else from a Ladin valley such as Badia, the home of a family of sculptors named de Rio, called Pacher in German documents. There is also a third theory, which was favoured for a long time and which some still regard as the most attractive: namely that Pacher originally came from Novacella and was related to the painter Friedrich Pacher, a pupil of his and, it has been ascertained, from Novacella. The vast archives of the convent of Novacella gave room to hope that this was a possible hypothesis, but the very lack of confirming documents in such a well-stocked archive, which provides detailed information on Friedrich and his family but nothing at all that indubitably refers to Michael, shows most clearly that Pacher had nothing to do with his namesake Friedrich or with the artistic life of Novacella. To the latter he contributed only later in his career and with only one work known certainly to be his, the altar of the Fathers of the Church. Friedrich Pacher, Marx Reichlich and the Uttenheim Master all played a much more important part in the artistic production in the monastery at this time. Pacher's failure to establish himself at Bressanone (Brixen), where Leonhard, a far less gifted painter, dominated the scene introduces another element of uncertainty; if Pacher, as it is suggested, had been born in the immediate vicinity he would certainly have become a citizen of this town. Finally, there remains an argument on artistic grounds: Pacher's art is a product of Pusteria as exemplified by the Master of the Ursulines at Brunico, and of the continuous contact of that region with the school of Padua. It has no antecedents in the Bressanone region, and was in no way influenced by the work of Leonhard and the Master of the third arcade of the cloister there, whom I would identify as Jacob of Seckau. The theory that Pacher originated from Pusteria, which all the known facts support, should not in my opinion be abandoned in favour of the hypothesis that he came from the Bressanone district.

But the question of Pacher's birthplace is of secondary importance. Factors which seem to be crucial are the environment from which the artist emerged, that is, the Veneto region, and the cultural and artistic background in which he was first nurtured, which was certainly that of Pusteria. Around the year 1400 conditions in Pusteria were particularly favourable for the flowering of its natural tendencies in the figurative arts, thanks to the prosperity created by the flourishing transit trade which brought closer contacts with the Styrian Alpine region and indirectly with Vienna and Bohemia, as well as with the Veneto.

In the course of the fourteenth century Paduan artists had developed a style along Giottesque lines which found ready acceptance in the hinterland and was soon emulated on the other side of the Alps; the pleasing and elegant versions of Altichiero which heralded the founding of an International Gothic style further spread the influence of this school. From Bohemia the echoes of the Soft Style in an Austrian modification more suited to the environment but still fundamentally linked with the Bohemian culture of the Luxembourg court of Prague and ultimately connected, despite some changes, with the French Rhineland, penetrated through the centres of Styria. This style with its exquisite figures in delicate draperies, emanations of a fabulous world long dreamed of and desired, a world in which even the most tragic sentiments are transformed into fables or elegies, was not out of harmony with the plasticity suffused with luminosity and blended with a serene and balanced narrative, which was favoured in the Veneto. Pusteria was thus the meeting-point of two stylistic tendencies which were opposed in their origins but which combined to arouse in the people of Pusteria a desire to develop their own artistic style, and brought about the first flourishing of artists in the area. Although little documentary information has been found in archives, those works of the time that have come down to us provide ample evidence.

John of Brunico may be considered the founder of the Pusteria school and his surviving works show him to have been a noteworthy painter. The basic features of his style are already discernible in a fresco depicting St. Mark painted in 1399 in the church dedicated to the saint at S. Lorenzo di Sebato, but reach their full expression in a series of works of remarkably high quality. Particularly fine are the frescoes in S. Nicolò di Stegona, near Brunico, in the church of the Saviour at Halle (*c.* 1406) and in the fourth arcade of the cloister at Bressanone (1417), those in the cloister at Novacella (1418) and the decoration of the church of the Hospital at Vipiteno. John of Brunico was still alive, although undoubtedly very old, in 1441, when Master Ambrose boasted, as a special claim to merit, of being his pupil; this we learn from an inscription which he added to the frescoes in S. Giacomo near Termeno (Tramin), which re-echo faithfully, although at a considerable distance of time, the pictorial decoration by his master in the cloister at Bressanone. Superimposed upon and harmoniously combined with John of Brunico's basic training in Pusteria is the Paduan style of Altichiero. This influence only seems possible if we assume John actually resided in Padua for a time. Certain episodes which are included in the religious paintings as independent motifs—such as the delightful incident of the oxen slipping under the weight of the cart in the Stegona fresco, reminiscent of the oxen in the Martyrdom of St. Lucy in Padua—give this painter a position of considerable significance; he played a prominent role in the painting of the Upper Adige, and by no means a negligible one outside that region.

Master Erasmus of Brunico, for whom we have documentary evidence covering the years 1398–1422, worked in Pusteria, first of all in collaboration with his brother Christopher and later with another pupil, Ludovic. He was active in the second decade of the fifteenth century and was probably one of the group of painters who worked on arcades IX–XIV of the cloister at Bressanone, where the unevenness of quality and draughtsmanship suggests the collaboration of various artists. However, the style which predominates in the tenth, twelfth and thirteenth arcades is recognizably that of the Master himself. His form derived from the Paduan school, probably through Master John, while his draughtsmanship is characterized by a northern delicacy. Here, then, we have an interesting artist but one who is a product of his locality and undoubtedly inferior to Master John. The Epiphany in the third arcade, which has a fairy-tale quality about it, is the work of another artist, on the whole less talented but belonging to the same school. This group of artists, who in all probability were working in Pusteria throughout the first half of the fifteenth century, must have been influenced during the 1430s by the presence of Hans von Judenburg. With the main altar in the parish church at Bolzano (Fig. 131)—which combines wood-carving and panel painting—and probably the frescoes there also, as well as other works in the Bolzano area, Von Judenburg brought about a profound stylistic revolution and, with the prestige of his name and his work, paved the way for his successors to spread the new style in art. The remains of the carving from the Bolzano altar permit us to judge his skill; he is the first clearly identifiable figure from the Austrian region and it is not surprising that he came from the town of Judenburg in Styria, the meeting-point of the principal routes across the Alps.

Hans von Judenburg and the Grosslobming Master, who takes his name from a place near the Styrian town, are so close to one another in style and accomplishment that it may be justifiably conjectured that their sculptured work represents two separate periods in the life of a single artist. Their carving is a triumph for the principles of the Soft Style of Bohemia, modified in a manner rather reminiscent of the Venetian style of the time and combined with a certain basic plastic solidity derived from the woodcarvers of Tuscany. The delightful carved figures of the choir stalls in St. Mark's in Venice are attributed to the Grosslobming Master, the great crucifix in S. Giorgio Maggiore to Hans von Judenburg. But Hans was also a painter. Although only pieces of carving have survived from his recorded work at Bolzano, the Cosmatesque motifs in the paintings on them show ample evidence of Italian influence, while the magnificent sinopes in the choir of the parish church, with scroll friezes reminiscent of Altichiero, are probably also his work and provide an example of his ability as a fresco painter. Moreover, from a comparison of styles it seems possible that he may also be identified with the Master of the St. Lambrecht Panel, a Styrian named Hans, who was working at the same time and in the same area, and who is as important in the field of painting as Hans von Judenburg is in that of carving. A strong plasticity characterizes the panel and is achieved by an accentuated chiaroscuro obtained through subtle transition rather than through violent contrasts of light. It shows an attempt to give the composition a solid construction, a problem which the artist tackled in a similar way in his carving, and it fits well into the contemporary European phenomenon of the exchange or rather "osmosis" of experience between Bohemia and Italy from which Giambono profited, perhaps also the Veronese school, and which influenced Donatello himself during his last period in the Veneto. Hans von Judenburg, who may be regarded as the leader of this new movement in which the traditions of Bohemia and the Veneto blend to form the basis of a new "Austrian" style, did not himself work either in Pusteria or at Bressanone, as far as can be judged from works of his which have survived. A close follower, the Master of the Altar of the Ursulines at Brunico, however, was clearly trained in Styria and worked in Pusteria during the third and fourth decades of the fifteenth century, his influence on his successors being noticeable up until the middle of the century. The reliefs in the Ursuline church, unfortunately spoilt some decades ago by being totally repainted and inserted into neo-Gothic constructions—which has discourgaed scholars from studying them—are among the most charming works in this style and period (Figs. 128, 129). They were probably executed for the main altar of the new church and consecrated with the altars in 1472, and therefore can be dated round about that year. The formal models adopted, albeit used in a mannered style, are the same as those for Grosslobming's carved figures and the altar at Bolzano, and their similarities to the fine St. Peter at Aflenz are so close that the possibility cannot be ruled out that the carver of the Ursulines was also responsible for the latter work.

Certainly attributable to the Master of the Ursulines is the sculptured group of Christ carrying the Cross with Simon of Cyrene, preserved in the parish church at Brunico. Prolonged exposure to the elements and clumsy repainting have considerably damaged it; none the less its craftsmanship is of a very high quality and its size is impressive (Fig. 130), providing us with a good example of the style.

The similarity between these works and the statue of St. Valentine at Falzes (Pfalzen), a village not far from Brunico, is so great that it is possible they are by the same artist, but separated by about a decade. The church at Falzes was consecrated in 1434 and the statue of the patron saint evidently adorned the main altar. This statue constitutes the most extreme expression of the Soft Style and heralds a reaction in favour of realism. There is still a delicacy in the features and form of the figure which places it in the unreal world of the Soft Style, but the drapery is organized with a severity and simplicity that reveal a desire to render plasticity and volume in a manner surpassing anything previously attempted by the artist or envisaged by the school in which he was trained. Roberto Salvini's tentative attribution of this work to the young Michael Pacher is significant, although unconvincing: the figure marks the final achievement of an artist of the old generation who anticipated and paved a way for the new perspectives, rather that the point of departure of a young man who would subsequently have had difficulty in freeing himself from the fetters of tradition which impeded the other artist (Fig. 132).

We have no definite examples of paintings by the Master of the Ursulines but a stylistic comparison enables us to attribute to him a devotional panel of the Madonna at prayer in the parish church at Casteldarne (Ehrenburg); the panel shows the same facial construction and the same draughtsmanship in the drapery that we find in the reliefs in the Ursuline church. Attributable to the same school, if not to the same artist, is a large votive fresco, painted probably in the fourth decade of the fifteenth century, which adorns the exterior of the church of St. Valentine at Falzes. These vigorous figures with their powerful chins and draperies spreading elegantly to give them a solid footing on the ground, are typical features which, as we have seen, had been passed on to the Master of the Ursulines from the Grosslobming Master and Hans von Judenburg.

Western Germany was also experiencing a violent reaction away from the Soft Style towards an emphasis on the massiveness of the body—this being forcefully achieved by breaking up the lines of draperies—and a realistic, even an expressionistic, ruggedness in depicting movement and faces. The most typical example of this trend in painting as well as in carving is perhaps the Wurzach altar (1437), together with the work of Konrad Witz, although the latter was also influenced by neighbouring France. In Bavaria the movement is represented by the Master of the Polling panels (1444), perhaps Gabriel Angler, and by the Tegernsee Master. The current of realism was introduced into Austria by Konrad Laib, a Swabian, who became a citizen of Salzburg in 1448 and whose influence soon spread to Styria as well as Pusteria. In Laib's dramatic scenes, fabrics, arms and individual objects are depicted with punctilious realism and accuracy; physical features are emphasized, and we find fierce and sinister faces even in figures where they are irrelevant, together with a delight in detailed descriptions of physical suffering that borders on sadism. Earlier, Hans von Tübingen had probably brought the new style to Vienna; he moved to Wiener Neustadt in about 1433 and worked there until 1462, frequently for the court of Vienna. The movement rapidly spread to Styria and thence, by the usual commercial route, to Bressanone. Some time before 1446 the painter Jacob of Seckau must have settled at Bressanone, for in that year he was already a citizen and master of a workshop; he was court painter to Bishop Hans Rottel of Hallein (1444–50), who may have invited him to come to the town, and then to his successor, Cardinal Nicolò Cusano. Jacob worked at Bressanone until the departure of Cusano, exercising a dominant influence in the revolution of taste which took place during those years. We can attribute to him the frescoes in the third arcade of the cloister, depicting the Ecce Homo and the Crucifixion, the latter probably commissioned by Canon Brandel (d. 1448). The frescoes are an abrupt departure from the earlier works in the cloister. They show a remarkably high quality, and a startling originality is revealed in the strong, continuous movement of the outlines of the figures—of fundamental importance to the dynamics of the scene, the picture being more drawn than painted—and in the heightening to an unrealistic degree of the dramatic poses, from the corpses of the two robbers contorted on the crosses to the expression of the faces, bordering on the grotesque in their violence. Such features are all in contrast with the paintings which had previously been produced here.

Before long this artist vanished from the scene—we do not know what became of him—and his place was taken by Master Leonhard, whom we find working from 1441 onwards. Leonhard may be regarded as a follower of the realist movement, but he compromised with the local artistic tradition, which evidently did not favour such harshness of style, and his version of the movement is moderate in every sense, although not of a very high quality. He worked in Bressanone until 1475 and his influence there was enormous and was rapidly spread by members of his school and workshop. His numerous works have yet to be clearly distinguished from those of his collaborators and imitators, and for the present he must be considered in terms of the overall production of his school.

The first and rather unimpressive product of the realist school in Pusteria, the panel of St. Ursula, stands midway beetween the styles of Jacob and Leonhard, and was produced in 1448 for the convent at Sonnenburg. It was commissioned by Verena, Abbess of Stuben, an implacable adversary of Cardinal Cusano, and it is unlikely therefore that she employed the court painters of Bressanone. It seems more probable, and stylistic factors support this, that the panel is the work of Leonhard at the beginning of his career, or of some other follower of Jacob. Jacob himself was certainly responsible for the fresco of the Crucifixion in the tabernacle erected behind the church at Millan, near Bressanone, now unfortunately in very bad condition.

It was the work of the followers of the Soft Style, together with the first products of the reaction in favour of realism, that Michael Pacher had before his eyes when he decided to choose the career of an artist.

The St. Thomas Altar and Michael Pacher's training in Padua.

Only vague conjecture is possible about the early training Michael Pacher received in his native town, probably between 1445 and 1450. From the direction he took later on it seems likely that he studied the finest examples of the Soft Style available to him in Pusteria, whereas the new tendency towards realism does not appear to have made much impression on him. Some of his carvings display links with the Bohemian tradition and especially with the school of Hans von Judenburg which cannot be accidental. One need only examine the models of ideal beauty realized in some of his carvings to find at once those connections with past tradition which in his major works are submerged in new stylistic features. What Pacher learnt about painting in Pusteria cannot have been impressive and in any case was completely overturned by his experiences in Padua.

Custom decreed that the young artist on completing his years of apprenticeship in a local workshop should leave his native locality and enlarge his experience and perfect his technique in one of the important cultural centres. Michael Pacher headed southwards. There were certainly reasons for his choice. At this time, about 1450, Bressanone was in a state of crisis, and the situation at Bolzano was little better. In Carinthia, Styria and Vienna the adherents

I Bull of St. Luke, from the inner side of a wing of the St. Thomas Becket Altar. Graz, Joanneum Museum

of the Soft Style had been displaced by the realist reaction, which at best could only offer the young artist the generally rather modest consolation of the paintings of Duke Albrecht's Master or the carvings of Kaschauer; nor was the prospect at Salzburg with Konrad Laib any better. It is not surprising, therefore, that Pacher chose to go south and stop at Padua, a city that had traditionally provided sound teaching since the days of Giotto and Altichiero, and whose art had been made familiar by echoes in the work of local artists such as John of Brunico, whom Pacher may have had the fortune to know.

Padua was the liveliest cultural centre in Northern Italy at this time because of the part it played, for the second time since Giotto's day, in spreading the innovations of Tuscan art. Filippo Lippi had left the city a short while before, leaving behind some of his best known works, such as the frescoes in the chapel of the Podestà and a Coronation of the Virgin in the Santo, which reflected the innovations of Masaccio. These paintings served as models for a whole generation of artists including Giovanni Storlato, Ansuino, Nicolò Pizzolo and Andrea Mantegna. Nor must Paolo Uccello's fresco of the Giants (c. 1445) in the Casa Vitaliani be forgotten, nor the works of Andrea Castagno, who was in Venice until 1445, and Pollaiuolo, whose drawings circulated among the artists in Padua. Of the sculptors, Pietro Lamberti had worked in Padua in 1430, works by Giuliano Fiorentino may also have become known there, and from 1443 Donatello was engaged on the Gattamelata monument and the altar for the Santo. Drawings and other works by these artists were passed around Padua and certainly seen by others than Squarcione. The younger generation turned their backs on the Gothic tradition represented by Antonio Vivarini and Giovanni d'Alemagna and welcomed with enthusiasm every reflection of the new movement in Tuscany. An intelligent young man like Pacher who entered this environment in about 1450 could no longer join the outdated exponents of a past, if not discredited, tradition, although there was no lack of German craftsmen and artists capable of giving him guidance and assistance. Meanwhile Francesco Squarcione was enjoying, with little credit to himself, the final fruits of his astute and unscrupulous policy of profiteering in talent at the expense of a new and by now emancipated generation.

Pacher took as his models the works of the great Tuscan painters, which were studied and imitated by all the young artists working in Padua. Jacopo Bellini had reduced Uccello's laws of perspective to elementary principles and explained them so that all could understand, though Squarcione boasted that he alone had inherited Uccello's geometric precision. Furthermore, Lippi's technique of using light as a concrete element which could support spatial recession, enriched by the superb experiments of the painters of the Veneto in the use of colour, endowed their paintings with that special atmosphere which filled the space provided by perspective and rendered it lifelike by implying the presence of air, and so subordinating colour to tone.

The Ovetari Chapel which, since the older artists had died or retired, had become the centre of the rivalries of the new generation, all followers of the Tuscans, must have aroused Pacher's admiration, particularly the work of Nicolò Pizzolo, who when still a young man was killed in a fight in 1453 while painting there. Pizzolo, a painter and sculptor, had also worked in collaboration with Donatello in the Santo, and it was through him that Pacher discovered Donatello and a new sculptural style unfamiliar to the north. To judge from the

II Burial of St. Thomas Becket (detail of Plate 4)

extent of their influence on his work it would seem that Pacher remained in Padua until 1453 and witnessed the production of Pizzolo's most mature work and the completion of Donatello's altar for the Santo. In that year Donatello left for Florence, leaving behind him one last but astonishing work of genius, the statue of St. John the Baptist in the Frari church in Venice. In this work Donatello adopted, in a totally unprecedented fashion, the style in which the German sculptors had traditionally excelled, producing a work which surpasses them all; one might say it is written in their own language, and that it is perhaps destined to remain incomprehensible to Italians.

The death of Pizzolo and the departure of Donatello seem to have indicated to Pacher that it was time to return to his homeland. He certainly saw the altar erected in the Santo and the *tondi* depicting the Fathers of the Church on the vaulting of the Ovetari Chapel, but it is unlikely that he witnessed the completion of the decoration, with the magnificent narrative scenes by Mantegna, now working on his own. It is inconceivable that Pacher's work, which displays so great a regard for artistic developments in Padua, could have remained uninfluenced by these paintings had he seen them.

On returning to his own region Michael Pacher had first of all to obtain a residence permit and the citizenship of Brunico, as well as authorization to practise the profession of mastercraftsman. Above all, he would have looked for a wife, without whom he could achieve little in a closed society with its rigid moral principles sanctioned by long tradition. His first work, the altar of St. Thomas Becket (Plates I, II, 1–5), was of modest dimensions and more suitable for private devotion than for use in formal worship in a church. It was probably executed for a regular canon of the Augustinian house at Novacella; Pacher may have hoped by demonstrating his talent to obtain the canon's assistance in finding more important commissions. In any case, it was there that the remnants of the altar came to light at the time of the Bavarian suppressions and despoliation. The middle section, which has disappeared, may perhaps have depicted, like the famous relief by Donatello in Padua, Christ in mourning supported by angels. The paintings of the symbols of the Evangelists (Plates I, 1) on the inside of the wings may allude to the same subject: they would have been seen at the same time as the centre painting, with the wings opened out. When closed, they displayed four episodes from the life of St. Thomas Becket, a regular canon and a venerated figure in Augustinian convents.

By 1808 the altar had long been demolished. All that survived were two panels representing the martyrdom and the funeral of the saint (Plates I, 2–5) on the outside, and two of the symbols of the Evangelists, the bull and the lion, on the inside. These may have been preserved in the treasury of the monastery, for here were kept the most precious remains of altars dismantled when Baroque alterations to the church were made.

The two panels had been selected and put in cases for dispatch to Munich Museum when they were mysteriously removed at the last moment; they only reappeared half a century later, in a private collection in Graz, from there they were subsequently taken to the museum of that city.

The symbols, as Winkler observed, were derived from the bronze reliefs on the altar of the Santo in Padua. Pacher's version, however, is a free interpretation strongly influenced by his recent experiences in Padua, and by the work of Lippi and Pizzolo, particularly the latter. These influences are of fundamental importance, but the work already reveals the dynamic vision peculiar to the artist. The bull (Plate I) is foreshortened and placed diagonally in space, an arrangement underlined and accentuated by the book lying open on the ground. This strengthens and clarifies the intention of the artist by giving the figure the dignity that Donatello had conveyed in his relief. Pacher fills the area of the picture, but at the same time seeks to convey the massiveness of the figure by creating a spatial recession which he accentuates by the precise and consistent side lighting. Another feature of this painting is the careful study of the bull, such as one might well expect from the youthful artist, who was undoubtedly of rural origin and must have had a familiarity with animals and nature in general, born of a deep and discerning knowledge far more direct and vivid than Donatello's. This is even more noticeable in his rendering of the lion (Plate 1), an animal rarely seen at that time and which the artist imagines as being closely related to the domestic animals with which he was familiar. The result is surprisingly realistic save for the heraldic stiffness of the muzzle, which is shown frontally. In the composition of the lion Pacher gives proof of the skill which which he is able to deal with similar problems by varying his methods: the lion is not foreshortened but on a plane parallel to the viewer and set back so that the book can be placed between the lion and the frame of the picture. The paws ingeniously connect the two planes, thus perfecting the careful spatial disposition of volume. The background of damascened gold and the grassy ground, flecked with gold highlights, create a vibrant atmosphere and an indeterminate depth of space in which the two animals seem to come life; it is as though one were looking at them through the frame of a window.

These two panels on their own would entitle the artist to renown, for with coherence and dexterity they formulate and solve pictorial problems of extreme difficulty, besides presenting to the observer two figures of animals which by virtue of their extraordinary vividness possess a majesty and a dignity which raise them to the level of emblematic and unearthly apparitions.

The paintings on the outside of the wing-panels present more complex problems, which the young artist was unable to solve with complete consistency: the problem of inserting into space several figures in unified dynamic action, and that of rendering space clearly in order to create a logical and convincing scene. Pacher was certainly helped by Lippi's frescoes (since lost) which are reflected, though not very impressively, in the frescoes painted in 1437 by Giovanni Storlato now adorning the walls of the chapel of S. Lucia in S. Giustina. Pacher had also carefully studied Pizzolo's forceful arrangement of perspective, emphasized by the sharp and well-defined lighting. He omits Renaissance features of costume and architecture, which would not have been known in Pusteria, adopting in their place ones which were more familiar in that region. Following the laws of perspective, which he has grasped but not fully mastered, he creates an architectural setting by carefully aligning the back wall along the axis of the painting and piercing it with a succession of openings of decreasing size, like a telescope, which are arranged in such a way as to give an impression of indefinite spatial depth. One of the side walls is foreshortened and set into the depth of the composition to join the back wall, a perspective which gives an illusion of receding space, further emphasized by openings through which there are glimpses of other rooms adjoining. The floor of marble squares reinforces the composition with its lines of perspective leading to a single point. This point is relatively high up, additional evidence that Pacher had not had time to learn Mantegna's technique but follows the way opened by the achievements of Lippi. Consequently, the ceilings and vaulting can only be imagined from the linear structure of the painting. The light, as usual, comes from the right, and separates each of the groups of figures, which diminish conspicuously in size as they recede. In the Martyrdom of St. Thomas (Plate 2), on the other hand, Pacher is unable to avoid an obvious weakness in the placing of the altar, which needs to be foreshortened in the foreground in order to give more prominence to the figure of the archbishop. This error is not repeated in the Funeral scene (Plate 4); here every detail is subordinated to the bier, which is handled with bold foreshortening and is evidently based on the carpentry in Pizzolo's Fathers of the Church. It acquires a material solidity in the structural and functional rendering of its individual parts, lacking in the altar, but which must have been naturally felt by a woodcarver. In the treatment of the drapery there is more sharpness and neatness than in Lippi's paintings which seem to imply a familiarity with some of Mantegna's works. Furthermore, the vanishing point is not in the upper half of the picture, as we find in Lippi, but in the lower half, and here we come to one of the achievements of the new generation of artists.

On the altar in the Martyrdom of the Saint (Plate 2) there is a wooden Gothic predella on which stand three carved figures (Christ on the cross between Mary and St. John). This motif, of startling iconographic originality, can only be explained as an individual interpretation, reduced to essentials, of the idea put forward by Donatello in the Santo altar. The group of priests who witness the tragic scene in stupefied grief, and yet also with a respectful curiosity, is easier to explain remembering the Trivulzio altarpiece, a youthful work by Lippi probably painted while he was in Padua. The priests are arranged in two rows, and those who stand behind are craning their necks to see over the shoulders of the others; similarly in the Trivulzio altar the angels behind the Virgin crane their necks to stare with an unrestrained and almost unseemly curiosity, expressed by the tension in their faces and half-open mouths, at the painter priest while he paints the Virgin, or at the worshipper praying before the picture (Fig. 138). The grimace on the half-open mouth of the assassin is a recurrent feature in Lippi's work, from the Trivulzio altarpiece to the last works such as the panel of the Death of St. Jerome in the Duomo at Prato (Fig. 137) and the sketch of a head, preserved on the back of the panel of the Virgin, in the Medici Palace in Florence. Another feature which can be traced to Lippi is the complex pattern of the marble floor in the Funeral scene. Lippi uses this type of paving in the *tondo* in the Palazzo Pitti, and had certainly provided other examples in Padua; it has precedents in Tuscan art but appears to be totally new to the northern tradition. The youth who looks out with a particularly intense expression from behind the shoulders of the assassin in the martyrdom scene could be a self-portrait of Pacher himself; after the portrait of the man who commissioned the painting, who kneels beside the bier, it is without doubt the most expressive head in the two Graz panels.

These paintings are rich in fine details, although not without certain touches of naiveté typical of a youthful work. Their originality is quite revolutionary in the context of the art of Pusteria. Instead of indulging in the dramatic style then in fashion thanks to Master Leonhard, Pacher tends rather towards the calm and balanced expression of dramatic feeling which is nearer to the ideals of the superseded Soft Style than to contemporary style, and suggests a return to traditional lines together with an additional emphasis on plasticity, colour and atmosphere which is completely new. His interpretation contained no unfamiliar elements from outside such as might have been found disturbing and, because of the conviction which resulted from the internal coherence of expression, was bound to please the instinctive taste of the people of Pusteria. Before long they recognized in their fellow-citizen the person best qualified to provide them with pictures which would cause them to reflect but which would not shock. Indeed they were not slow to focus their attention on him and choose him to execute the main altar for the parish church of S. Lorenzo, the old centre of Pusteria which had been built on the ruins of a Roman settlement at the mouth of the Badia valley, a few miles from Brunico, the episcopal seat.

The St. Thomas altar, as already noted, seems to have been intended for private devotional purposes rather than for formal worship, and was probably executed for a canon of Novacella—perhaps resident in Pusteria to administer the extensive properties the convent owned there—with the object of soliciting his patronage and support.

Hitherto, the theory that the panels constitute the remains of an altar erected in the tower chapel at Novacella in the course of repairs completed in 1465, when the church was reconsecrated, has prejudiced consideration of other possible datings. A closer examination of the tower chapel, however, leads to the surprising conclusion that the Romanesque niche above the altar, decorated with frescoes datable to the beginning of the thirteenth century, was renovated by the superimposition of a new fresco, the work of Master Leonhard, which can be dated to about 1465. It is most unlikely that the niche would have been redecorated with new paintings and then half-hidden by a wooden altar with wings. We can therefore discard the theory that the St. Thomas altar was originally in the tower and dates from about 1465. From the paintings themselves, we can deduce that they belong to the period before the St. Lawrence altar, which was probably begun in about 1460, and also before the installation of Hans Multscher's altar at Vipiteno in 1458, for the latter work had a strong influence on Pacher which is not yet in evidence in this altar. It appears therefore that the altar dates from about 1455, not long after Pacher's return from Padua but some time before the altar at S. Lorenzo.

The St. Lawrence Altar

In 1507 the administrator of the parish church of S. Lorenzo di Sebato (St. Lorenzen) presented himself before the judicial authority in a final attempt to recover a bequest made 44 or 45 years earlier on his deathbed by a certain Maurice, court tailor to the influential knight Balthazar of Welsberg; the latter, despite all the solicitations that had been made, had steadfastly refused to pay the sum involved and by this time had himself died. The legacy had been intended by the devout tailor as a contribution to the cost of the main altar of the church, on which Michael Pacher was at work. We do not know the outcome of this episode, but it is doubtful whether the church received the amount to which it was entitled. The document concerned is of vital importance because it gives the identity of the artist and the date of the old altar of St. Lawrence; the altar was dismantled and largely destroyed during the Baroque period, but some parts of the carving and painting have survived (Plates III, IV, 6, 7, 10-20).

The problem of the date of the altar merits some attention, for the text of the document, as well as the qualities of the remaining parts of the work, show indisputably that it is by Pacher. The documents states that the bequest was made in 1462 or 1463, the commission for the altar already having been given to Pacher. We can therefore assume that the altar was begun in about 1460 and completed not later than 1465. The first of these dates receives some confirmation from the fact that the episodes from the life of Mary show the direct influence of the paintings on Multscher's altar at Vipiteno, which was erected in 1458. In the years between the St. Thomas and the St. Lawrence altars, Pacher must have undertaken other works that would have made him known and appreciated in the area, for the parishioners of S. Lorenzo would not have entrusted this important commission to an inexperienced artist.

Only the Virgin Enthroned with the Infant, which dominated the centre of the shrine (Plates 6, 7), remains of the carving of the altar, and it was unfortunately extensively restored and completely repainted during the last century. It is the first definite example of Pacher's wood-carving and reveals an assured sculptural technique combined with a softness of surface which have caused no little trouble to students of the chronology of Pacher's *oeuvre*. In this carving, in fact, Pacher displays his artistic qualities to the full and shows that he has completed his development as a sculptor, so that only a very close examination will reveal stylistic differences from the works he produced in succeeding decades. The face of the Virgin has a classical line, with a firm, rounded chin, a clearly but gently defined mouth with dimples at the corners, a rounded forehead, and straight-set, strongly-delineated eyes. All these features have the classical regularity we find in Donatello's figures of the Virgin and Saints in Padua. They contrast sharply with the traditional treatment of the subject in Styria and Pusteria as exemplified by the reliefs on the altar of the Ursulines or the Virgin of the St. Sigismund altar. On the other hand, this idealized but solidly carved face has nothing in common with the faces of Multscher's figures, whose features are strongly individualized with flat foreheads and noses either too pointed or too rounded. Similarly, the face of the Infant displays unmistakable connections with Donatello's putti on the altar at Padua; it has the same facial structure, the same straight-set eyes, the same mouth, half-open as though speaking. In the drapery there are more definite signs of Pacher's original training in Styria and Pusteria, and also, perhaps, some traces of Multscher's influence; but the strong rhythm of the folds and the clear indication of the volume of the body underneath lead us once again to Padua. Yet Pacher's interpretation is no copy; it bears the stamp of an artist who selects and uses only such elements as will suit the requirements of his own style and subject. Making allowances for the deterioration caused by attempts to restore it, the St. Lawrence Virgin can be considered one of Michael Pacher's finest pieces of sculpture; perhaps because his genius is most fully displayed midway between the influences of Padua and the North, perhaps also because he worked with special care on this his first important commission (which the St. Lawrence altar certainly was), particularly on the central figure, and did not trust his workshop with any part of it.

At this point we must look at a statue of St. Lawrence which, because of its iconography and style, and its similar dimensions, may be considered not only as the work of Pacher and contemporary with the St. Lawrence Virgin, but also as having originally been part of the same altar. It is preserved in the Ferdinandeum Museum in Innsbruck, and its provenance is unknown. In his left hand the deacon saint formerly held a book, now missing, and his right hand probably rested upon the gridiron, also lost. The position of the figure, which leans slightly to one side and does not stand well in isolation, indicates that it was originally placed in a shrine to the right of a central figure, which could well have been the Virgin described

III St. Lawrence before the Prefect (detail of Plate II)

above. There a
ing of the pai
affect appraisa
preserves intac
ful face; his e:
unseeingly ahe
the Santo at P.
prototype in b
can be regardo
present be pro

Of the pain
the Virgin, the
with the patro
preserved at M
as a result of

In the scene
by Hans Mult:
in the Death o
although with
even Christ wi
the interrelatio
of St. Peter, w
in the small bu
Peter. The Vir;
the bedhead tl
in the backgro
apostles. In on
turned which
to reinforce an
a linking elem
from the right, v

A purely Pa(
which emphasi
Multscher had
effect of his pai
the dramatic so
recreates the so
such as the hal
one of the func
stands out in th
painting shows
suffers from a
atmosphere the

the armour against the background of the open window. In the Arrest of Pope Sixtus (Plates IV, 10) the light bursts in through the doorway where the Pope is about to pass, imparting to his figure a chiaroscuro underlined by the pallor of the youthful faces of the two deacons standing behind him, thus creating an impressive contrast further accentuated by the strong counterlight of the figure of the guard who stands on the right in the foreground. Pacher's rendering of this story also deserves a mention. St. Lawrence stretching out his hands towards the Pope as he is dragged away by the guards, is deliberately isolated against an architectural structure that recedes into the distance; on the other hand, the group in which the Pope stands is enclosed at either end by the two soldiers whose position and glinting armour make the group a distinct and compact unit. The moment of drama is thus conveyed not so much by outward signs, these being limited to the meeting of the eyes of the two men and the timid movement of the saint's hands, as by the expressive lines of the composition itself. Pacher significantly makes the drama felt rather than narrates it, which shows his affinity with Italian art and contributes to his isolation from the German tradition. Unconsciously, he revives in this scene the solemnity of the inner drama which Giotto had expressed earlier in the Kiss of Judas. The same treatment, subdued and devoid of comment—almost submissive—occurs in the Saint before the Prefect (Plates II, 11); no one speaks, and the whole drama is expressed in the glances exchanged between the protagonists of the scene and in the eloquent, though not emphatic, gesture of the saint, who points to the poor crowding behind him. Perhaps the weakest of the scenes is the Distribution of Alms (Plate 12), probably because of the necessity to include two kneeling figures who must be the men who commissioned the altar—one of them, I like to think, may even be the benefactor, Maurice the tailor.

Even in as dramatic a scene as the Martyrdom (Plates 14–17) Pacher maintains a subdued, restrained tone and refrains from exaggerating physical suffering and ugliness. He had undoubtedly studied Multscher's two Vipiteno panels depicting the Flagellation and the Crowning with Thorns, and took certain characteristic motifs from them, such as the man in armour with the retroussé nose in the Saint before the Prefect, obviously derived from one of the flagellators of Christ, and the guard on the left in the Martyrdom, whose fierce profile is also to be found in the Flagellation panel. Comparing the panels on the Vipiteno altar with the St. Lawrence panels, we must conclude that Pacher deliberately avoids any note of exaggeration in his portrayal of the human figure and its emotions. The very guard who is holding down one of the saint's arms against the hot gridiron with a pitchfork has a sorrowful expression—more that of a pitiful wretch than of a criminal—and his tormented, bony face reflects nothing of the brutality of his action (Plate 15).

Particular prominence is given in the Martyrdom of the Saint to the northern type of city depicted in the background, an adaptation in German Gothic style of an architectural model obviously derived from the Venetian style, perhaps even the Doge's Palace in Venice: the building has a portico with arches on the ground floor, open loggias on the first floor, and a solid wall on the second, which is crenellated at the top and has simple mullioned windows.

In the St. Lawrence altar, then, as our analysis of the work shows, Pacher has fully assimilated all that he had learnt at Padua: the new *rapport* between the figures and the architectural background (Plates 12, 15), the firm placing of the figures themselves, and the use of vibrant colour in tonalities which convey the all-pervading light and atmosphere. These are the

IV Arrest of Pope Sixtus (detail of Plate 10)

principal innovations which enabled Pacher to gain ascendancy in his own locality, and which served to spread his reputation further afield.

As we have seen, Pacher's sources of inspiration are drawn mainly from the Paduan tradition of Lippi and Donatello, and the recent direct experience of the Vipiteno altar. Some have professed to see in Pacher, probably because of his emphasis on plasticity and colour in fabrics and armour, a reflection of the work of Witz. However, emphasis on materials was a tendency throughout Europe at the time, and in Pacher's work there is no feature of composition, perspective, form or colour, that could suggest even the slightest influence of Witz.

We find the style of the St. Lawrence altar paintings further matured in four panels which must have belonged to the predella of an altar of considerable size, probably forming its wings. On the inner sides the heads of St. Peter and St. Paul were depicted against a background of gold (Plates 21, 24), and on the outer sides those of St. Catharine and St. Barbara against a blue background (Plates 22, 23). These pieces came from the convent at Wilten and are now divided between the Österreichische Galerie in Vienna, the Ferdinandeum Museum at Innsbruck, and a private collection. Their origin is unknown, but we can discount the possibility that they belonged to any altar in the monastery itself; it is far more likely that the panels were taken there during the first few decades of the nineteenth century, following the notorious depredations of the Bavarians, and that they originate in the Alto Adige. In any case, the panels prove that there formerly existed an altar by Pacher, executed not long after the St. Lawrence altar, but before the Gries altar (1471). There are obvious similarities with the St. Lawrence panels in the colouring, the brushwork, and several conspicuous details such as the hands, with their rather short, stiff fingers. On the other hand, the greater assurance and freedom of design, and the tendency towards a more precise characterization of physical features, suggest that the artist had devoted further study to the works, and particularly the carving, of Multscher. The contrast between the facial types of the two saints recalls similar antitheses in the saints and in the angels of the Vipiteno altar, although Pacher tends towards idealization whereas Multscher favours a more realistic portrayal.

We can date to the same period a piece of carving of exceptional interest because of its intrinsic beauty as well as its remarkable stylistic features: the figure of St. Michael in the Bayerisches Nationalmuseum in Munich (Plates 8, 9). This figure was discovered in 1875 in the Bressanone valley in North Tyrol; on being purchased and subsequently removed to the castle of Matzen it was transformed according to contemporary neo-Gothic taste, into a St. George. Later it was sold and taken to Cologne, having by this time been separated from the parts which had been added, and changed back into St. Michael. In this process, although less violently handled, it suffered further ill-treatment. Finally it was moved to Munich, where in 1967 it was again restored and all the modern additions removed.

It is commonly held that the statue was originally the centre figure of an altar executed by Pacher between 1482 and 1484 for the parish church at Bolzano, but no evidence has ever been produced in support of this theory. Stylistic considerations, the only valid ones in this case, suggest that it was produced at a much earlier date, between 1460 and 1470. The structure of the head is still that of the St. Lawrence Virgin (Plates 6, 7) and the hair with its Mannerist curls reflects the style of Hans von Judenburg and his followers. In the Gries and St. Wolfgang altars the saints' hair falls in flowing locks, with none of the stylized compactness characteristic of Pacher's youthful work. The draperies too, in so far as they have survived, are much closer to the St. Lawrence Virgin than to those of, let us say, the Salzburg Virgin. The Munich figure is of appreciably higher quality than the St. Lawrence Virgin at Innsbruck; this could be because the latter belongs to an earlier period, or else because the Munich figure is a surviving piece from an altar which, like that from which the Wilten panels come, was executed after the St. Lawrence altar and is therefore the product of a more mature reflection.

1 Lion of St. Mark, from the inner side of a wing of the St. Thomas Becket Altar. Graz, Joanneum Museum

2 Murder of St. Thomas Becket. Graz, Joanneum Museum

3 Murder of St. Thomas Becket (detail of Plate 2)

4 *Burial of St. Thomas Becket. Graz, Joanneum Museum*

5 Burial of St. Thomas Becket (detail of Plate 4)

6, 7 Virgin and Child, and detail, from the former high altar. S. Lorenzo in Pusteria, Parish Church

8 St. Michael. Munich, Bayerisches Nationalmuseum

9 St. Michael (detail of Plate 8)

10 Arrest of Pope Sixtus. Vienna, Österreichische Galerie

11 *St. Lawrence before the Prefect. Vienna, Österreichische Galerie*

12 *St. Lawrence distributing alms. Munich, Alte Pinakothek*

13 *St. Lawrence distributing alms (detail of Plate 12)*

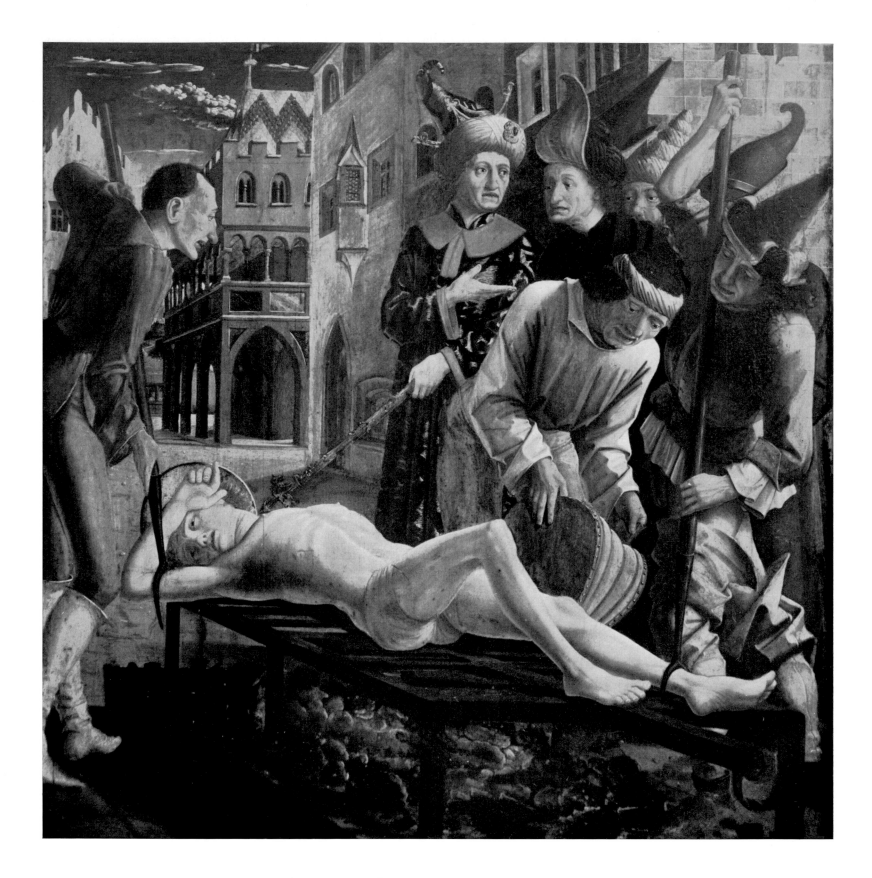

14, 15 Martyrdom of St. Lawrence, and detail. Munich, Alte Pinakothek

16 Martyrdom of St. Lawrence (detail of Plate 14)

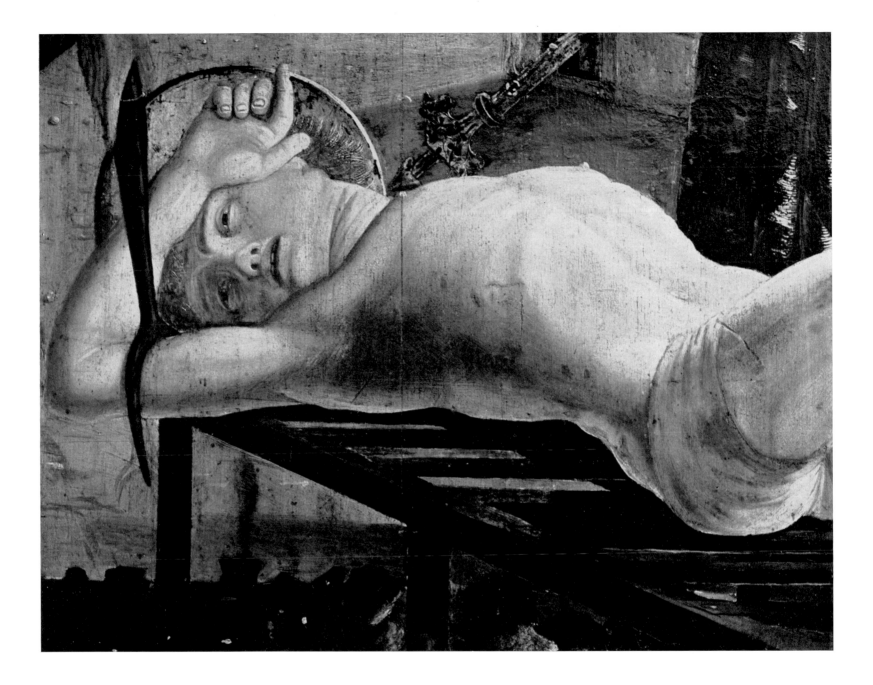

17 Martyrdom of St. Lawrence (detail of Plate 14)

18 *Annunciation, the St. Lawrence Altar. Munich, Alte Pinakothek*

19 *Death of the Virgin, the St. Lawrence Altar. Munich, Alte Pinakothek*

20 Death of the Virgin (detail of Plate 19)

21 *St. Paul, predella panel from Wilten. Vienna, Österreichische Galerie*

22, 23 *St. Catharine, and detail, predella panel from Wilten. Innsbruck, Ferdinandeum Museum*

24 *St. Peter, predella panel from Wilten. Vienna, Österreichische Galerie*

CHAPTER TWO

The Gries Altar

What we know about Michael Pacher and his work, as is invariably the case where medieval art, especially in the Alpine region, is concerned, we owe to the fortuitous preservation of various documents in archives, and of certain works which, because of the element of chance involved in the ravages of time, are not always the most significant. From the St. Lawrence altar little more has survived than a few small panels of the wing-paintings and a document which provides, if only as indirect proof, a basis for the attribution and approximate dating of the work. But we do not know how the shrine was made, nor have we any knowledge of the character or the style of the complete structure of which the remaining fragments formed part. It has already been noted in connection with the St. Lawrence statue how difficult it is to understand a fragment divorced from the setting in which and for which it existed and served a logical purpose. To restore, at least theoretically, the original function of the fragment—in other words, to understand it—is one of the most difficult tasks confronting the art historian; often he has to proceed by the methods of induction and deduction used by archaeologists.

With the disappearance from the chapel of Castel Novale, near Bolzano, of a panel depicting the Pietà which, according to those who saw it around the year 1860, bore the signature of Michael Pacher and the date 1465, a piece of evidence of fundamental importance for the chronology of Pacher's *oeuvre* was lost. This work would probably have shown that having completed the St. Lawrence altar, Pacher then made his way to the liveliest and most prosperous town in the region, the commercial centre of Bolzano. There he produced work that gave proof of his talent and which must have made him known and appreciated. It was on the strength of this that when, not long after, the decision was made to build the main altar for the parish church at Gries, Pacher was thought to be the man most worthy of the task. It can therefore be assumed that the panel had been executed with special care if (no doubt in conjunction with other works by him) it secured for Pacher the favour of the people of Bolzano. His connections with the town, which then had extensive links with the trading centres of Europe, also make it probable that the young artist found there the opportunity of joining a group of merchants and of undertaking the journey to the Low Countries that must have played so important a part in broadening his artistic horizons.

The Castel Novale panel having disappeared, however, nothing is known of Michael Pacher after the completion of the St. Lawrence altar for a period of more than five years. During this interval he clearly underwent experiences that were of vital importance, for in the Gries altar we find him completely transformed. We must infer that between 1465 and 1471, besides producing various works probably in Pusteria, Pacher also made another journey abroad. The presence of frescoes in the style of Pacher on the vault (constructed in 1468) of the Abbey of St. Paul in the Lavant valley in Carinthia, suggests that Pacher went there and received an important commission, perhaps even for the main altar of the church, which occasioned him to entrust the execution of the decoration for the vault to his pupil, Friedrich Pacher. It is most unlikely, however, that this remote valley, which led into a territory desolated by Turkish incursions, could have inspired the innovations evident in Pacher's art in 1471. It seems more probable that the work executed for the abbey in Carinthia provided him with the means for a journey, even if only a brief one, in the direction indicated to him by the Vipiteno altar, namely Ulm, thence through the Rhineland to the great artistic centres of Flanders. Only there, through contact with the Van Eycks and Van der Weyden, and, above all, with Hugo van der Goes (whom he may have met) could he have assimilated those features which led him for a time to forget what he had learnt in Padua and from Multscher. Nor were these influences confined to painting; in the field of carving too, the Low Countries, having not long before given Europe a sculptor of stature in Nicolaus Gerhaerts, certainly had something to teach him.

On returning from this journey, fresh from new experiences and perhaps somewhat bewildered by them, the young artist at once sought to secure commissions. By now his reputation would have been carried far and wide by travelling merchants and—although their importance is invariably underestimated—by the various convents and monasteries whose communications were primarily religious in character, but also economic and cultural. Thus it was not long before Pacher received two opportunities for work: the execution of the main altar for the parish church of Gries, near Bolzano, and that of the main altar for the sanctuary of St. Wolfgang, in the Salzburg area. He accepted both offers, one of which was to be begun at once; the other had to wait as the choir was still under construction, but it was of far greater interest because of the magnificence and ornateness required, and because of the financial reward it would bring the artist. Consequently on 27 May 1471, he signed the Gries contract and on 13 December of the same year the contract for St. Wolfgang. Both contracts were preserved, but the Gries contract, which Koch discovered and drew attention to in 1846, was later removed by an unscrupulous scholar and never found again. We have to be content, therefore, with the copies made by the few people who had the good fortune to see and study it, which although not perfect are generally reliable on the fundamental points. The contract for the St. Wolfgang altar was discovered in 1912 by Zibermayr in the state archives at Linz, and is still kept there.

By the Gries contract the artist was bound to produce the altar within four years for a fee of 350 marks in good Meranese coin. He had to install it on the site at his own expense, but while he was at Gries the men who commissioned it would have provided food befitting a person of his standing. As regards the system of payment, they gave him an immediate advance of ten florins and undertook to pay him the sum of 50 marks within the year and 32 marks annually thereafter until the fee agreed upon had been paid in full. The agreement specified that the niche of the predella must contain sculpted busts of Saints Blaise, Leonard, John the Baptist, and Vigilius; there were to be reliefs of St. Wolfgang and St. George on the inner sides of the wings, and on the outer sides paintings of St. Barbara and St. Catharine on panel. In the shrine a sculptured group was to represent the Coronation of the Virgin—the measurements corresponding throughout with those of the main altar in the parish church of Bolzano—flanked by statues of St. Michael and St. Erasmus. Reliefs on the wings would depict the Birth of the Virgin and the Adoration of the Magi on the left, the Annunciation and the Death of the Virgin on the right; on the outer sides would be paintings of scenes from the Passion: on the left, Christ in the Garden and the Flagellation, on the right, the Crucifixion and Resurrection. Statues of St. Sebastian and St. Florian were to be placed at the sides of the shrine, with Christ on the cross between Mary and St. John in the centre of the cymatium, and in an edicule at the top, a statue of the Virgin and Child.

Only on 8 December 1488 did Pacher draw up his final receipt, showing that he had been paid exactly 950 Rhenish florins for the altar. There had evidently been difficulty in finding the sum due to him for the work; this had probably discouraged the artist, who was not in fact responsible for the painting at the back of the altar—that task was entrusted, probably during these same years, to an unknown artist of a completely different school.

The altar dominated the main apse of the church until 1736 when as a result of the change in artistic taste it was dismantled and removed, and replaced by an altar in stucco lustre made by the Carinthian stucco-worker Hannibal Bittner in the Roman style. This consisted of an altarpiece on the back wall and an altar with a tabernacle flanked by worshipping angels free-standing in the centre of the choir. In 1846 the shrine of Pacher's altar, without the predella, wings, cymatium and the statues at the sides, was discovered in the side chapel of the church, now dedicated to St. Bartholomew. It was returned to its position of honour, where it has remained to the present day. Unfortunately, not long afterwards, it was restored and completely repainted in a manner strongly criticized by Messmer in 1857 and in 1862 by Atz. In the course of restoration a very high neo-Gothic predella was added, which contained a fifteenth-century statue of the Virgin from the area; at the sides were placed two reliefs representing St. Barbara and St. Catharine dating from the end of the fifteenth century and although they may have been found in the church, they obviously cannot be identified as the paintings mentioned in the contract. Above the shrine was another altarpiece of the late fifteenth century, the provenance of which is not known, and over this were neo-Gothic pinnacles with Baroque statuettes from various places. The two surviving reliefs from the wings of the altar, depicting the Annunciation and the Adoration, were fixed to boards and hung on the side walls of the chapel. An attempt to identify a statue of the Virgin and Child with the one formerly on the centre pinnacle above the Crucifixion group has been unsuccessful because the statue itself, which still stands in one of the niches in the church—not the place for which it was originally intended—is not the work of Pacher. But this does not, in my opinion, preclude the possibility that the statue originally formed part of the altar. Although of somewhat inferior quality—not surprising in view of its location—it has the character of a work produced at that time and in the workshop of Pacher.

When the shrine was reassembled in the church in or around 1950, all the extraneous elements were removed under the supervision of the Italian Soprintendenza delle Belle Arti, and it was set on a predella which reproduces as simply as possible the form of the original, with the wings, to which the two surviving reliefs were affixed, restored to it. The nineteenth-century repainting which had disfigured the statues, especially the areas representing flesh, was also to a large extent removed.

These is little that can be said about the genesis of the architectural composition (Plates V–VII, 25–54) because apart from the St. Sigismund altar, which is too far removed in time, there are no examples from which to deduce the characteristics of the wooden altars that Pacher might have seen in Pusteria during the years 1450–55. However, the altar erected at Vipiteno in 1458, which, as we have already seen, also exercised a decisive influence on Pacher's painting and culture, undoubtedly played an important, indeed a fundamental part in the development of his architectural ideas. Of the architectural elements of the Gries altar only fragments have survived, sufficient to pose and to formulate the problem of how the altar should ideally be reconstructed, but not to solve the problem completely. It was certainly from the Vipiteno altar that Pacher took the motif of the angels holding the curtains in the background of the shrine (which in the Gries version are painted and not carved), and the statues on either side of the shrine were undoubtedly suggested by those of St. George and St. Florian at Vipiteno. But apart from these and similar features which are mainly formal and iconographic, where the architectural elements are concerned, it may be claimed that Pacher, taking as his point of departure principles completely different from Multscher's, reached conclusions that were original and independent.

His achievement was in keeping with the formative training he had received in Padua and, above all, with his own sensibility, which led him to adopt an approach characteristic of the art of that school, giving importance to the creation of volume and of space. In Multscher's altar, as later in the Tiefenbronn altar (1469) or in the choir-stalls of Ulm cathedral (1468 and following years), we find that the architectural forms tend to be arranged on superimposed planes which are clearly separated and measurable, but which lack depth and are thus conceived more on the surface than in space. The pinnacles are still soaring and decorated, the arches are generally ogival and do not disrupt the scheme, which is concerned not with the suggestion of space rendered subjective and vibrant by the presence of light and atmosphere, but with a real situation, fixed and immutable. Pacher, preoccupied with the problem of translating into northern terms what he had learnt while at Padua, attempts in his shrine to convey depth and dimension so as to achieve in carving the effects which in painting were achieved by the laws of perspective, light and tonality. Accordingly he constructs settings designed to suggest space, either by creating a niche in the central part or by giving the illusion of greater depth by ingenious use of the overhang of the Gothic canopies. To heighten the effect, the projecting canopies are set an angle producing the optical illusion of accentuated perspective, and are isolated and detached by the insertion of pinnacles which create contrasting areas of shadow of unmeasurable depth. In this way the slight recession of the shrine acquires an infinite depth which transforms the effect of the grouping. In order to translate pictorial and spatial elements into architectural terms, Pacher curves the arches so that they become pliant branches, adorned with patterns of lilies and foliage, rising upwards to take the place of architectural features and even the pinnacles; they become decorative motifs which fluctuate

V Angel playing a musical instrument, from the shrine of the Altar of the Virgin (see Plate 25)

between light and shadow, and so lose all architectural solidity. Not only do the pinnacles and canopies become transparent, even the pedestals upon which the saints stand are pierced so that they produce both light and shadow. In this subjugation of architecture to effects of light and atmosphere—characteristic, it should be remembered, of the art of the Veneto—Pacher never fails to sustain the clarity of the composition, with straight and precise lines which are sensed rather than seen, corresponding, in this unusual Gothic rendering, to the framework of lines of perspective whereby spatial depth is created in his paintings. Within the setting thus created by the illusion of space, atmosphere and light, Pacher places his figures firmly, giving them an integral solidity and using simple effects. He arranges the figures of the central group in three planes of recession: in the middle plane the kneeling Virgin is turned slightly sideways so that the figure encroaches into the further plane, where the hands of Christ and of God the Father reach forward in the act of placing the crown upon her head. These figures are also slightly angled to increase the illusion of spatial depth. The dove poised above the Virgin's head has, *mutatis mutandis*, the same function as the egg suspended in the apse in Piero della Francesca's famous altarpiece: it marks the ideal centre of a three-dimensional space in which the atmosphere circulates. The two angels set in the foremost plane hold the edge of the Virgin's mantle and by their gesture emphasize, or rather convey, the break between the nearest plane and that beyond. Smaller angels playing musical instruments are set in open niches in the pillars which divide the space into three parts, and serve a similar purpose, the projecting trumpets they hold (Plate VI) having the same function—that of measuring space—as the dove. Thus Pacher has produced an entirely original composition in an attempt to convey perspective and atmosphere by the application of all that he had learnt through his contact with the school of the Veneto.

Let us now pass to Pacher's use of colour. Anyone familiar with Multscher's figures at Vipiteno knows that here colour is an objective not a subjective element, unchanging and so not influenced by atmospheric factors. The effect sought by Multscher is purely one of chiaroscuro and colouring. The statues may be set inside an altar or in isolation as desired: the colour does not change, whereas the plastic effect, which was Multscher's prime concern—being an architect and a sculptor in stone rather a painter and a woodcarver—can indeed alter.

Pacher's approach, based on what we might call the scenic principle, is entirely different: the backgrounds of gold damask, the gilded tracery and garments give an exceptional intensity to the vibration of the atmosphere. The setting thus created resembles a theatre stage illuminated by strong arclights, where an actor would be obliterated and absorbed by the intensity of light, and his face would acquire a cadaverous tinge if he did not take the precaution of covering his skin with heavy make-up, sufficient to compensate for the effect of the stage-lighting. Pacher, whose gifts as a great colourist we are learning to recognize, realized the almost theatrical situation of his figures and therefore gave their faces the flushed and heightened colouring, full of contrasts, needed in order to make them stand out amidst the brilliance of the gilded background. When the figures are removed from the altar and shown in normal light against a neutral background, their colouring becomes quite unacceptable. The face of St. Erasmus has a vivid reddish tone shading into violet which passes unnoticed in its usual setting against the background of gold cloth and amidst the gilded garments and architectural framework; isolated from these, however, it becomes improbable and illogical,

VI Angel playing a musical instrument, detail, from the shrine of the Altar of the Virgin (see Plate 25)

like an actor walking in the street without having removed his make-up. The same applies to the Virgin and to all the other figures. It was precisely the inability to understand this fact which led the neo-Gothic restorers of the nineteenth century to paint every single face the same shade of pink, even though the original colouring was still intact, so as to give the statues a bland, uniform tint which they believed would correct a serious fault in their original conception.

Now we come to the execution of the individual parts of the altar; in particular let us try to determine the direction in which Pacher's art was moving at that time. It is at once noticeable that the structure of the face of the Virgin (Plate 34) is quite different from the classical structure of the S. Lorenzo Virgin (Plate 7), it is longer with a childish rotundity in the prominent chin, the rounded forehead and the small irregular nose. The eyes are distinctly carved, in a very gentle almond-shaped curve, giving the face an expression of dreamy ingenuousness reminiscent of the delicate North European images of the Virgin, among which this is immediately ranked; and likewise the adolescent face of St. Michael (Plates 42–45), with its slightly upturned nose, rounded, delicate and projecting chin and full-lipped mouth, and the faces of the angels. One of these (Plate 48), however, radiates an energy and vitality which is not to be found in the angel figures of North Europe: the beautiful angel who turns towards us with a sharp movement of the head and an animated almost mischievous expression, is reminiscent once again of the Paduan school.

Only the six angels holding the curtain have survived of the painted parts of the altar since the wings have disappeared. There seems no doubt about the attribution of these paintings to Pacher, although over-hastily denied by some, if one notes the rapid assurance with which they are sketched, rather than executed, and how these sketches have none of the mechanical quality of a craftsman or a workshop assistant, but display in every stroke the decision, the energy, the conciseness and, in short, the maturity of the artist. It is enough to examine the magnificent hands, summarily sketched, without correction or retouching. It is this sketch-like quality that gives so personal a stamp to the painting, making it one of Pacher's most genuine and remarkable works. The details, such as the elongated faces, pointed chins, even the curling or wavy hair and the long slender necks, immediately bring to mind the paintings of Hugo van der Goes and his school. In fact, the treatment of the angels constitutes the principal grounds for suggesting that Pacher had recently made a journey to Flanders. Newly returned and fired with enthusiasm, the painter would have been very likely to exaggerate in his memory the characteristics of the art which had so excited and impressed him.

A comparison between the face of the Virgin and the fine fragments of Nicolaus Gerhaerts' sculpture in the Liebighaus at Frankfurt shows Pacher's admiration for the great Flemish master and his school; but precisely because of the similarity of formal features, it also points to the magnitude of the conceptual differences between them. With his powerful grouping of sculptural masses and with a physiognomical penetration which is exploited to express an inner drama, Gerhaerts exemplifies an uncertain unity caught in a fleeting equilibrium but none the less firmly balanced between formal expression and inward drama—just as we gain a better understanding of the spirit of the great Erasmus from the portrait (or self-portrait?) in the Strasbourg Museum than from the famous portraits by Holbein. Pacher, on the other hand, brings out the plastic and formal features but, as we have seen in an earlier comparison

VII Third and fourth angels holding curtains, from the background of the shrine of the Altar of the Virgin (see Plate 25)

with Donatello, he makes use of them in a way calculated to show us not so much the image of a particular personality as an element of an all-embracing vision. During the period of the Gries altar, Pacher was still elaborating on what he had learnt in Padua by a thorough study of the disposition of forms in space. The need for this space to be clearly measurable and plausibly defined dominates all his original experiments and prevents him from exploring forms for the sake of their physical or psychological characteristics. It was only later, in the period of the St. Wolfgang altar, that the mighty fusion of Donatello's teaching with that of Gerhaerts, for which, as we have seen, Pacher's familiarity with Multscher's work had in a sense paved the way, reaches maturity. With this comes the liberation of the individual characters within a compact architectonic and compositional unity, in which they become integrating parts of a new dynamic generated by the interaction between formal connections and spiritual suggestiveness. This is clearly the prelude to the emotional conception of a work, which the great artists of the sixteenth century were to realize.

The attempt to resolve problems of perspective and composition so apparent in the Gries altar, particularly when it is compared with the naturalness of the more mature solutions to be seen in the St. Wolfgang altar, is shown clearly in the two surviving reliefs of the altar wings, the only reliefs by Pacher that have come down to us. The wings are executed in very low relief, yet more than other parts of the work they appear to be constructed according to principles of perspective which predominate over those of plasticity; and these, in fact, with their contribution to the atmosphere of the piece, were suggested by the subtle interplay between the carved part and the painted background which is now unfortunately lost. In comparison with the St. Lawrence panels the figures in the Gries reliefs are placed more harmoniously in their setting, which acquires greater conviction from being the central theme of the composition rather than a feature of the background. In the Adoration of the Magi (Plate 54) the perspective design of the cattle-shed conveys the impression of a clearly defined spatial depth. The figures are deliberately set on a sequence of planes: the last of the Magi, who stands upright on the threshold in the foreground is clearly separated from his companion within, while the third king, who is kneeling, forms a link with the group of the Virgin and Child: St. Joseph, who is bending forward towards the three Magi, continues the link and thus closes the curved movement of the composition. The flying angel outside the cattle-shed in the front plane enhances the impression of depth and seems to be a preparatory experiment for the painting of the Death of the Virgin at St. Wolfgang (Plate 95), where Christ receiving the Virgin's soul performs the same function, and the two apostles, one in the right foreground and the other kneeling within the chamber, serve the same purpose as the Magi in establishing the depth of the composition as a whole.

The Annunciation (Plate 53) suffers from the loss of its painted background, which must have played an important part in the composition. But here too one senses the tendency to build the composition around elements conveying spatial recession—a tendency suggestive of Donatello's reliefs which Pacher must have had in mind. Again we are faced with the difficult task of reconstructing from the surviving fragment Pacher's original conception, evidence of which is clearly provided by the perspective of the reading-desk and the mantle of the kneeling Virgin which gives added depth. The foreground is indicated by the dove and the Infant bearing the Cross, both descending from the sky. On the same plane as the Virgin is the angel whose wings are partially concealed by the arch.

It is impossible to make a full theoretical reconstruction of the reliefs because the painted backgrounds are lost; furthermore, the altar is now in a side chapel where the light no longer falls across it from the right as Pacher had envisaged when he conceived the work, and as it had done when the altar was in its original place in the apse of the church.

Nevertheless, the two pieces, in spite of their fragmentary state, are of outstanding significance in the study of the north's interpretation of Donatello's reliefs. Through the agency of Pacher, Donatello's conception was spread among local carvers although their work lost the inner coherence which the Gries prototypes, and particularly the more fully developed reliefs from Salzburg, now lost, must have possessed.

A panel (Plate 55) which was discovered at Bressanone in the last century and recently exhibited at the National Gallery, London, should be mentioned at this point by way of concluding the discussion of the Gries altar and of introducing the examination of the altar of the Fathers of the Church at Novacella. Whether it should be included in Pacher's *oeuvre* is a complex question; its remarkable quality and its similarity to some of his work make it imperative at least to consider the possibility of the attribution. The obvious North European features suggest a dating to the period following his stay in Flanders, while on the other hand, some features of the figures are excessively attenuated and there are weaknesses in their placing which contrast with Michael's style and the essential solidity of his work. In short, the architectural composition seems to reflect the mature style of the Fathers of the Church altar, but lacks its assurance. In composition, colour and chiaroscuro it reproduces the effect of a shrine containing three figures, namely the Virgin enthroned and two saints, St. Michael and an unidentifiable bishop saint, and suggests a *modello* submitted to those who had commissioned an altar. But the possibility that it is a straightforward exercise cannot be ruled out.

One hypothesis is that it may be a work not of Michael Pacher but of his son Hans, who was born in about 1460, or earlier. Hans would have been at a formative stage at a time when his father was under strong Flemish influence and executing the Gries altar and the fresco in the parish church at Bolzano, which I believe also dates from these years. He must have attained his majority in about 1480, but it may reasonably be assumed that, having naturally been initiated into his father's craft at an early age, he had by then assisted him for some years. If a dating to the period of the altar of the Fathers of the Church is accepted, the London panel is clearly the work of someone well acquainted with this altar and also with the Gries altar. A certain graceful fragility in the work, or more precisely a failure to combine a convincing solidity with delicacy of execution, is certainly characteristic of Michael Pacher's son, as we shall see later. He was an intelligent and willing young man, but not a genius; an able painter and carver with the kind of ability that can be acquired by starting young and working hard, but as uncertain and as slow to change as his father was decisive and rapid. The perspective composition in the niches does not bear close scrutiny; these is no feeling of an enveloping atmosphere, and the figures, despite rather timid attempts, do not stand out from their background. It seems to me therefore that his delightful little painting can be regarded not as an original work by Michael Pacher but as a piece specially undertaken by his son, possibly produced on his reaching the age of 21 and presented at Bressanone or Brunico as a test piece in order to secure, prior to his marriage, permission to practise his profession as an independent artist. Although executed some twenty years later, the Thyssen panel at Castagnola, which I consider to be the work of Hans, seems to show the same fundamental characteristics in a more mature form and, like the earlier panel, lacks any possibility of development. The Castagnola panel too is a charming, careful, diligent piece of work, full of attempts, albeit unsuccessful ones, to detach the figures from the background. It is, in effect, a touching demonstration of the narrow but impassable gap that separates ability from genius.

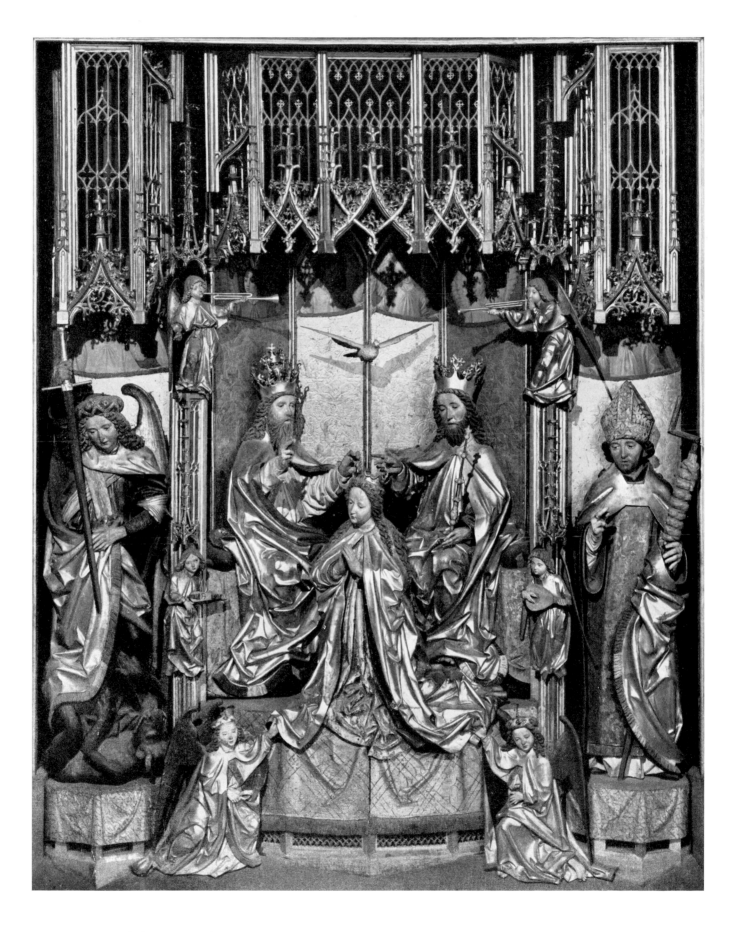

25 *Coronation of the Virgin, shrine of the Altar of the Virgin. Gries (Bolzano), former Parish Church*

26, 27 *Detail showing open-work of a canopy of the shrine;*
head of the second angel from the background of the shrine (see Plate 25)

28 Detail of the first angel holding a curtain in the background of the shrine (see Plate 25)

29 Detail of the sixth agel holding a curtain in the background of the shrine (see Plate 25)

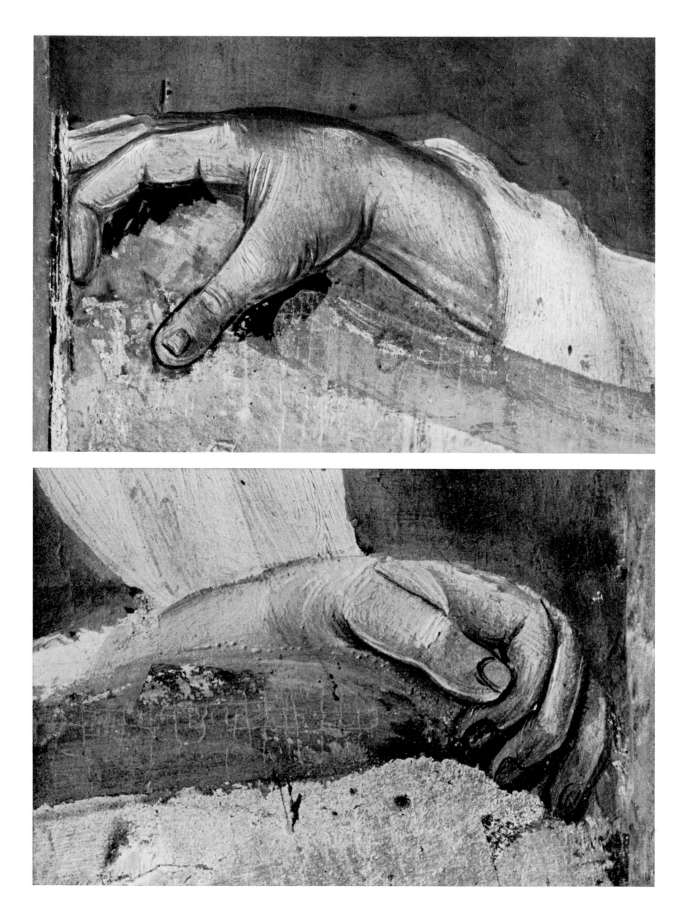

30, 31, 32 *Hand of the first angel; hand of the sixth angel; head of the fifth angel;
from the background of the shrine (see Plate 25)*

33, 34 Statue of the Virgin in the shrine, and detail (see Plate 25)

35 Statue of God the Father in the shrine (see Plate 25)   *36, 37 Statue of Christ in the shrine, and detail (see Plate 25)*

*38, 39, 40, 41 Statue of St. Erasmus in the shrine, and details
(see Plate 25)*

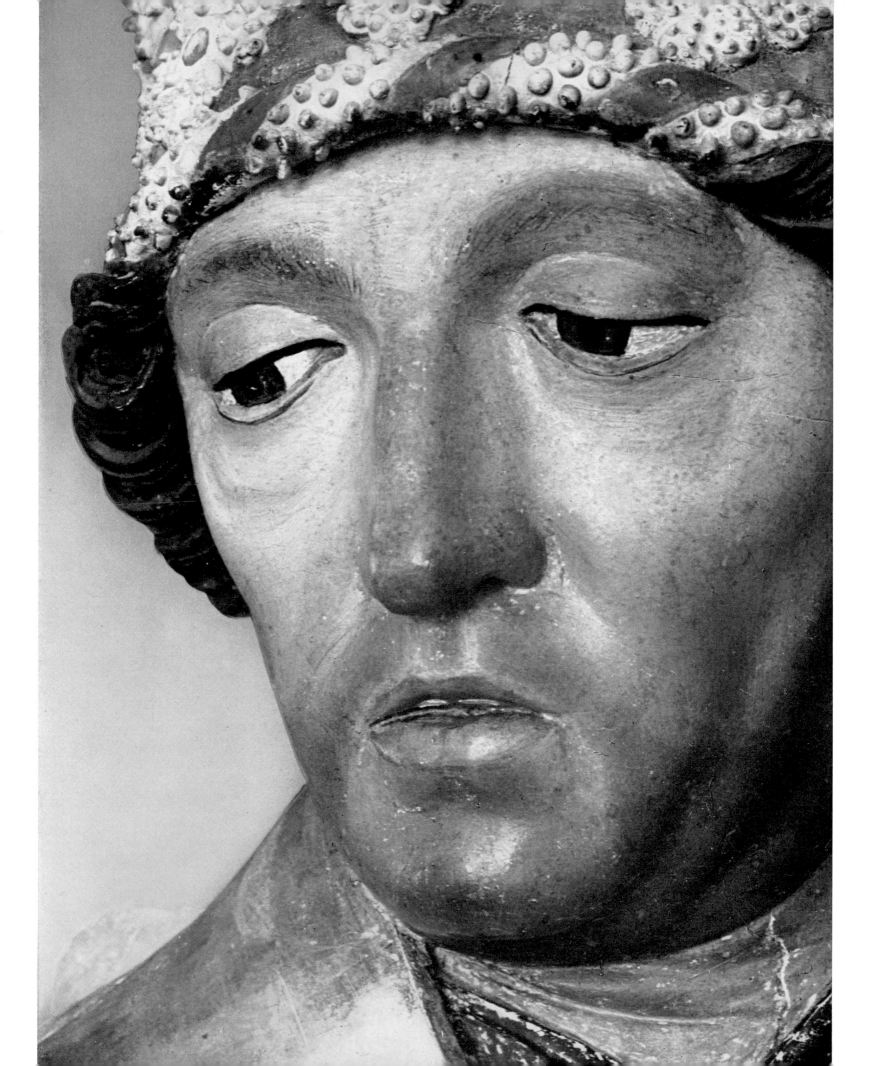

42, 43 *Statue of St. Michael in the shrine, and detail*
(see Plate 25)

44, 45 *Statue of St. Michael, details*

*48, 49, 50 Angel holding the Virgin's robe (detail)
and angels playing musical instruments,
from the shrine (see Plate 25)*

51 Angel playing a musical instrument (detail), from the shrine (see Plate 25)

52 Angel playing a musical instrument, from the shrine (see Plate 25)

53 Relief of the Annunciation (on modern ground),
on the right wing of the shrine of the Altar of the Virgin. Gries (Bolzano), former Parish Church

*54 Relief of the Adoration of the Magi (on modern ground),
on the left wing of the shrine of the Altar of the Virgin. Gries (Bolzano), former Parish Church*

55 *Virgin Enthroned between two Saints (Hans Pacher?). London, National Gallery*

CHAPTER THREE

Michael Pacher at Novacella: the Fathers of the Church Altar

In the contract for the Gries altar no provision was made for painting the back of the shrine which, as we have seen, was done by an artist of a quite different school who had no connection with Pacher's workshop. Evidently Pacher was not prepared to add the painting of the back to the work already agreed upon, but, in any case, as this was a secondary feature of an altar it was generally assigned to the workshop. It is probable that the artist refused, not because he lacked assistants but because the system of deferred payment would not have made this commission an attractive one, particularly if others of greater importance and with a better guarantee of prompt payment were calling him elsewhere.

In and around 1475, in fact, Pacher was not yet being pressed by the men appointed to commission the St. Wolfgang altar as they were preoccupied with the construction of the choir of the church in which it was to be erected. The choir was still unfinished when it was consecrated in 1477. Judging by the two dates inscribed on the altar itself, 1479 and 1481, it would seem that the main part of the work was carried out between these two years, although it is possible that some preparatory work had been done previously, particularly for the carvings for the shrine, which required efficient workshop organization and numerous assistants as well as the personal participation of the artist himself.

During the period that intervened between the completion of the Gries altar and the execution of the St. Wolfgang altar Pacher probably first made contact with the convent at Novacella. The altar of the Fathers of the Church which resulted from this contact was commissioned by the provost, Leonhard Pacher, who was elected in 1467 at the age of 67. Leonhard had formerly been parish-priest at Falzes and Chienes, in the immediate vicinity of S. Lorenzo in Pusteria and Brunico, and could have known of Michael Pacher from the time of his earliest works. It is not impossible that between 1465, or earlier, and 1471, Leonhard Pacher had commissioned altars from him in his own parish, which was then very extensive and had many churches, and that some fragments of these are among those we have identified. It seems very likely that the newly elected provost had at once formulated an ambitious scheme to renovate the church at Novacella in the Gothic style and therefore turned to the brilliant local artist with the proposal that he should produce an altar as part of this scheme. Although not as important as the altar which was to dominate the new choir of the church then under construction, this altar would by no means be insignificant, being dedicated to the Fathers of the Church and so including St. Augustine, the patron saint of the Order.

There can be no doubt as to when work on the altar began, for Pacher was not available until 1475. Moreover, the sacristy was built at the same time as the choir of the church, and completed in the same year, 1478—a date provided by an inscription in the vaulting of the choir itself. Frescoes on the keystone, clearly painted when the sacristy was built, depict the Virgin surrounded by the Fathers of the Church. These figures are iconographically related to the figures of the altar (Plate 72; Figs. 147–149). Hempel attributed them all to Michael Pacher but Pächt entirely rejected them as his work. The frescoes have not been repainted, as some have thought, but are fundamentally untouched. A close examination reveals disparities in their quality suggesting that the workshop was involved in their execution. Some of them could well be the work of Friedrich Pacher who, when he was working with Michael used the latter's sketches, and almost succeeded in concealing the limitations of his artistic talent which later was to prove rather mediocre. Probably, therefore, the altar of the Fathers of the Church was produced between 1475 and 1479. Four years would be more than sufficient for its completion since it was of moderate size, without carving, and required neither large-scale workshop organization nor a great deal of time, even if we assume that it was executed in its entirety by Michael Pacher himself, and that he had to work at the carvings for the St. Wolfgang altar at the same time. We can date the panel to about the end of this period (1478–9), thereby accounting for the traces of the influence of Antonello da Messina which could not be expected before 1475.

Hitherto the altar has been assigned to the period between the completion of the St. Wolfgang altar in 1481 and the retirement of Provost Leonhard in 1482, whose munificence, the earliest sources claim, was responsible for the work. However, quite apart from certain stylistic elements which make this dating unlikely, there is the fact that the provost at that time had been compelled to abandon his grandiose scheme for the total reconstruction of the church and to resign himself to consecrating only the choir and the *mensa* of the high altar. Furthermore, the manoeuvres of the dean had so divested Leonhard of authority that in 1482 he had to retire and his advanced age brought him to the threshold of death, which finally brought him release on 10 March 1484. In these circumstances it does not seem possible that Leonhard could have commissioned a subsidiary altar in 1481 or 1482 when all the resources of the monastery were undoubtedly directed towards the completion of the main altar. This indeed was the first preoccupation and responsibility of his successor, who consecrated it in 1485. We must also remember—and the importance of this should not be underestimated—that it was in 1481 that Pacher completed the St. Wolfgang altar and at once accepted a commission for the construction of an altar dedicated to St. Michael for the parish church at Bolzano, which kept him occupied until 1484, when he signed the contract for the Salzburg altar. During these years, then, he was busy on other undertakings and could not have devoted his time to the Novacella commission.

In the course of the Baroque transformation of the church in 1735, the Fathers of the Church altar was removed from its original position and placed in the convent treasury, a kind of museum where in 1750 it was seen and admired by a Tyrolean scholar, Anton Roschmann. Roschmann remarked that "in particular the infant in the cradle beside St. Ambrose and the lion with a thorn in its paw are executed with incomparable skill". The altar was included among the works of art belonging to the convent which the Bavarian government removed in 1812, and it was never returned. Now sawn into four parts and without the outer wing paintings it is displayed in the Pinakothek in Munich.

The altar (Plates VIII–XI, 56–59) formerly comprised a central panel with figures of St. Augustine and St. Gregory, and the wings opened out to reveal those of St. Jerome and St. Ambrose beside them. When closed the outer side of the wings showed four episodes from the life of a bishop saint hitherto identified as St. Wolfgang. St. Wolfgang, however, has no connection with the altar, or the church, or the Augustinian Order, and I believe that the saint depicted is St. Augustine himself, who is also portrayed in the place of honour on the central panel, to the right of the Pope, St. Gregory.

St. Jerome is depicted as about to extract a thorn from the paw of a lion with his pen; St. Augustine, his right hand raised in benediction, points with his left hand to a young boy squatting at his feet who is trying to drain the sea with a spoon. St. Gregory is delivering the soul of Trajan from Hell, and St. Ambrose is examining the point of his pen, while at his feet lies a child in a cradle, a reminder of the story of his miraculous birth. The four scenes painted on the outsides of the wings represent episodes in the life of the saint. They deal with his moral character and his evangelical work rather than with his actual life story: the saint miraculously curing a sick man, the saint disputing with heretics, the saint disputing with the devil, the saint in ecstasy.

The four Fathers of the Church are set within Gothic niches and the light falling upon these from the right gives a particularly strong effect of relief enhanced by the extremely

Schema for the perspective plan of the Fathers of the Church Altar

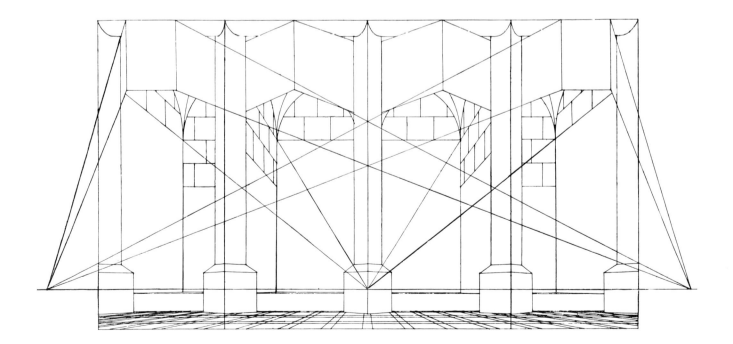

skilful perspective arrangement. The two central figures are shown frontally, and we can see glimpses of the back walls of their cells, and respectively the left wall of one and the right wall of the other. In contrast, the two outer figures are portrayed in profile and their cells complete the architecture of the whole piece, showing the points at which the outer walls meet the back walls. The cells are separated by pilasters with niches containing statues of various saints. In the first from the left are Saints John the Baptist, Mary Magdalene, John the Evangelist and Philip; in the second, Saints James, Peter and Andrew, and a fourth who is hidden by the reading-desk; in the third, Saints Paul, Simon and Bartholomew, and another also hidden by a reading-desk; in the fourth, Saints Thomas, Matthew, Matthias and Catharine.

The floor is common to the central panel and the side-wings when opened; it is composed of multi-coloured marble squares and its design is the same as the one in the St. Thomas Becket altar, ultimately derived from the prototype introduced to Padua by Filippo Lippi. It is shown in centre perspective, with an extremely low horizon and a vanishing point corresponding to the exact centre of the middle panel. This is also the meeting-point of the lines of perspective that run from the niche walls and hence from the Gothic canopies. The two middle canopies have two projecting planes whereas those at either end have three; the effect of *sotto in su* thus obtained enables us to see the rib-vaulting. The scheme has the same rhythmic clarity we find in the architectural framework of the Gries altar canopies. Here, however, the artist, chiefly by means of perspective, created a more complex effect with projections and recesses, so that the composition appears to project over the frame of the altar—an effect which is difficult to produce with an actual architectural structure, even one which, as in the Gries altar, was devised with optical illusions. At St. Wolfgang the artist continues along the same lines and in the carved architecture of the shrine achieves this effect of overhang which he had suggested at Gries and developed fully at Novacella by the use of perspective.

A variety of devices are used to emphasize the setting of the figures in spatial recession. In the first cell the lion, shown from behind and skilfully forehortened, marks the passage from the foreground into the second plane. In the next two cells it is the lecterns, or reading-stands, placed symmetrically at either end of the centre panel, which convey depth; their pedestals, it should be noted, are equal in volume but different in height. The shaft of one has a square cross-section and accordingly is supported by four struts, while the other is hexagonal and has three. A perspective plan of the two lecterns would show to what lengths the artist went in his enthusiasm for the logical arrangement of forms in space. In the niche containing the figure of St. Augustine, to whom Pacher wished to give special prominence, the child at the feet of the saint (Plate 57) is strongly lit from the right and stands out against the cope in the shadow of the saint who is extending his hand towards us in blessing; this gesture serves to indicate and measure the space around the saint, and undoubtedly derives from Masaccio. Through Mantegna perhaps, or more probably Antonello da Messina, who in turn had learnt it from Piero della Francesca—upon whom it had made an especially strong impression—the gesture came down to Pacher. The receding planes in the niche containing St. Gregory are created by the figure of Trajan (Plate 58), who rises from the ground in the front plane. He is linked with the background by his profile presentation and by the gesture of the saint as he grasps Trajan's arm to help him up. In the last niche it is the cradle, executed with astonishing skill and boldly foreshortened, which performs an analogous function.

VIII St. Gregory (detail of Plate 56)

The arc of the cradle stands out sharply against the background, and is both an element in the perspective of the composition and a device for attracting attention to the head of the infant, rather like a halo.

It was Pacher's intention in this magnificent composition to show the degree of skill he had attained in the rendering of perspective. But Pacher combined these miracles of perspective with other miracles, harder to analyse but no less evident. He created the atmosphere for the scene by means of colour, made vibrant and transparent by lighting and transformed into tonal entities of unsurpassable refinement. In the diaphanous faces of the saints (Plates VIII, IX), there is a delicacy and subtlety of colouring which makes these idealized portraits of thinkers and scholars vivid and unforgettable images.

No less important for the study of Michael Pacher's art are the scenes on the outer wings of the altar. In the picture of the miraculous healing (Plates 66, 67), we are shown a room in striking perspective: light enters through three windows on the right and against one of these windows there is a bed with an open-work headboard. Beneath the coffered wooden ceiling hang horizontal bars on which blankets, clothes and bed-linen are hung. These bars are used by the artist to measure and emphasize the space and depth of the composition. The door in the left wall is open, allowing a glimpse of distant landscape. The bed stands on a floor made up of marble squares, an effective device for rendering perspective and accentuating the impression of depth. The young man sitting on the bed is just about to rise, and with his legs towards us he reaches into the foreground. He is linked with the saint, who stands behind him, by the hand with which the latter grasps him in order to raise him. To find a comparably convincing setting in a painting we should have to turn to the Flemish painters; but to find a similar combination of careful description and skill in perspective we must look to the works of Antonella da Messina, Carpaccio or Dürer.

The panel depicting the Ecstasy of the Saint (Plates 62, 63) again contains the favourite device of a door in the wall at the back opened to reveal a splendid landscape receding into the infinite distances of the sky. On the left is the end wall of the presbytery of the church, with two stone altars each in a canopied stone niche. The vanishing point is extremely low, resulting in a strong foreshortening which adds drama to the scene. An angel descending vertically lifts the monstrance from the altar and with one hand lightly touches the saint, who is kneeling in prayer with his face buried in his hands. From the right a strong light falls on the figures of the saint and angel, and they stand out against the shadowy back wall. An astonishing effect of plasticity is thus produced. The painting is also remarkable for the realism of the few details it contains, such as the very beautiful altar-cloths and the monstrance.

In the third scene (Plates X, 64–65) the vanishing point is equally low so that the figure of the saint, who stands on the right disputing with the heretics, fills the whole height of the panel. The imposing effect thus achieved is heightened by lighting that gives emphasis and mass to the body enveloped within the cope. On the left side of the picture the heretics are arranged in front of the saint on a horseshoe-shaped dais and in such perspective that the man in the foreground, although seated, occupies the full length of the picture: the difference between his height and that of the other seated figures reveals the spatial recession of the scene. The lines of perspective are clearly indicated by the marble floor and by the beams on the ceiling of the adjoining aisle which, like the aisle in which the scene is taking place, runs parallel

IX St. Ambrose (detail of Plate 60)

to the spectator. In this case the artist has not considered it necessary to include a foreshortened side wall in order to convey recession, for he had achieved his purpose satisfactorily by other less obvious but more telling means.

This favourite device of a wall running parallel to the spectator with a side wall in perspective, recurs in the final picture (Plates XI, 68, 69). Here, however, it has undergone an ingenious transformation: in place of the left wall there is a row of houses which jut out in varying degrees, as in the St. Sebastian panel by Antonello da Messina at Dresden. The background is pierced by a double gateway which is open and allows us to see the continuation of the street up to the walls and fortified gates of the city. Above the double gates is an uncovered passage-way from which some people are looking down. The idea has its precedents in the painting of the Martyrdom of St. Christopher in the Ovetari Chapel at Padua, and in the Dresden St. Sebastian, a later work which may have directly influenced Pacher. Perspective tricks and skilful lighting are used to give the impression of depth and airiness. Standing in the foreground, and occupying the full height of the picture, the figures of the saint and the devil face each other. The majesty of the saint's figure is enhanced by the deliberate fullness of the folds of his mantle and by the crozier, which rests firmly and vertically on the ground, strong and impassable. The figure of the devil is thin and crooked, and he bends towards the saint in a diagonal which is reinforced by the book he is holding.

Comparing these figures with those painted ten years earlier for S. Lorenzo di Sebato—unfortunately we have very few examples from the intervening period—we find that in general the artist has kept to the principle of employing perspective devices to give emphasis to the figures but he has meanwhile refined and perfected these means. The vanishing point has been lowered and sometimes brought down almost to the level of the floor, making the figures more imposing; the treatment of architecture shown in perspective has been altered in some particulars so that its purpose is not so obvious; the use of colour has undergone further refinement and there is an increasingly noticeable tendency, which will culminate in the St. Wolfgang altar, to create settings of impressive proportions. His acquaintance with the Flemish painters has taught Pacher not only the value of representing certain details precisely but also how to vary the faces of his figures, and give them greater elegance by elongating their features and their slender, sensitive hands. Gone is the thinness of the Gries angels and the bodies are solid as well as supple and alert. The artist has turned once again to considerations of plasticity, which suggests that he may have undertaken a journey to North Italy in about 1475, or not long after, to counterbalance the Flemish influence, and have come into contact with works by Mantegna and Antonello.

Because of its moderate size, Pacher himself was able to execute the whole of the altar of the Fathers of the Church. Intending as he did to make it a worthy example of his artistic talents with a view to the possibility of obtaining a commission for a large-scale work—such as the main altar in the newly-built choir of the church must have been—there can be no doubt that he wanted it to be something of a *tour de force*.

Unfortunately Michael Pacher's hopes were to be disappointed: for after the retirement of the old Provost Leonhard who had entrusted him with the commission for the Fathers of the Church altar and who would probably also have chosen him for the main altar—which would have been at least the size of the St. Wolfgang altar—his successor in the provostship,

X Disputation with Heretics (detail of Plate 64)

Lucas Härber, preferred another artist. If we are correct in identifying this artist as Marx Scherhauf, son of the painter Leonhard of Bressanone and brother of one of the canons of the Novacella house itself, he would have enjoyed considerable local support; and being connected with Pacher's circle he could guarantee a good piece of work, perhaps on more favourable financial terms.

If, as I believe, the panel depicting St. Anne, now in the picture gallery of the monastery, is the sole surviving fragment of the altar commissioned from this painter in about 1483 and installed in 1485, then it certainly cannot be said that the convent lost little by the change of artist.

The Bressanone area was full of artists who were inferior to Michael Pacher but who enjoyed protection against outside competitors because they were of local extraction. The path to success was still barred to him here, and even at Novacella he was generally less highly regarded than Leonhard, the Uttenheim Master and even Friedrich Pacher. In these circumstances Pacher had no choice but to move northwards, beyond the Alps. So it was that the St. Wolfgang altar came to be followed by the altar for the parish church at Salzburg, the last the artist was to make.

The Monguelfo Tabernacle, and collaboration with Friedrich Pacher

Förster in 1853 was the first to declare that the Monguelfo tabernacle (Plates XII, 70–71; Figs. 150–152) was by Pacher, and simultaneously attribute to him other works which later authorities have rightly rejected. Nevertheless the attribution of the tabernacle was accepted, with the reservation that an assistant was perhaps involved. All discussion, however, was cut short when the tabernacle was destroyed as a result of flooding in 1882. Since then the frescoes have been assigned without reservation to Michael Pacher alone. The sole remaining record of them is some sketches made by Blachfelner, which are insufficient to permit any stylistic analysis. These sketches constituted the only basis for the incorporation of the surviving fragments in the new tabernacle in 1893, and for Melicher's reconstruction of the missing parts in 1895. Melicher worked largely from his imagination and furthermore repainted such parts as had survived, thus depriving scholars, as Semper lamented, of any chance of examining or judging them. In 1943, however, I unexpectedly found in the archives of the Museo Civico at Bolzano photographs of the four sides of the tabernacle, taken before it was destroyed, which had previously been unknown to scholars. Such was the importance of this discovery that I at once had copies made, and this was a fortunate precaution for while alterations to the museum were being carried out between 1943 and 1945 the photographs themselves disappeared.

An examination shows conclusively that the frescoes of the Monguelfo tabernacle, although executed entirely from designs by Michael Pacher and under his direction, are in part the work of Friedrich Pacher. The two principal sides of the tabernacle (Plates 70, 71) depicting the Crucifixion and the Virgin Enthroned, were indeed painted by the master himself, but the other two sides are by his pupil (Figs. 150, 151).

The subjects depicted on the walls of the tabernacle were as follows: on the east wall, in the niche, the Crucifixion, flanked by St. Peter and Paul and on the ceiling, St. Gregory and

XI Disputation with the Devil (detail of Plate 68)

the eagle of St. John the Evangelist; on the north wall, in the niche, the Virgin Enthroned, on either side St. Barbara and St. Catharine, on the ceiling, St. Jerome and the lion of St. Mark; on the west wall, St. Sylvester and St. Stephen, with St. Leonard and St. Florian on either side and St. Ambrose and the angel of St. Matthew on the ceiling; on the south wall, St. Margaret with St. James and St. Ulrich on either side and St. Augustine and the bull of St. Luke on the ceiling.

Unfortunately, the Fathers of the Church and the symbols of the Evangelists are only just visible, and some cannot be made out at all in these old photographs. This is a serious loss, for their bold foreshortening might have been the most interesting and novel feature of the tabernacle, at least from the point of view of clarifying Pacher's connection with the Renaissance art of Padua.

The fresco of the Virgin Enthroned (Plate XII) is the best preserved of the fragments and is the only one that permits of a sound stylistic judgement. The disaster ruined the head of the Virgin but spared the figure of the Infant, while the composition of the whole is clearly visible in the old photograph. The great delicacy of the colouring—the rosy flesh of the Infant against the white robe of the Virgin—and the draughtmanship with its extreme refinement of detail executed with the tip of the brush, not to be found in any of the other frescoes attributed to Michael Pacher, prove not only that it is the work of the artist's own hand but also that he devoted particular care to the painting. The composition is reminiscent of the fresco of the Virgin on the façade of the parish church of Bolzano (Figs. 171, 174) but it is of undoubtedly higher quality, as a comparison of the heads of the Infants shows: the Bolzano head has heavy delineated eyes and a huge, mis-shapen ear like a cabbage leaf, whereas the ear of the Monguelfo Infant is small and delicate. We may infer from this that the Bolzano painting is certainly not by Michael himself. Nevertheless, the face of the Virgin recalls some of the angels in the painted background of the shrine of the Gries altar, notably the fifth one. There is also a definite similarity between this Virgin and the one in the London panel; but, as I have already said, the thinness of the figures there suggests that it is the work of another hand.

The background architecture is particularly interesting. The interior of a church is shown in centre perspective, with the vanishing point in the middle. The rib-vaulting can therefore be admired in full detail as well as the lines of the floor. As usual, the light enters from the right and creates a clear dividing line at the centre of the vault. It should be noted that this impressive perspective conception, which is not found in the Fathers of the Church altar nor in any of the earlier works, was to recur: in the panel of Christ and the woman taken in adultery in the St. Wolfgang altar it is carried to its extreme conclusion. This detail alone suggests that the Monguelfo tabernacle dates from the period after the Fathers of the Church altar and before that of St. Wolfgang.

The two female saints on either side of the Virgin are only visible in the photographs. They are also set against the background of a rib-vaulted church. The edge of St. Jerome's robe descends from the fresco above to cover part of the left margin of the painting, and being lit from the left casts a shadow on it. In the painting opposite, however, the lion of St. Mark was lit from the right, as we can tell from the magnificent opened book which rests on the lower fresco; this book is reminiscent of its counterpart in the St. Thomas altar, but here the composition is even freer. A fragment of St. Jerome remains, which includes the hand, and

XII Virgin and Child (detail of Plate 70)

the right side of the lion, with the open book.

The fresco of the Crucifixion is virtually completely ruined, since the upper part, which up to 1882 was in a good state of preservation, disappeared in the disastrous flood, while the lower part, which still remains, had by then already been severely damaged by the elements, and today it is almost impossible to make it out. The powerful depiction of Christ upon the cross recalls Donatello's version at Padua, especially in the fluttering loincloth. In Pacher's version there is a restrained drama in the interpretation which is peculiar to northern art, as is also the anatomical realism which is toned down sufficiently to produce an equilibrium between the inner drama and the expression of physical suffering. The cross stands out against a very delicate landscape background, with a blue sky and a view of mountains, and a distant city where the inspiration of Paduan iconography is translated into local terms by means of the steep roofs of the towers and a soaring Gothic structure with spires, clearly northern in origin. The flanking figures of St. Peter and St. Paul were already badly damaged before 1882, except for their beautiful heads—particularly striking is St. Paul's look of compassion. Both show signs of the influence of the Wilten panels and perhaps also of recent contact with Mantegna's work. From the painting on the vault St. Gregory's robe (he can be seen almost intact, Fig. 152) hung down into the picture below, close to the head of St. Peter, throwing a shadow against part of the frame. The book held in the talons of the eagle of St. John also projected over the frame, casting a shadow on the fresco beneath. The frescoes on the other two walls were conceived on similar lines and were undoubtedly designed by Pacher himself, but the stiff and heavy manner of their execution clearly shows they are the work of Friedrich. The frescoes on the vaults display the influence of Pizzolo's frescoes on the vault of the Ovetari chapel in Padua (Fig. 139). Pacher had grasped their essential quality and interpreted it in a personal style of his own. Again, the perspective rendering of the Gothic vaulting from below, here introduced by Pacher for the first time, is but an ingenious adaptation of the perspective views of Renaissance ceilings found in Pizzolo's frescoes.

The Monguelfo tabernacle marks the renewal of contact between Pacher and his Paduan inspiration after his preoccupation with Multscher and Flemish painting. Now, however, these influences are reshaped by Pacher's own personality and combined with the others so that they are merely evocative suggestions within a style that is coherent and personal.

In connection with this group of paintings arises one of the most discussed problems: the nature of the link between Michael and Friedrich Pacher. At Monguelfo it is shown on a practical level as a working collaboration between master and pupil, but as we shall see, the partnership continued at St. Wolfgang in the execution of several panels, mainly from drawings by Pacher. In 1481 it ended for good, and in 1483 Friedrich signed his name in full on the altarpiece in the Hospital at Bressanone as if to show that he had won his freedom as an artist and set up a workshop of his own, and now wished to go his own way. He never again worked with his teacher, and in a short time had squandered the heritage of experience and of formal motifs acquired in the workshop of the master, and sunk to producing those last miserable efforts which are so bad that some have considered them the work of another artist.

Much fanciful information has been invented concerning Friedrich Pacher. He has been said to have been born in about the same year as Michael, if not earlier; he has been considered to be his brother; and his work, owing to the over-hasty interpretation of documents, has been so inaccurately dated as almost to justify scholars (for example, Pächt) who held that he was senior to Michael and assigned to him the position of pre-eminence, which he could not have had and in fact does not hold. If, as seems logical, he is to be identified with the painter named Friedrich who in 1474 was a citizen of Brunico and was paying taxes on a house in that town, we may place the beginning of his career as an independent artist to that date, perhaps a few years after he had completed his apprenticeship in Michael's workshop and had started to work in collaboration with him. Hence we suggest that he was in fact born about 1450. That he was a native of Novacella or at any rate had strong family ties there seems certain from the studies and discoveries made by Schrott. In 1486 the painter Friedrich Pacher became the owner of the "Pömergut" at Novacella, which he inherited from a relative; he sold it to his sister Dorothea and her husband Hans Reintaler, but granted to another sister, Juliana, the right to lodge there. This little family holding was previously owned by a certain Leonhard, probably the father of the painter, who in turn had inherited it from his father, Friedrich. Then, in 1487, the "Pömergut" was handed on to Christina, daughter of Elizabeth, another sister of the artist, and her husband Urban Almperger. It is noteworthy that Dorothea Oedenhauser, the artist's wife, came from a wealthy Novacella family. However, documentary references to Friedrich Pacher are found with increasing frequency only from 1478 onwards, and are mostly concerned with transactions made while he was living at Brunico; they continue to the time of his death, which occurred around 1508.

As for the beginning of his career, it is not impossible that Friedrich served in Michael Pacher's workshop even before 1471. Between 1468 and 1471 Pacher may have been engaged on the execution of an altar for the church of St. Paul at Lavant, where the reconstruction of the vault had in 1468 just been completed. The vault itself is decorated with quatrefoil frescoes painted by Friedrich, who was certainly working under the partial supervision of Michael Pacher. It seems likely that Friedrich had at that time recently completed his years of apprenticeship and had perhaps stayed on to work with his teacher. On returning from St. Paul it is probable that Friedrich painted a second fresco from sketches by Michael and under his direct supervision. This was the fresco of the Virgin Enthroned in the parish church at Bolzano, which has many points of similarity with the best elements of the vault at St. Paul's, and must date from the same years as the Gries altar. Next comes the decoration of the vault of the sacristy at Novacella and of the archive above it, which has characteristics suggesting it was executed under the direct supervision of the master and indeed is partly by his hand. It can be dated to about 1478, at which time Michael was working on the Fathers of the Church altar and Friedrich himself on the altar of St. Catharine which Provost Leonhard had commissioned from him. After this followed Friedrich's collaboration with Michael on the Monguelfo tabernacle, described above, together with various fresco commissions which Michael, who was evidently too busy to undertake them, passed on to him or reserved for him. As with the St. Catharine altar the master himself undertook no responsibility for these commissions, neither for directing their execution nor for the production of designs or *modelli*. In my opinion, the last product of the period of their collaboration which preceded the St. Wolfgang altar, was the fresco in the collegiate church of St. Candidus (Figs. 153, 158). The commission was given to Michael and was in part painted by him; the rest was executed by Friedrich under

Michael's close supervision, and with such care that it is barely distinguishable from those parts which are the work of the master. Nevertheless there is a clear difference in the brushwork which would appear to establish that Michael worked on the head of St. Candidus; whereas in the head of St. Corbinian, with its stiffer and more mechanical features, it is easy to distinguish Friedrich's hand. It was undoubtedly Michael who designed the St. Candidus fresco, which is a relatively late example of his work. It contains a presentiment of Renaissance forms in the compositional linking of the three figures by means of a single rounded arch in the background, a feature which appears to derive from a well-known drawing by Jacopo Bellini of a Roman aqueduct.

The remaining frescoes to be examined are a group of fragments preserved in the Academy Museum in Vienna. Their extremely high quality suggests that Michael Pacher had a hand in their production, and was at least responsible for the carrying out of the commission, although the work was executed by other artists and dates from the 1470s. The poor state of the fragments does not allow us much scope for discussion which, in any case, would not bring us nearer to solving the problem of their relationship to Pacher. The same is true of the small fresco of the Virgin at Tesido (Fig. 143) which was commissioned for the funerary chapel of Balthazar of Welsberg who, it will be remembered, withheld the bequest made by Maurice the tailor for the altar for S. Lorenzo di Sebato and who died in 1470. This tiny, delicate fresco is in the style of Pacher, but does not look like the work of the master himself.

It is certain that the collaborative partnership between Friedrich and Michael Pacher entered a critical period during the execution of the St. Wolfgang altar and came to an abrupt end. The temperaments of the two men were definitely not well-matched and it was only possible for them to collaborate on commissions of secondary importance and on frescoes, which Michael, it seems, did not willingly undertake. While the youthfulness of the pupil determined his relationship with Michael as one of direct and absolute dependence they could work together. Friedrich's impetuous and unreflective character, his tendency towards the more violent excesses of expression and the inconsistency of the execution of his work, which is sometimes careful but often negligent and hasty—none of these things could have been pleasing to Michael, whose temperament was balanced and thoughtful, and who tended not to emphasize the outward expression of a drama, but rather to concentrate on the psychological situation and convey the drama simply by restrained gestures and moving but not emphatic expressions.

The St. Wolfgang altar, fortunately preserved intact, is assured of its well-deserved fame and contains some of the finest and most significant examples of the art of Michael Pacher. Furthermore, it offers proof of his talent in planning and organizing a large-scale commission which combined architecture, painting and sculpture. At the same time his partnership with Friedrich, whose work became more and more hasty, uneven and careless, must have caused him recrimination and profound dissatisfaction. In some of Friedrich's paintings, such as that of St. Wolfgang building a church, the draughtmanship is so shaky and the execution so slovenly that the great Pusterian artist cannot but have suffered and felt ashamed. He must have regretted the happy times when he was working by himself on the Fathers of the Church altar, whose small dimensions and absence of organizational problems made it unnecessary for him to have recourse to outside collaborators. Indeed, this altar represents the most successful and enjoyable period of his career.

56 *Centre panel of the Fathers of the Church Altar, with St. Augustine and St. Gregory. Munich, Alte Pinakothek*

57, 58 *Details of the centre panel (see Plate 56)*

*59, 60, 61 St. Jerome, on the left inner wing; St. Ambrose, on the right inner wing; and detail;
from the Fathers of the Church Altar. Munich, Alte Pinakothek*

62, 63 *The Saint in Ecstasy, on an outer wing of the Fathers of the Church Altar, and detail. Munich, Alte Pinakothek*

64, 65 Disputation with Heretics, on an outer wing of the Fathers of the Church Altar, and detail. Munich, Alte Pinakothek

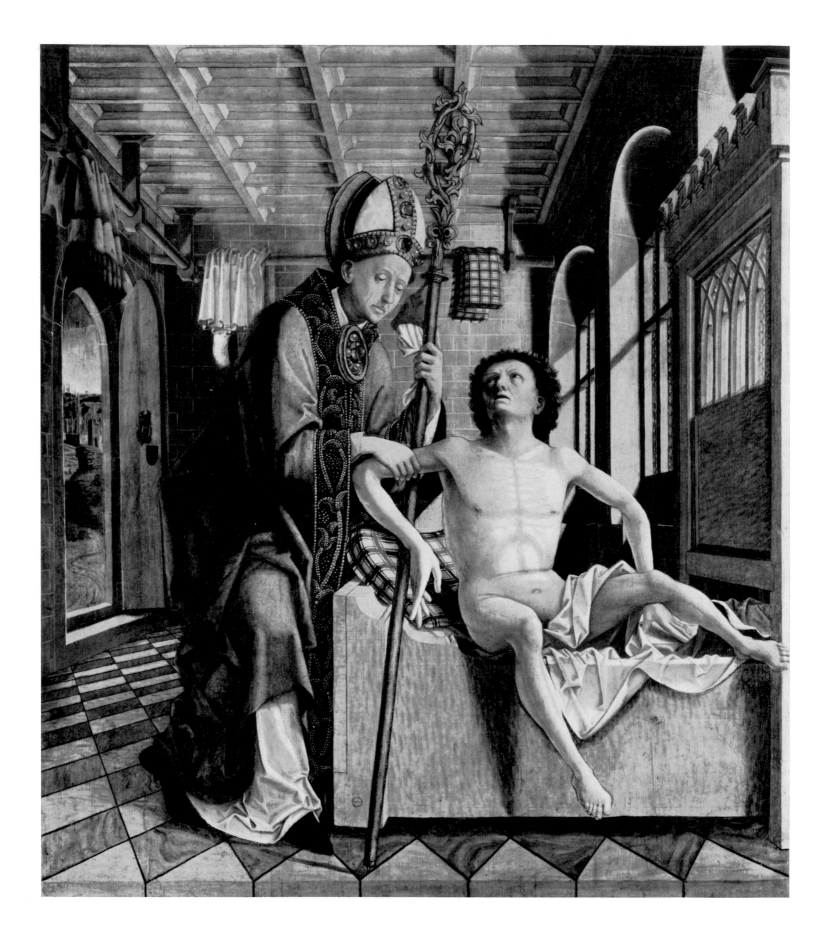

66, 67 A Miraculous Cure, on an outer wing of the Fathers of the Church Altar, and detail. Munich, Alte Pinakothek

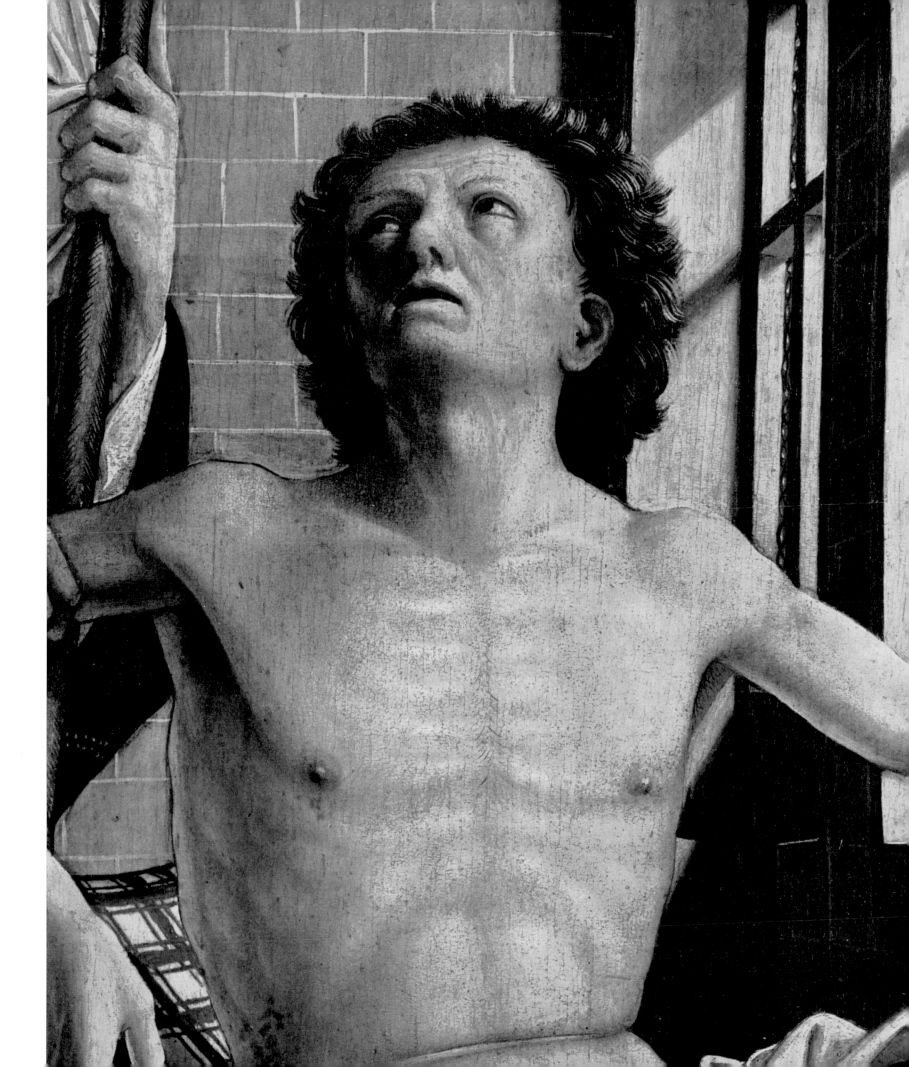

68, 69 Disputation with the Devil, on an outer wing of the Fathers of the Church Altar, and detail. Munich, Alte Pinakothek

70 Frescoes on the north side with the Virgin Enthroned (from an old photograph). Monguelfo, Tabernacle

71 *Frescoes on the east side with the Crucifixion (from an old photograph). Monguelfo, Tabernacle*

72 *St. Jerome. Novacella, Sacristy*

The St. Wolfgang Altar

The St. Wolfgang altar (Plates XIII–XVIII, 73–111; Figs. 159, 166–168, 189), is the only altar by Michael Pacher—and one of the few purely Gothic altars—which has been preserved intact. Considering the high quality of its execution it is deservedly celebrated. Furthermore, the conception of the whole piece is the fruit of the artist's full maturity and demonstrates the extent of his skill as an architect, sculptor and painter combined. On the other hand, precisely because it was produced during a period when Pacher's work was sought after and it was therefore necessary to work at a faster rate, the altar possesses many faults. Some are due to hasty execution, others to the participation of artists who were not sufficiently supervised by the master or else were incapable of creating figures which could merit a place beside the work of Pacher himself. His most successful period, represented by the Fathers of the Church altar, was now past; with the St. Wolfgang altar he begins to lapse into workshop production, a decline which was to become complete with the Salzburg altar. Already we sense that the master is losing control over his collaborators and tending to assume the role of manager rather than of artist. Although this judgement may sound harsh and even unjust, especially since this is Pacher's most famous and widely known work, it is a necessary preliminary to discussion. We can then select and isolate from the whole those parts which constitute the highest expression of Pacher's art, and draw a veil over those others which do him no honour.

The contract for the altar was concluded with Benedict, the abbot of Mondsee, on 13 December 1471, after the artist had drawn up and agreed upon a basic plan. The fee fixed for the work was 1,200 Hungarian florins, but neither the conditions nor a time for the completion of the commission and the payment of the fee were laid down. Moreover, even the description of the projected altar was rather vague when compared with that given in the Gries contract, being confined to an indication of the subjects chosen for the shrine and the predella, the number of wings, and little else.

All this can be explained, however, when we consider certain circumstances. Firstly, Pacher was unable to commit himself to execute the altar at once, having already signed a detailed agreement a few months previously under which he was obliged to start on the Gries altar immediately and to complete it within four years. Furthermore, Abbot Benedict was not ni a position to receive the altar within a short space of time, since the choir in which it was to be installed was still under construction. In fact the choir was only consecrated in 1477, while apparently still not completely finished.

This document, the only one that has come down to us, is perhaps not so much a contract as a preliminary statement, useful to both parties, whereby the abbot secured the best artist then available to carry out the work dear to his heart. So great was his concern for the undertaking that he gave Pacher an immediate advance of 50 florins without any of the normal conditions usual in such transactions. The artist for his part was on the crest of a wave, and there were certainly many extremely good commissions open to him; but he was also anxious to ensure his future security with a commission that was both financially rewarding and not excessively binding with regard to the date for its completion. The agreement was therefore in both their interests.

The problem of producing the work became pressing only in, or rather after, 1477. Probably, the preliminary outline agreement was followed some time during 1477 by a definite and detailed one which laid down precise conditions for the completion and assembly of the work. In the meanwhile, however, Pacher had certainly committed himself elsewhere, and was showing reluctance to begin this commission, or was working on it without enthusiasm; indeed, we may infer that the shrine, made and finished in 1479, as the date on the painting shows, remained unassembled and empty until 1481, when the individual parts of the altar were brought from Brunico. Generally, the shrine was made *in situ* because of its size. In this case it was also painted at St. Wolfgang by a local painter not of Pacher's school, while the predella upon which it was to rest was painted in Pacher's workshop and probably transported from Brunico together with the other pieces of the altar.

The Fathers of the Church altar has been attributed to the years between 1475 and 1479, but we may perhaps place its execution nearer to the latter date and assign to the intervening period a journey made by Pacher to Italy, bringing fresh experiences and contacts with Mantegna at Verona and Mantua, and with Antonello da Messina in Venice. We could then assume that work on the St. Wolfgang altar did not begin until after 1477, alternating with work on various other commissions until 1479; from that year onwards the work proceeded at a feverish pace until the altar was completed. The altar itself shows signs of the haste with which it was finished, being the fruit of the collaboration of a team of artists of a variety of schools and of uneven, and sometimes poor, quality. The artist himself was without doubt responsible for the principal sections—the shrine and the four inside panels of the outer wings, which would be seen at Mass and solemn ceremonies. He decided on and supervised the collaborative work on the inner panels of the wings, on the predella, the figures of the warrior saints on either side of the altar, and the painting of the lower row of the group of saints portrayed on the back of the altar. He gave a free hand to the assistants who carved the upper parts of the cymatium and who painted the outside panels, parts of which are mediocre productions and hardly acceptable, even bearing in mind that they were visible only during Lent and on non-feast days.

There is very little to be said about the fortunes of the altar from that time onwards. In 1675 it was miraculously saved despite proposals to remove it and replace it with a Baroque altar; fortunately, it not only survived the mania for renovation of the Baroque period and even the suppression of the Benedictine abbey, but also, unlike the Gries altar, emerged almost

XIII Detail of the Virgin, in the shrine of the high altar. St. Wolfgang, Parish Church (see Plates 75, 76, 77)

unscathed from the harmful attentions of the neo-Gothic restorers of the nineteenth century. The proposed restoration work was in fact rejected by the Austrian authority responsible for works of art, which itself undertook the task of renovation and carried it out with a degree of care exemplary by the standards of the time, completing it in 1861. Further measures for the conservation of the altar were taken in 1908 under the supervision of the same authority.

The condition of the work as a whole is good. Although there are signs of early repainting of the carved sections, there is a general darkening of colour in the panels, which have become desiccated in places. Woodworm have also left abundant traces of their destructive activity. Fortunately, so far they threaten only the cymatium carvings, which were made on the spot by local carvers in limewood and were thus an easier prey for woodworm than the sections made in pine at Brunico, which are the best parts of the altar.

The architectural composition of the shrine is the most advanced example we have of Pacher's experiments in this field, since the Salzburg altar has disappeared and left no evidence of its form. We can take as a basis for comparison the altar at St. Sigismund, a work which although not on the whole impressive does reflect the forms which were in general use in Pusteria around the middle of the fifteenth century. In that altar we find the same three canopies, identical in shape and with a square cross-section, together with buttresses decorated with pinnacles containing figures of angels with musical instruments, which we have seen in the Gries altar. They constitute a spatial entity which, although it is restricted and can be measured optically, did imply an attempt on the artist's part to convey an impression of volume. Michael takes as his point of departure forms of this kind, resisting the attraction of Multscher's Swabian interpretations, which were of no use to him in his attempt to achieve the creation of spatial effects. In the Gries altar he succeeded in deepening the concavity of the shrine and in arranging the canopies on lines of perspective accentuated by optical effects so as to suggest a depth of space greater than it actually was. He followed this up in the Fathers of the Church altar by adding further to the illusion of spatial depth, not only in the recession of the niches but also in the projection of the canopies, simply by using perspective and lighting effects. In this way he started, with great lucidity, a new interaction, imparting to the forms in his work a dynamic tension which was balanced and resolved by equating the thrust of opposing movements. This interplay is less obvious in the St. Wolfgang altar, but it penetrates and pervades the whole of the architectural structure with a dynamic intention that is no longer stated in the individual parts but fused and sensed in the work as a whole. The basic structure is the same as that of the Gries altar—a large central canopy between two smaller canopies. The perspective scheme is also the same, though modified as a result of the experience of the Fathers of the Church altar: the two lateral canopies project at an angle, as they do there, but the most important innovation is in the centre canopy, which appears to jut out into a sharp angle, an effect reinforced by the centre pinnacle which repeats the form of those on either side but contains a dove in place of the angels. In this way a dynamic tension is created and is transmitted through the high curved arches of the pinnacles on the buttresses and thence to the canopies on either side, through which the movement of the springing intersecting arches is absorbed, to be taken up again in the spatial depth which opens behind the figures. The projection of the canopies is gently, but with intentional emphasis, echoed in their pedestals. Pinder's definition seems appropriate to this highly original architectural conception: "a work of architecture

XIV Presentation in the Temple (detail of Plate 92)

composed of movement", or what today one would call dynamic architecture.

The concept of the dynamic equilibrium of architectural masses is of fundamental importance in understanding the contribution made by the art of the Cisalpine region. This art acted as intermediary between the Tuscan concept of monumentality, based on the clear definition of surface and mass, using optically measurable horizontal and vertical lines, and the northern concept based upon the *ad infinitum* dynamism of dominant vertical lines, or else upon a vortical movement that is resolved within itself.

Pacher's architectural setting for the St. Wolfgang altar, notwithstanding its vibrant dynamism, creates a clear and precisely defined space within which the figures, of sculptural solidity, serve to produce a rhythmical reciprocal release of tensions, giving the feeling of an exploding but controlled vitality. They have a sureness and naturalness which to some have appeared cold, hard and arrogant, compared with the figures of the Kefermarkt altar. These rather sentimental figures lack substance and in spite of the skill of execution, a skill which is an end and not a means, seem to be in need of protection and support for the "pathetic simplicity of their souls" (Oettinger). The powerful figures of the saints in the St. Wolfgang altar are far from being simple souls: they are representatives of superior and heroic humanity, to whom one might well turn to ask for help and guidance. They know and understand all, and before them one need only kneel and ask for intercession and grace.

Pacher placed the group of Christ blessing the Virgin (Plates XIII, 76–78) in such a way that it receives full light from the right and the face of the Redeemer dominates the group. By setting the faces of the two saints in the shadow within the recessed niches he intended to produce a contrast that would place them on a different plane without robbing them of prominence. In this use of psychological contrast Pacher was perhaps remembering the fine examples in the work of Multscher: the face of the bishop saint Wolfgang (Plate 79; Fig. 135) is marked with lines of sorrow and the weariness of one who has lived in continuous contact with human misery, whereas the unblemished face of St. Benedict (Plate 80; Fig. 136) suggests a vital force and energy as he gazes with understanding and compassion from the remoteness of his voluntary renunciation of the world. It cannot be a coincidence that during the same period Giovanni Bellini was similarly expressing the contrasting ideals of the active and contemplative life in two pairs of saints in the polyptych for the Frari church, Venice. Dürer used the same idea and produced a Germanic version, more dramatic and extreme but remarkable for its terseness of expression, in the two pairs of saints which are now in the Pinakothek, Munich.

From the faces of the two principal saints of Pacher's altar it emerges clearly that the artist was acquainted with similar figures by Donatello (Fig. 134). If we examine the very fine casts (Figs. 135, 136) in the reproductions published by Stiassny (the casts themselves were unfortunately destroyed), the absence of colour makes it easier to recognize the similarity.

In the statues of the magnificent warrior saints on the outer sides of the shrine (Plates 82, 83) Pacher concentrated on solidity of construction, and in the faces upon a more penetrating rendering of physiognomy. The figures in the pinnacles above them, however, are executed with noticeably less care, and indeed parts of them are not Pacher's own work. The lower row of figures on the cymatium (Plates 86, 87) are still passable, being the larger and more visible ones, but those in the upper rows are the hastily produced work of a mediocre sculptor

XV Circumcision of Christ (detail of Plate 94)

representing a superseded style and incapable of the standards demanded by Pacher's art (Plates 88, 89).

The Adoration of the Magi group in the predella (Plates 84, 85) deserves to be discussed separately. While each detail is carefully hand gracefully executed, the group as a whole lacks coherence, and the individual figures are heavily proportioned, a fault which is exaggerated by the unconvincingly arranged draperies. The faces are childish and expressionless, and the Child, with eyes myopically half-closed, stretches out two disjointed arms. All in all, it is manifestly the work of an apprentice, whose hand may perhaps also be detected in the figures of St. Catharine and St. Margaret on the cymatium. In the writer's opinion, this artist is the son of Michael Pacher and we shall be returning to him later on.

To turn to the panels: those which were to be seen during solemn ceremonies when the shrine was open are the most carefully planned and executed. The panels on the left depict the Nativity and the Circumcision of Christ, those on the right the Presentation of Christ in the Temple and the Death of the Virgin. The Nativity (Plates 90, 91) certainly draws on what Pacher had learnt years before in Padua; the traditional wooden stable is reduced to a load-bearing structure and therefore to pure architectural values. Its perspective uses all the devices known to the artist through the lively drawings of Jacopo Bellini. In Pacher's version the precise and accurate carpentry of the building demonstrates the ability and strict logic of the artist. The angels, whose wings interweave with the beams, appear, as Hempel

Perspective plan of an architectural composition for the St. Lawrence Altar

observed, to be derived from a painting by Hugo van der Goes. In the background, the distant city and the shepherds on the right (Plate 91) are painted with a harshness and limitation of palette that stamp them as the work of an assistant, probably Friedrich Pacher. A comparison with the luminous background of the Novacella panel (now in Munich) depicting St. Augustine and the Devil (Plates 68, 69), underlines the difference. The foreshortening of the ox and the ass allowing the eye to judge the depth of the two central spans of the stable and providing a deep background to the kneeling figure of the Virgin, is a device typical of Pacher.

The Presentation in the Temple (Plates XIV, 92, 93) repeats with a few variations the architectural structure of the Ecstasy of the Saint in the Novacella altar (Plate 62). Here, however, the basis of the composition is enlarged and perfected by the inclusion in the perspective scheme of the vault of the church; scarcely hinted at in the Novacella altar, this idea was openly used in the Monguelfo tabernacle (Plate 70), and is now fully and daringly resolved to impressive effect. The human figure, enlarged by perspective devices and effects which are perhaps a little overdone, acquires an imposing presence while remaining in proportion to the setting.

Of all the paintings of the St. Wolfgang altar the Circumcision (Plates XV, XVI, 94) is perhaps the one to which Pacher devoted most care; in fact, it can be considered to have been executed entirely by his hand. The scene is the interior of a Gothic church viewed in centre perspective with three aisles and an ambulatory around the choir. It displays not only Pacher's

Perspective plan of an architectural composition for the St. Wolfgang Altar

keen awareness of the architecture of his day, but also his ability to create an accomplished and spacious building, and his great skill in transforming the gold of the background into a source of light. Two groups of onlookers who stand to the right and left of the priest control the spatial depth of the composition while the cavity formed by the vault of the great nave emphasizes the spatial values of the figures and re-echoes their symmetrical arrangement, skilfully achieved by subtle variations of pose. The colour tones are exceptionally brilliant and include features of magical beauty, such as the face of the onlooker on the right seen against the light, which reflects the whiteness of the clothes in which the Infant is wrapped, and the bronzed face of the spectator on the left, wearing a white hood (Plate XVI).

In the Death of the Virgin (Plate 95) the spatial problem is resolved by the use of new techniques: the composition is in centre perspective, to correspond with the previous scene, and the spatial depth of the field of vision is divided into two units by the round arch of a marble doorway. Between us and the arch stand two apostles, while a third kneels with his back turned towards us, marking the transition to the scene that is taking place beyond the arch. The group with Christ supported by flying angels and bearing the Virgin's soul into Heaven is placed high in the foreground in front of the arch, as if outside, or passing outside, the picture. Behind the doorway and illuminated by an extremely strong light from the right, the Virgin's body, surrounded by the apostles, is laid out upon a bed. The bed, which is completely fore-shortened, distantly recalls the bier of St. Thomas Becket (Plate 4), but is more closely reminiscent of Hugo van der Goes' plan in his panel of the Death of the Virgin in the Museum at Bruges, both in the foreshortening of the Virgin and in the group of Christ borne by angels. The difference between the two versions lies in the spatial distinction expressed through the laws of perspective in Pacher's panel, but unknown to Van der Goes. In addition, the use of the marble archway framing the scene and the placing of the figures in the foreground recalls, as Oscar Doering pointed out, a similar device employed by Rogier van der Weyden in the St. John altar. The panel depicting the Birth of the Baptist is particularly relevant in this connection. However, Pacher's assimilation of style is so complex a process that certain problems remain unanswered, and it is difficult to prove the real sources of his inspiration. In this case, for example, there are just as many arguments to support the hypothesis that Pacher saw and studied a composition by Mantegna of the same type as the Madrid Death of the Virgin, where not only is the scene similarly set behind an archway with some apostles in the foreground, but we even find corresponding figures: the apostle with his back turned, and the group of God the Father. There is a similar composition in the Mascoli chapel in St. Mark's, Venice, which seems to be derived from a painting by Mantegna.

Eight episodes from the life of Christ (Plate 74): the Baptism, the Temptation, the Marriage at Cana, the Miracle of the Loaves and Fishes, the Attempted Stoning, the Cleansing of the Temple, Christ and the woman taken in adultery, and the Raising of Lazarus, can be seen when the outer wings are open. This series of panels shows signs that the workshop was playing an increasingly important part, working under supervision in the four central panels but almost alone on the other pictures, with the exception of the fifth. Friedrich was responsible for the execution and probably the composition, of the Baptism of Christ (Fig. 159). The Temptation (Plate 101) was more carefully supervised, and some of the finishing touches, especially in the figures of the two protagonists in the foreground, are undoubtedly by Michael. The blessing of the wine at

XVI Circumcision of Christ (detail of Plate 94)

the Marriage at Cana (Plates 102, 103) is a superb composition, designed by Michael; it was weakened in the process of its execution by the workshop, and then Michael added the finishing touches. Both the design and execution of the Miracle of the Loaves and Fishes (Fig. 160) are certainly by Friedrich, and it is a particularly mediocre painting. The Attempted Stoning of Christ (Plates XVII, 100) is obviously based upon a wonderful design by Michael, traces of which are to be found in the two men, one bending towards us and the other away from us, who are throwing stones. They are both seen in a similar pose, an idea taken from Pollaiuolo, though perhaps indirectly through a drawing, which is fully exploited by the Tuscan master in his Martyrdom of St. Sebastian in London. The final touches can be attributed to Michael, but unfortunately Friedrich was responsible for the execution of the greater part of the painting. The same is true of the Cleansing of the Temple (Plates 96, 97); behind the doorway leading into the church, the narthex is shown in bold perspective, emphasized in depth by the steps which lead the eye through a wide open door and towards the vanishing point in the arches of the cloisters. This device, and the confused flight of the merchants in the entrance, provide us with an unforgettable example of Pacher's art, for although its brilliance is diminished through its execution by Friedrich it was supervised and finished by Michael himself. In the episode of Christ and the woman taken in adultery (Plates 98, 99), it can be seen that the master and his assistant collaborated in a similar way. The composition shows a majestic Gothic church in centre perspective, and the clearly defined division in the symmetrical perspective creates an impassable gulf between the group containing the adultress and her attackers on one side and Christ on the other. Its forced, unnatural composition and careless execution show the Raising of Lazarus (Fig. 161) to be entirely the work of Friedrich; even the colours here are inadequate and lacking in atmosphere.

When both the outer wings of the altar were closed (Plate 73) the worshippers would have seen four episodes from the life of St. Wolfgang. Friedrich was left to produce these paintings on his own, having been given some general instructions and perhaps two complete sketches. The first scene, the devil interrupting a sermon of St. Wolfgang, descends to the level of popular art on account of its careless execution and mistakes in the arrangement of perspective and in the figures. The lady on the right in the foreground may be derived from a figure by Paolo Uccello, seen long before by Michael. Possibly some of the other figures are from Michael's drawings, but Friedrich's slovenly work has caused general confusion. That Michael was responsible for the composition of the Distribution of Alms episode (Fig. 162) is evident from the disposition of the lines of perspective and the intelligent placing of the figures in groups to the left and right, which permits the eye to measure the spatial recession of the scene; the execution by Friedrich, however, had disastrous consequences, for the whole painting is flattened out and rendered awkward. The height of grotesqueness is reached in the scene depicting St. Wolfgang engaged in building his church (Fig. 164): the landscape leans in all directions as though it were in the middle of an earthquake, and the saint's face is so lacking in the slightest gleam of intelligence that it comes as no surprise to find that he is laying a stone of the wrong size. As for his robes, they are as stiff and wooden as the handle of the spade. Two black ducklings swimming in the water are the only parts which survive unscathed. The painting of the Woman possessed by the Devil (Plates 104, 105) is passable on the strength of its composition which is by Michael—in particular, the church under con-

XVII Attempted Stoning of Christ (detail of Plate 100)

struction in the background is an extremely fine detail. The paintings on the predella wings, compared with the panels painted by Friedrich, are of reasonably high standard. In the delightful paintings on the inside of the wings, the Visitation (Plates 106, 107) and the Flight into Egypt (Plates XVIII, 108, 109), we have in my view the results of a successful collaboration between Michael and his son. The composition of the Flight is taken from a Flemish model, as can be seen from the hooded nightgown worn by the Infant Jesus—a similar garment is found in a relief of the same subject in the Rijksmuseum, Amsterdam, dating from the late fourteenth century. It was unknown in Italy, however, and reappears in the celebrated panel by the Mondsee Master only because it has obviously been taken from Pacher's painting. Various features of the Flight into Egypt reveal the hand of an assistant—Pacher's son, Hans— at work. The landscape is marred by its rigidity, and the artist is incapable of conveying the volume of the figures, which are covered rather than clothed in wrinkled draperies rather as if they were worked in bas-relief. As usual, the light comes from the right, but instead of creating contrasts and blocks of shadow it is distributed throughout the picture with depressing uniformity. The short hands with stiff fingers are reminiscent of an old and super-seded style. Nevertheless, while there are clear signs of the artist's connection with Michael, there are no similarities with Friedrich to be found.

The same artist is also in evidence, less closely supervised, in the portraits of the Fathers of the Church on the outer wings (Figs. 165, 166); these are copied unimaginatively from Michael's compositions for the Novacella altar (see Plates 56–61), but the colours are dull and heavy; and also in the four Evangelists (Figs. 168, 169) behind the predella, which contain Flemish echoes frequently found in the work of this artist. The paintings on the back of the shrine, as we have already seen, were painted in 1479, probably on the spot and therefore by a local artist who had to conform with a general design by Michael Pacher, but otherwise worked with a fairly free hand. An attempt has been made to identify this artist as Georg Stäber, but a discussion of this attribution would not be appropriate here. The figures are accurate and the execution is competent—the sad and moving faces of the saints in the lower row (Plates 110, 111), are in fact, very carefully rendered—but summary, as was usual in a painting on the back of an altar. Of all who assisted Pacher with the paintings for the altar this artist is undoubtedly the best, although his style is the furthest removed from that of Pacher himself.

We have already spoken of Friedrich Pacher. His hasty, careless work prejudices one's enjoyment of many parts of the altar that must have been produced from designs by Michael. As yet, no careful and illuminating analysis has been made of the work of Friedrich Pacher, and so his contradictory character remains confused and uncertain. In the dating of his individual works, too, there is often a margin of uncertainty. As for his influences from outside Michael's school of painting, we may observe a certain receptiveness on his part, due to temperamental inclinations, towards exaggerated formal elements acquired perhaps from the study of works by Jacob von Seckau and Leonhard of Bressanone. It is also possible that Friedrich travelled in the Veneto, perhaps immediately after the completion of the St. Wolfgang altar, and there came into contact with the school of Bartolomeo Vivarini and Crivelli. The motif of the window-sill with its small birds and fruit in the Baptism of Christ, painted in 1483, suggests such contacts. Work on the St. Catharine altar at Novacella must have begun only

XVIII Flight into Egypt (detail of Plate 108)

a short while before the St. Wolfgang altar, for the Annunciation on the wings already reflects the architectural backgrounds of the St. Wolfgang altar and, indirectly, of the Monguelfo tabernacle. Another work that must date from this period is the Pacully panel now in Vienna; it is probable that this panel was produced for a church in the Veneto mountains, for it was at one time purchased on the antiquarian market in Venice. Certainly later than the St. Wolfgang altar is the altar of St. Peter's at Vipiteno—now divided up so that part of it is in Innsbruck and part in Jerusalem—which is one of Friedrich's finest works. Thereafter the standard of his work sank so low that an attempt has been made to invent a "St. Corbinian Master" in order to explain the mediocrity of the paintings produced in Friedrich's workshop during the latter part of his career when he had been made a judge and executed little of the work himself, leaving most of the commissions for the workshop to produce. It is in the field of fresco painting that Friedrich has a certain importance, for in his frescoes he shows great technical ability and produced his best work. Examples are the composition of the Rich Man in the cloisters at Novacella, the fresco of St. Gregory's Mass at S. Martino in Pusteria, and the cycle of frescoes in the cloister of the Dominican convent at Bolzano, which was painted in about 1494 and is one of his last works. Nor should we forget the frescoes, probably painted under Michael's supervision, at Novacella, Monguelfo and St. Paul in Lavant. Friedrich Pacher's style poses complex chronological problems but it is clearly recognizable and has for some time been generally distinguished from that of Michael.

We shall discuss later a pupil and assistant of Michael Pacher whose style is recognizable in various works dating from 1471 onwards, but whose precise identity has yet to be established. The chronological links between this artist and Michael lead the present writer to believe that he is to be identified as Hans Pacher, the son and successor of Michael, who evidently worked in his father's workshop almost all his life, for he died in the first decade of the sixteenth century.

73 *High altar closed. St. Wolfgang, Parish Church*   74 *High altar with outer wings open. St. Wolfgang, Parish Church*

75 High altar open. St. Wolfgang, Parish Church

76 *Coronation of the Virgin, detail of the shrine of the high altar*

*77, 78, 79, 80 Christ blessing; the Virgin Crowned; St. Wolfgang;
and St. Benedict (details of the shrine, see Plates 75, 76)*

81 *Angels holding curtains in the shrine (see Plate 75)*

82, 83 St. George and St. Florian, from the sides of the shrine (see Plate 73)

*84, 85 Adoration of the Magi, and detail, in the predella of the high altar
(workshop of Michael Pacher; Hans Pacher?). St. Wolfgang, Parish Church*

86 Cymatium, high altar (Michael Pacher and workshop). St. Wolfgang, Parish Church

87 St. Michael on the cymatium (detail of Plate 86)

88, 89 St. Ottilia and the Virgin of the Annunciation on the cymatium, details (workshop).
St. Wolfgang, Parish Church

90, 91 Nativity of Christ, and detail, from the high altar (Michael Pacher and workshop).
St. Wolfgang, Parish Church

92, 93 Presentation in the Temple, and detail, from the high altar. St. Wolfgang, Parish Church

94 Circumcision of Christ, from the high altar. St. Wolfgang, Parish Church

95 Death of the Virgin, from the high altar. St. Wolfgang, Parish Church

96, 97 Christ Cleansing the Temple, and detail, from the high altar. St. Wolfgang, Parish Church

98, 99 Christ and the Woman taken in Adultery, and detail, from the high altar (Michael Pacher and workshop). St. Wolfgang, Parish Church

100 *Attempted Stoning of Christ, from the high altar (Michael and Friedrich Pacher). St. Wolfgang, Parish Church*

101 Temptation of Christ, from the high altar (Michael Pacher and workshop). St. Wolfgang, Parish Church

102, 103 Marriage of Cana, and detail, from the high altar (Michael Pacher and workshop). St. Wolfgang, Parish Church

*104, 105 Curing the Woman possessed by the Devil, and detail, from the high altar (Michael and Friedrich Pacher).
St. Wolfgang, Parish Church*

106, 107 The Visitation, and detail, from the predella of the high altar (Michael and Hans Pacher).
St. Wolfgang, Parish Church

*108, 109 Flight into Egypt, and detail, from the predella of the high altar (Michael and Hans Pacher).
St. Wolfgang, Parish Church.*

110, 111 St. Erasmus and St. Elizabeth, on the back of the shrine of the high altar.
St. Wolfgang, Parish Church

CHAPTER FIVE

The Last Years

Two documents preserved in the archives of the convent at Novacella attest that in 1481, after the completion of the St. Wolfgang altar, Michael Pacher possessed financial assets, presumably as the result of the payment of the money which was due to him. We are told that on 12 July and 25 November of that year he deposited sums of money in cash with one Sigismund Mor of Brunico.

Meanwhile he had not of course omitted to look for another commission. On 14 November 1481 he was at Bolzano negotiating with the vestry board of the parish church the contract for the execution of an altar to be dedicated to St. Michael, for which he shortly afterwards received 15 marks, perhaps as earnest-money. That we have any record of the altar is entirely due to the fact that an old woman named Ganznerin, evidently so-called after the Ganzner farmstead at Cardano (Kardaun), had left the sum of 36 marks towards its execution; the heirs paid the money over to the church in various instalments during the following years, and the church had therefore to keep a record of the payments in its registers. Evidently the remainder of the money required to pay for the altar was acquired in some other way, for no record of this is preserved in the parish archives. The final payment, amounting to 10 marks, was paid to Michael Pacher in 1484, following delivery of the receipt and probably in settlement of the commission.

The altar was described with some precision in the Visitor's Records for 1674, which have hitherto been neglected: it contained a shrine with two shutters and inside were three statues of gilded wood—the Virgin in the centre and St. Michael and St. Martin on either side. It was placed "in cornu epistolae in medio ecclesiae", that is, against one of the pillars in the south aisle of the church. In 1686 it was taken down and placed against the wall near the south door of the church. In 1687, however, the altar was removed altogether, and the Rottenpucher family, who in 1620 had endowed it with a benefice, arranged at their own expense for the replacement of the Gothic structure by a stucco altar in Baroque style with an altarpiece by the painter Alberti. This altar in turn disappeared in 1786; and thereafter the only remaining sign of the cult of St. Michael in that part of the church was a fourteenth-century fresco of the saint, which was found in 1945 underneath a fresco of the same subject dating from 1400. The remains were detached and transferred to the Museo Civico.

There is no trace of the Gothic altar. A statue of St. Michael purchased on the antique market in the last century was believed to be a surviving fragment but both the shape and the stylistic features of the statue render this hypothesis, which has no evidence to support it, unacceptable, as explained earlier. Nor has any greater favour been accorded Benesch's recent suggestion concerning a statuette of St. Michael preserved in the Palazzo Venezia, Rome.

While completing the St. Michael altar at Bolzano, Michael Pacher was negotiating with the Salzburg civic authorities about the execution of a high altar which they intended to place in the parish church. Unfortunately we do not possess the contract; but from the surviving correspondence it emerges that the artist, who at the time was detained at Bolzano—presumably in order to put the finishing touches to the altar there—was invited in a letter of 26 August of that year to deliver plans for this altar to a certain Hans Pichler of Salzburg, who would be in Bolzano for the fair of St. Vigilius. Another letter of the same date shows that the proposal to award the commission to Pacher came from Virgil Hofer of Salzburg, a resident of Rattenberg in the Tyrol, who had also promised in case of need a remarkably generous donation of 1,000 florins; and in view of his right to be informed, a copy of the contract made with the artist was sent to him. It would appear that it was this promise of financial aid that resulted in the decision to entrust the work to Pacher; negotiations had earlier been started with Rueland Frueauf of Passavia. This is not difficult to understand when it is considered that the sum paid for the entire St. Wolfgang altar had amounted to little more. In a letter dated 9 September 1484 Hofer communicated to the city council of Salzburg that he had already sent Pacher 100 florins in part payment, and that he was willing to make further payments as the need arose up to the limit he had specified; he stated that his object was that the altar should be produced with all possible speed. By this date Pacher had already negotiated with the master carpenter, Leonhard, and the cabinet-maker, Ulrich, for shaping the wood needed for the work; the execution of the shrine, which was to be entrusted to Ulrich, was under discussion. But Pacher had not delivered the plans of the altar as requested, so that on 18 November he received a pressing letter from the Salzburg city council expressing anxiety at the fact that, although the necessary woodwork had by now been cut it was impossible to proceed further with the work without designs for the altar. Furthermore, since the goldsmith engaged to gild the shrine was unable to start work, he was in danger of not meeting the time-limit prescribed in the contract. Another letter, similar in tone, was sent to Hofer with the intention that he should put pressure on the artist who, evidently engaged elsewhere, was protracting matters. Finally, it appears, the work was begun; it is likely that the sculptures were carved in the workshop at Brunico and then transferred to the site in the normal way. By 1495, in any case, the greater part of the work was done, and Pacher, together with his skilled workmen, then moved to Salzburg in order to assemble the various parts of the altar and to execute those parts which it had not been possible to produce in the workshop in Brunico. Presumably he remained in Salzburg until his death, which occurred in 1498 while he was putting the finishing touches to the predella; the altar had been installed shortly before, and had probably already been in use.

It seems strange that the execution of a single altar should have taken so long a time, about fourteen years in fact. We must remember, however, that financial problems of no little importance arose in connection with this commission, and that these problems caused temporary suspensions of work on the altar when the artist was forced to undertake other commissions in order to live and to provide his assistants with work. By a piece of good fortune records survive of one of these minor commissions undertaken by Pacher while he was in Salzburg and engaged on the task of assembling and finishing the imposing piece in the parish church. The work in question was an altar, or high altar, for the church of St. Michael am Aschhof, undertaken on behalf of Peter, Abbot of Salzburg; but apart from two records of payment we have no precise information concerning this altar.

From the accounts for the Salzburg parish church we learn that the altar was finally set up and displayed to the congregation in the summer of 1497. During the course of the following year the church's remaining estates were sold off, and further payments were duly made to the artist—the last of these on 7 July 1498. The payments that followed were handed over to Caspar Neuhauser, Pacher's son-in-law who was a judge at Chiusa (Klausen), on 14 August and 17 November 1498. By this time the artist had died, probably towards the end of July, judging by some documents that have recently been discovered. On 10 December 1502 Neuhauser, as guardian of the interest in the estate which had passed to his daughter Margaret upon the death of his wife, also called Margaret and the daughter of Michael Pacher, issued the final receipt. This showed that the total cost of the Salzburg altar was 3,500 Rhenish florins—an exceptionally high figure even for those times, particularly bearing in mind that a deduction had been made from the agreed price because the predella had not been finally completed.

The altar was first cleaned and repaired in 1515. In 1605 a tabernacle was added to it in accordance with the ordinances of the Council of Trent, and in 1603 it was again cleaned and restored. At the beginning of the eighteenth century the altar was demolished and in 1710 its place taken by the present altar. The Father Guardian of the Franciscans, to whom the church now belonged was responsible; he destroyed all the wooden carving except for the central figure of the Virgin, so as to extract the gold and silver. This barbarous operation, which incidentally was less uncommon in those times than is generally believed, yielded the impressive sum of 512 florins—not much less than the total cost of the Gries altar—owing to the thickness of the gilding and the high quality of the gold used for it. This gives some idea of the colossal size of the Salzburg altar. Parts of the panel paintings were used by the carpenters of the convent for making furniture, while other parts were perhaps still considered useful because they portrayed conventional religious scenes, and were probably hung for a time in the church or in the corridors of the convent; later on these panels too disappeared. It is entirely due to the studies carried out during the past few decades and to a recent fortunate discovery by Theodor Hoppe, Superintendent of Monuments at Salzburg, that some fragments of the panel paintings have been found and identified. From these we are able to gain a rough idea of the dimensions of the altar and the principal subjects that were portrayed on the panels. Unfortunately we know nothing about the shrine except that it was dominated by the figure of the Virgin in the centre. Demus, to whom we are indebted for the most convincing attempt at reconstructing the iconographic scheme of the altar, has suggested that a figure of a saint may have stood on either side of the Virgin. The inner wings, according to Demus, were decorated in relief, as in the Gries altar, and probably depicted four scenes from the life of the Virgin. Possible subjects that come to mind are the Annunciation, the

Nativity, Pentecost, and the Death of the Virgin, but these are only conjectures intended to give a general idea of the scheme. As in the St. Wolfgang altar, when the inner wings were closed eight panels were seen, depicting four episodes from the Passion of Christ, together with their Old Testament equivalents according to the tradition of the Biblia Pauperum. It is likely that the figure of Job corresponded to the Flagellation of Christ, and Joseph in the Well to the Descent from the Cross. We have no clues as to the subjects of the other four pictures, but Demus suggests Christ carrying the Cross and the Sacrifice of Isaac, the Resurrection of Christ and Samson at the gates of Gaza. When the altar was closed the viewer would probably have seen four scenes from the life of Mary: her Birth, Betrothal, perhaps the Presentation in the Temple, and the Visitation. Finally, Demus argues convincingly that the fragment depicting the Flight into Egypt now preserved at Basle comes from one of the wings of the predella. The same scene was in fact also depicted on the St. Wolfgang predella.

As for the dimensions of the altar, suffice it to say that the figure of the Virgin which has survived measures 1.46 metres, whereas the figure of Christ on the St. Wolfgang altar measures only 1.15 metres, excluding the crown. The height of the individual panels was at least 2.61 metres, as can be seen from the surviving fragment, which was being used as part of a cupboard when it was found. This measurement would bring the height of the shrine up to about six metres and that of the whole altar, assuming that the proportions corresponded to those of the St. Wolfgang altar, to about 17 metres. At St. Wolfgang, however, Pacher had been forced by the restricted height of the choir to reduce the proportions of the altar and even to cut off part of the main pinnacle when it was assembled on the site. But the proportions of the choir in the church at Salzburg, with its remarkable and regal loftiness, would have permitted Pacher to elaborate on some particularly adventurous pinnacles. When we consider that the St. Wolfgang altar is 11 meters high, Stoss's altar at Cracow 13 metres, the Kefermarkt altar 13.50 metres, and Schnatterpeck's altar at Lana, the largest in existence, 14.10 metres, we get some idea of the colossal enterprise with which Michael Pacher crowned his career; it may perhaps have been the very largest Gothic altar ever constructed.

The only remaining figure, that of the Virgin Enthroned (Plates 112, 113) has suffered greatly from defacement and thoughtless restoration work even in the not so distant past; it is therefore impossible to pass judgement on the carved part of the altar. Comparison of the head with that of the St. Wolfgang Virgin suggests that Pacher had revised his ideas in the interval. The face is unlike that of the St. Lawrence Virgin, with its solid, classical features, or the dreamy Flemish face at Gries, nor does it resemble that of the St. Wolfgang Virgin, in which the return to the earlier solidity is balanced by the retention of elongated facial proportions. The Salzburg Virgin has a broad face and a small chin; the composition is both forceful and gentle, as can be seen in the strong turn of the neck as the Virgin bends to gaze at the Infant whom she holds sitting in her lap. It can be said that the interpretation of the figure has become dramatic; it is that of a mother who, absorbed in admiration and concern for her child, can think of nothing else. Unfortunately, the figure of the Infant has disappeared; in the St. Lawrence altar this figure was an element of only secondary importance whose absence would not disturb the composition as a whole, but the Salzburg Infant forms a unity with the Mother and is as necessary to her as she herself to him. In contrast with the

XIX Fragment of the Flagellation (detail of Plate 114)

St. Lawrence statue, the group broadens out at the bottom where the drapery is arranged so as to form a wide base.

By the blind folly of the Father Guardian of the day who destroyed this unique art treasure we have been robbed of the most noble and dramatic moment of Pacher's artistic achievement.

As we have already seen, the greater part of the carved work was in all probability produced at Brunico, like the St. Wolfgang altar, and taken to Salzburg in 1495. For obvious practical reasons it would not have been possible to transport painted panels either together or in pieces, and these must have been painted on the spot at Salzburg. If transporting the panels of the wings of the St. Wolfgang altar, measuring 1.65 by 1.36 metres, across the Alps on narrow and often impassable roads presented practical problems of some difficulty, it would not have been feasible to make the same journey with panels that were at least 2.60 metres long and of corresponding breadth. It seems reasonable, therefore, to say that the panels were painted *in situ* between 1495 and 1497, designs for them having perhaps been prepared at Brunico, and that the shortage of time at his disposal compelled the master to make extensive use of various collaborators.

The remains of the altar exhibit variations of style, some of them very obvious. The Flagellation of Christ (Plates XIX, XX, 114, 115) seems to me to be entirely the work of Pacher, but the Betrothal of the Virgin (Plates 116–118) may be by another artist working in collaboration with the master, from his composition and under his supervision. The same is true of the fragment depicting the Birth of the Virgin (Plate 119), in which, however, the hand of the master predominates. The Joseph fragment (Plates 121, 122) is apparently a composition by the master but drawn and painted by the workshop. Finally, the fragment of the Flight into Egypt (Plate 120) appears to be entirely by the workshop, although painted from the master's drawing.

First of all, therefore, it will be necessary to examine Michael's ideas of composition during the Salzburg period, as suggested by the surviving fragments of the altar. The Flagellation scene is dominated by the figure of Christ in the centre; Christ is bound to a pillar, but so high is the pedestal on which his feet rest that the flagellators are scarcely able to strike the upper part of his body. Foppa used a similar device in his Martyrdom of St. Sebastian now in the Castello Sforzesco, Milan, and so did Pollaiuolo in his version of the martyrdom in London. It can therefore be said that Pacher's interpretation is strongly influenced by Italian artists, or, that even if independent of them in its origin, it bears a close resemblance to them. The device borrowed from Pollaiuolo that we noted in discussing the Attempted Stoning of Christ from the St. Wolfgang altar is too obvious to be used here. Instead, the artist prefers to arrange the three ruffians in different ways and to give them different functions: one is administering the flagellation, another is fastening the ropes to the pillar and the third is bent over to the ground, repairing the scourge. Two of these figures are set in the foreground and serve to measure the distance between the front plane and the figure of Christ, while the third figure stands between the pillar and the stairway in the background. The stairs lead up to a balcony from which a doorway leads into a room with a mullioned window on one wall. Two figures on the balcony, perhaps Pilate and Judas, indicate the spatial depth of the balcony itself. The wall of the room receives light through a large window with Gothic tracery on the left, which looks out over the countryside. The perspective devices, then, are those which we

XX Fragment of the Flagellation (detail of Plate 114)

have come to expect, but here, in contrast to the St. Wolfgang altar, the lines of perspective are less emphasized in the background architecture. More attention is given to the disposition of the human figure in spatial recession. Although a strip is missing from the upper part of the panel so that we see only glimpses of the vaulting of the building, the vault performs no special function in the picture. The figure of Christ dominates the scene not so much by being viewed at a striking angle from below as by the careful composition which places him in a raised position.

In the Betrothal of the Virgin the foreground is dominated by the two protagonists, linked by their joined hands. Behind them in the second plane the gesture of the priest forms a connecting link with them: his left hand is held above the hands of the betrothed couple while he blesses them with his right. The background is set diagonally to the group, and is emphasized by the architecture of the church interior. Frey's reconstruction, in which he attempts to complete the bottom of the panel, is unacceptable because the floor is left with an empty space such as would never be found in any composition by Pacher. In my view we should include in the reconstruction one of the suitors in the act of breaking a rod, bending down to the floor in front of the couple. The diagonal arrangement of the background architecture serves to underline and emphasize the frontal presentation of the main group of figures. In comparison with the St. Wolfgang altar the artist has made noticeable progress in the arrangement of perspective, which is less accentuated and conveyed more effectively and naturally.

The panel of Joseph being lowered into the well contains a wooden hut, a motif which we have already seen used in the St. Wolfgang Nativity (Plate 90); in this picture the hut appears particularly firm and solid. Rather than using Mantegna's method—that of drawing the horizon low down in the picture to ensure that the scene is dominated by the human figures—Pacher achieves the same effect by the far more substantial device of setting the figures on a raised platform. In this way it was possible to place the horizon on a level with the mouth of the well, so that the figures are made imposing without the need to resort to any more obvious contrivance. Once again a variety of appropriate elements are skilfully used to measure spatial recession, such as the man slaughtering a lamb over a trough in the foreground. This figure takes in almost the entire depth of the scene, his right leg coming forward to the margin of the picture while his back is almost resting against the parapet of the well. Because seen at eye level, the well is not viewed in perspective; its volume is indicated by the figures surrounding it and by the foreshortening of the figure of Joseph who is being lowered into it. Beyond the wooden beams of the roof of the shed—a feature well suited to the measurement of spatial depth—stretches a background landscape with paths, meadows and trees.

In short, it appears that whereas at St. Wolfgang Pacher had placed the figures in a setting whose dimensions and proportions he indicated by means of the recession of lines of perspective, in the Salzburg altar he restored to the human figure the role of protagonist and, abandoning the contrived effects achieved with perspective, strove to make the figures dominate in their own right rather than by indirect means. This is Pacher's final point of arrival, and that of European art in general at the beginning of the sixteenth century. From the study of perspective effects and the principles of foreshortening, the artist had progressed to the spatial disposition of the human figure in a way that is more natural and less contrived; his figures are now given an unforced position in the setting of the picture and an inherent dignity such as they had previously possessed, if at all, only as the result of contrived formal devices.

In the execution, too, Pacher shows proof of having looked ahead of his time. Christ and the three ruffians in the Flagellation scene possess a plastic energy within an extremely sensitive functional line reminiscent of Pollaiuolo, of Antonello and even, it could be said, of Bramante's crystalline volumetric constructions. In this work Michael Pacher reveals himself as aligned beside the greatest Italian artists of his day, no doubt because he maintained his connections with them and so followed the course of artistic events in Northern Italy until the end of his life; but also, in addition to this, because he was following the same path as they were, the achievements which he reached independently were similar to theirs. Compared with the Flagellation, the Betrothal panel is formally inferior; the dull, expressionless faces—especially those in the background—look as though they were painstakingly but not well finished by a pupil of Pacher. The Joseph episode gives the same impression, but even more strongly: the young man on the right of the picture, with the thinness of his crossed legs, incapable of supporting him, and his stereotyped and lifeless face, can only have been painted by the workshop. Even the drawing, parts of which are visible beneath the painting, although interesting, does not in my view resemble the firm and energetic yet delicate line of Pacher. To appreciate the difference one need only look at the extremely fine brush-point drawing of the Virgin in the Monguelfo tabernacle and compare the ear of the Infant Christ with the hesitant, mis-shaped ear of the man killing the lamb. Nor, in my opinion, is the Flight into Egypt fragment the work of Pacher himself. Its similarities with the St. Wolfgang predella paintings suggest it is by the same hand. Here the artist is less closely supervised by the master but has become more mature and more self-confident in some manneristic traits that are clearly visible; not long afterwards he painted on his own the panel depicting the Mystic Marriage of St. Catharine, now at Castagnola.

However this may be, the fragment of the Flagellation panel is sufficient indication of Pacher's greatness and of the advanced point that he had reached on the eve of the sixteenth century. This painting alone would be enough to bring fame to an artist.

Pacher's collaborators

In examining the works of Michael Pacher I have continually borne in mind the necessity of presenting a clear image of the artist, and I have excluded everything which did not seem to me to be executed by him or which was predominantly the work of his assistants. In some cases this was an easy task because the artists concerned were recognizable minor figures whose works are known to us, Friedrich Pacher for example. One such artist who assisted Pacher but has remained unidentified, has been aptly described by Rosci as "a clearly distinguishable figure who worked under the aegis of Michael first on the St. Wolfgang altar (on the predella), then later, in works that are sufficiently individual, he emphasized the Flemish side of the master's art without, however, turning from the style of the St. Wolfgang which as Hempel observed, is continued in the Lugano panel formerly in St. Peter's church at Salzburg".

It is now time to examine this artist, and we must begin with the principal work attributed to him which is the Lugano panel mentioned above, originally in St. Peter's, Salzburg, and now in the Rohoncz Collection at Castagnola (Plates 123, 124). It portrays the Virgin Enthroned with the Infant Christ; Christ is offering a ring to St. Catharine, who is accompanied by St. Margaret. The painting belongs to the circle of Pacher's closest followers and dates from about 1500, the period immediately after the Salzburg altar. It is executed with the most careful attention to every detail and displays an extremely thorough grasp and abundant use of all the devices employed by Michael Pacher in the spatial disposition of a composition with figures. The figures, arranged on various planes, are linked together and, like Pacher's, have weight and volume. In the best tradition of the master the light clearly falls from the right and lends life to the figures and colours. From a practical point of view, the dragon of St. Margaret and the wheel of St. Catharine in the foreground, though ably foreshortened and correctly lit, fail to indicate the distance between the two saints and the edge of the picture; this is because they lack any effective connection with the figures or any solid anchorage on the ground, which they completely cover. The robes of the two saints seated in the second spatial plane fall symmetrically and meet in the centre, but the folds do not sufficiently emphasize the saints' knees, which are almost impossible to discern. Brilliantly illuminated against the background of the Virgin's robe which lies in shadow are the gold cross held in St. Margaret's right hand and her raised left hand; the intended plastic effect, however, is lost because the foreshortening of the cross is indecisive and the gesture of the hand quite meaningless. St. Catharine fares no better: in her left hand she holds a book on her knee; the artist, however, has not had the courage to open the book completely and the half-open volume fails to achieve the effect he wanted. Her right hand reaches into the background towards the Infant Jesus, and instead of being foreshortened as the artist intended, it appears stiff and cramped. An attempt is made to link the outstretched arms of the Infant to the figures of the saints but the movement seems strained and affected. Magnificent gold brocades, reminiscent of the priest's robes in the Circumcision, glitter in the light without adding substance to the bodily forms beneath them; the golden crowns look bizarre and unreal and do not sit naturally on the heads of the saints. To sum up, this artist has an excellent grasp of techniques but a timidity in applying them which renders his virtuosity useless, if not actually harmful. The absence of logical coherence and conciseness in every gesture and detail are clearly shown up by this irresolution.

Certain affinities with the Betrothal of the Virgin (Plate 116) of the Salzburg altar are revealed, such as the face of the Virgin and the heads in the background which are the inferior parts of this composition and which I have attributed to collaborators from Pacher's workshop. One need only look at the heads which appear behind the main figures in the Presentation in the Temple (Plate 92) or the Circumcision (Plate 94) to understand at once how Pacher would have painted the characters of the Betrothal picture had he done it himself. Nor can it be a question of Pacher's decline, for the Flagellation scene shows us that he was still able to produce magnificent work. A figure which displays no conspicuous stylistic differences from those in the Betrothal painting is the Colli St. Barbara in the Österreichisches Museum, Vienna. The painting has previously been attributed to Michael Pacher but should in my view be assigned to the artist under discussion and to a period earlier than the panel from St. Peter's, Salzburg.

Two small panels depicting St. Sebastian and St. Barbara (Figs. 172, 173), originally from Brunico and now preserved at Innsbruck, are attributed to Michael Pacher. However, on close examination of these two delicate figures, which are resplendent with colour and carefully executed, we are compelled to make the same kind of reservations as have been made about the Betrothal painting; painted by the same artist after the St. Peter's panel, they form an obvious link with the Colli St. Barbara. If we compare the Innsbruck St. Sebastian with the Salzburg panel of Joseph (Plate 121) we at once notice a similarity in the features, in the brushwork and in the inconsistency of volume, which suggests that the assistant who worked on this panel probably also painted the Innsbruck panel. Finally, there is another work which must be by the same artist and dates from the exact period in which the Salzburg altar was made. This is the panel of St. Andrew and St. Catharine originally in St. Peter's, Salzburg, and shown at the Innsbruck Exhibition of 1950; it forms a pair with a small panel depicting St. Benedict and St. Scholastica which recently came to light on the antiquarian market.

Let us now turn to the physical characteristics of these figures. Their faces are long, with round, prominent chins, narrow and often half-open mouths; the eyes, when looking downwards, seem distorted by being excessively curved, whereas when raised they curve in the other direction, with a characteristic swollen appearance of the lower lids which gives the faces a drowsy expression. The draperies are arranged on the surface as though carved in bas-relief, the figures are inconsistent in their proportions and are either too long or too short, and their hands are generally short and badly jointed, with somewhat rigid fingers. If one wished to include these works in the chronology of Pacher's *oeuvre* they would have to be assigned to the period when he was most strongly under Flemish influences, that is, the time of the Gries altar or shortly afterwards.

At this point we are confronted with the problem of the London panel (Plate 55), already discussed at some length, which cannot be included among Michael Pacher's works. Comparing this panel with the one from St. Peter's, Salzburg, we find that, although separated in time by perhaps two decades, they exhibit some surprising similarities. The London panel seems to reflect Pacher's style of the period between the Gries and the Fathers of the Church altars, the St. Peter's panel the style of the Salzburg altar. There are many points of contact between the two works suggesting that both are by the same artist: the narrow, half-open mouths and the essential thinness of the figures, and the indecisiveness in the rendering of perspective and of volume in relief. None of these stylistic elements would exclude *a priori* the theory that these works were painted by Michael himself during his formative years, that is before about 1460.

We have, then, collected together a reasonable number of works which can be assigned to an artist trained in Pacher's workshop at the time of the execution of the Gries altar (1471–5) when Pacher was most influenced by the Flemish artists. This artist stayed on as an assistant in the workshop until the master's death without undergoing any radical change, and conforming as far as possible to Pacher's requirements. Though not lacking in ability, he is a minor artist, who loses his individuality in the presence of Pacher. When working on his own he is able to give expression to his own noteworthy talents, and in particular his commendable skill in execution. He is first found as a collaborator with Michael in the predella paintings of the St. Wolfgang altar (Figs. 165, 166, 168, 169), copying without much imagination elements of the Novacella Fathers of the Church altar; on the back he painted the four Evangelists with rapid and hasty strokes of the brush, again making use of the formal ideas of Flemish artists. Even in the beautiful paintings of the Flight into Egypt and the Visitation, on the inner wings of the predella (Plates 106–109), his hand can be detected working under the master's supervision. In my opinion the flattish arrangement of the drapery and the background landscape, which is hard and rather lacking in airiness, are his work; certainly, however, the execution was extensively supervised by Michael and he was responsible for part of it.

The Basle fragment (Plate 120), which Rosci has correctly linked with a panel in the style of Pacher depicting St. Barbara, now in a private collection at Novara, is definitely not by Michael. On the other hand, it does contain certain stylistic characteristics of the pupil and collaborator whose works we have been trying to distinguish from the paintings of Pacher's school.

So far we have limited our discussion to the paintings; in the field of sculpture we encounter a carver who can probably be identified with the unknown painter. We already notice some features reminiscent of this artist in the figure of the Virgin thought to have originally been on the highest pinnacle of the Gries altar. In contrast with the stylistic similarities between the Virgin and the other statues there are elements of formal harshness in the former, such as the stiffness of the Infant's arms and the roundness of the Virgin's head with the characteristic double chin, which suggest that it is the work of an assistant who has yet to develop fully. It dates from around 1475. In the painting of the Adoration of the Magi on the predella of the St. Wolfgang altar (Plates 84, 85) of about 1481, I believe we can again distinguish the same artist at work; his style has become finer and more mature in the interval, but the fundamental characteristics are identical. The shortness of the figures, which are poorly enveloped in the draperies, the uncertainty of their facial expressions, the jointless arms of the Infant and the narrow, half-open mouths recall the panel from St. Peter's, Salzburg. By the same hand are the well-known elegant figures of knights and ladies on the predella frame, and probably also the statuettes of St. Margaret and St. Catharine in the pinnacles. The statue of St. Michael in the Palazzo Venezia Museum, Rome (Fig. 170), which Benesch unconvincingly attributed to Michael Pacher, has very close similarities with the reliefs on the frame of the St. Wolfgang predella and can be assigned to the same artist. Last of all, the delightful little figure of the Virgin Enthroned in the Ursuline convent at Glasenbach, near Salzburg (Fig. 167), which was analysed with great acuteness by Demus, seems to represent the artist's ultimate stage of development which he reached, in about 1500, at the end of the Salzburg period. Demus rightly considers the face of the Virgin in the Betrothal panel "as a pictorial projection of the face of the Ursuline Virgin" and points to resemblances with the Colli painting of St. Barbara (Fig. 175) and the Innsbruck St. Sebastian (Fig. 173), which he suggests is the work of a young assistant of Pacher. He further notes the contrast of types between the Ursuline Virgin and Pacher's Virgin from the Salzburg altar (Plate 113). The first of these has "a high forehead, a nose which is spoilt by the extraordinarily sharp angle of its projection, and a receding jaw with the hint of a double chin", whereas the other has a regular, almost classical profile. Finally he observes that the Ursuline statue is more closely related to the works dating from the Gries altar period than to those of the Salzburg period.

We have now given an adequate description of this artist who, although his work lacks the compositional and volumetric solidity of his master, still shows considerable ability as a sculptor. The conclusions we are trying to draw are obvious: the artist was first Pacher's pupil and later his collaborator, he received his training during the period which produced the Gries altar and his style continued on much the same general lines. He can be none other than Michael's own son, the young Hans Pacher, master painter and citizen of Brunico. Hans had a workshop of his own by 1484–5 at the latest; in 1490 he was in all probability living in Michael Pacher's house. On the death of his father he returned to Brunico, where from 1504 to 1506 he worked as a collector of episcopal tithes, and in 1507 or 1508 he died, leaving an only child, Anna. When the latter attained her majority in 1512 she requested from Caspar Neuhauser, the executor of Michael Pacher's will, payment of the money due to her from the fees for two altars which her grandfather had executed.

The main facts of Hans Pacher's career, then, are as follows: he studied under his father during the Gries altar period, came of age in about 1480 or a little earlier and continued to work in his father's studio, occasionally undertaking works on his own account; upon Michael's death he returned to Brunico, where he again worked for a number of years. The two panels at Innsbruck came originally from Brunico, and these are undoubtedly the remaining parts of an altar made by Hans Pacher at the very beginning of the sixteenth century.

Hans cannot have left behind many other works, for he worked in collaboration with his father for nearly the whole of his life. A Crucifix preserved in the chapel of Castel Lamberto near Brunico may be an example of his carving surviving in Pusteria. Badly repainted on several occasions, all fineness of detail has been lost, but in the half-closed eyes and the treatment of the beard one can see it possesses features remarkably similar to those of the figures of the St. Wolfgang predella, and must be by the same artist dating from between 1481 and 1485. Careful research in this direction might lead to the identification of further works by Hans in the Brunico region. Besides the characteristic features of Michael Pacher's school such works would also have to contain elements akin to those which we have tried to isolate in the paintings and sculptures attributed to this artist.

But the surviving parts of the Salzburg altar, Michael Pacher's last work, cannot be explained in terms of the collaboration of his son alone. It is quite possible that Marx Reichlich was engaged as an additional assistant. Reichlich was probably born at Novacella, perhaps around 1465; that he recieved his early training under Friedrich Pacher is clearly shown by the Mentelberger altarpiece, signed and dated 1489, which was formerly at Wilten. In a slightly later work, the altarpiece at Valdaora di Mezzo (Mitter-Olang) in Pusteria, the young artist already displays his orientation towards Michael Pacher. He had probably been admitted as an assistant in Michael Pacher's workshop when he became a citizen of Salzburg in 1494; presumably he stayed with the workshop until the master's death, but he must also have worked independently during this time since in 1499 he received payment for an altar panel for the abbey of St. Lambrecht in Styria. However, he returned to his native locality shortly after the death of Michael Pacher, scarcely leaving it again although he remained a citizen of Salzburg. In 1499 Reichlich painted a votive panel for Christoph von Thurn, canon of Bressanone, which fully indicates the artist's conversion to the style of Michael Pacher and the proximity of his art to that of Michael's last period. This panel is exceptionally important both because of the care with which it is executed and because it allows a reconstruction of the influences which Reichlich underwent. Comparison of the panel with the surviving parts of the Salzburg altar suggests that the artist assisted with the finishing touches of the painting of the Betrothal of the Virgin—mainly the heads in the background, but perhaps also the head of the Virgin. The artist may also have collaborated, along with Hans Pacher, on the painting of the Flight into Egypt, now in Basle; this picture is probably a remnant of the predella wings, which were completed after Michael Pacher's death.

The remains of the Waldauf altar in Hall made in about 1500–2 show that at this time Reichlich was still under the influence of his training with Michael Pacher; he later tended towards a greater emphasis on the lively expressionism characteristic of his work which had been encouraged by his contact with Friedrich. In 1506 he executed the altar of St. Stephen and St. James for the abbey of Novacella, the greater part of which is now in Munich and the remainder at Novacella. This work displays a renewed enthusiasm for dramatic emphasis in which the influence of Michael Pacher is by no means absent, and indicates that the artist had observed and studied the Fathers of the Church altar. In 1508 Reichlich, by now considered the greatest artist living in the area, was entrusted by the Emperor Maximilian with the task of restoring and in part repainting the frescoes on chivalrous themes at Castelroncolo, near Bolzano, for the sum of 300 florins. While staying in the Adige valley he must have made contact with artists of the Italian Renaissance, and probably as a result of this decided to make a journey to Italy, where he saw works of the Umbrian school and perhaps by Raphael himself. His admiration for the new forms led him to reform his own style, as is already evident in the altar of the Virgin at Novacella, painted in 1511, and at a later stage in the Lubiana altar, painted in about 1513, and originally in the Knillenberg residence at Merano.

Only uncertain and contradictory information remains concerning the last years of Reichlich's life. A rather weak version of his style is present in the panel paintings of the Heiligenblut altar which date from 1520; they are probably by the painter Wolfgang, whose signature is found in the well-known and much-disputed inscription. Reichlich was also a capable portraitist, a fact which is attested by the panel painting of Canon von Thurn, an early work, and by that of Waldauf. In my view this confirms the attribution to Reichlich, which I have previously proposed, of the self-portrait in the Ferdinandeum, the splendid portrait of Canon Angerer in the same museum, and some other portraits closely linked with it.

Because of his adoption of architectural and stylistic elements from artists of the Italian Renaissance, Marx Reichlich is included in the group of German artists who forged new links with Italian art. Basically, however, he remained a German artist, creating his own dramatized version of the figurative world of Michael Pacher, interpreting Pacher's perspective innovations in terms of line and transposing them onto the surface of the picture. Pacher's exemplary use of colour taught him the importance of the careful observation of objects and prompted him to develop certain refinements of expression. He is one of the most important figures in the diffusion of Pacher's influence in Austria, and, according to some, one of the key figures in the development of the "Danubian style" of painting.

The Uttenheim Master and the Coronation of the Virgin at Munich

In these pages I have endeavoured to give a clear and coherent picture of Michael Pacher's artistic personality, taking into account the latest discoveries and eliminating those works which cannot be considered as by his hand. I have also attempted to provide a more precise account of the personality of his collaborators: his son Hans, Friedrich Pacher and Marx Reichlich, who worked under him at Salzburg. Now we are left with the task of clarifying the character of an anonymous artist of the Upper Adige region and assessing his importance in the school of Pacher. Known as the Uttenheim Master from the place of origin of one of his finest paintings, this artist was probably neither a pupil nor an assistant of Michael Pacher but merely a fellow-countryman, an imitator and very likely a rival. In 1929 Pächt raised a question concerning this painter, later regarded as solved, especially after Hempel's detailed researches; but now, after an interval of almost forty years and with the return of Pächt to Vienna, the problem has been taken up once more. It is restated in its original terms in a recently published study written under Pächt's guidance by a pupil of his, Irmlind Kmentt, at the University of Vienna.

Pächt's theory is that during his formative years the anonymous artist was in contact with Witz and thus with the current of realism prevalent in German art around 1440. He later became acquainted with the Paduan art of the Reinassance, and on returning home he founded the Pusterian school and therefore became the true teacher of Michael Pacher, who (according to Pächt) was also influenced by Friedrich Pacher. The panel which, still according to Pächt, attests to the nature of his early influences, a painting of the Birth of the Virgin in the Innsbruck museum, has in fact long been dismissed as possible evidence, for it has nothing in common with either the Uttenheim Master or the art of the Upper Adige. The next works assigned to him by Pächt are the eight scenes from the life of St. Augustine at Novacella, which already display a knowledge of the laws of perspective; these are followed by a panel depicting the Holy Family, also at Novacella, which Pächt believes could be identified as the St. Anne altarpiece and dates to the year 1453, the year in which the *mensa* of the altar dedicated to that saint was consecrated. After this, in Pächt's view, the artist underwent Multscher's influence, evidenced in the years around 1460 by the Uttenheim panel and by the Moulins panels and finally, circa 1470, by panels depicting scenes from the life of the Virgin and from the Passion. Leaving aside the fact that the dates Pächt gives are too early and so appear improbable in the context of the art of this region, his chronological arrangement of the works of the artist comes up against certain special difficulties. It is impossible to conceive how the painter could have demonstrated a knowledge of the laws of perspective at Novacella in 1450–53 (and if this date were confirmed be would have to be considered among the first perspective painters in Europe outside Tuscany!), then perfected his knowledge by 1460, as attested by the Uttenheim panel, and immediately afterwards, in the Moulins panels, show that he had completely forgotten those laws to the extent of violating their most elementary principles—or how he could have turned into an expert in perspective once more around 1470. Furthermore, if he was an erratic and often careless painter possessing only a sketchy understanding of perspective even when he demonstrated his familiarity with it, how could he have instructed Pacher in its principles? Again, some of the formal motifs of the Moulins altar are identical with those of the St. Lawrence altar, considered by Pächt to be the later of the two works. Could the "pupil" then feasibly have copied from the "master", correcting his mistakes and showing vastly superior ability in perspective, which he had allegedly learned from the latter, as well as in the rendering of light and colour?

In 1931 Hempel's fundamental study appeared, and some discoveries of works and documents were also made about this time, among them the document proving that the St. Lawrence altar was executed around 1462. We need not discuss here the studies on the beginnings of North Italian Renaissance art, which have entirely revolutionized our previous knowledge of the artistic scene in that region, nor the researches and discoveries in the field of medieval art in the Alto Adige. But the position taken up then remains practically unchanged. According to Kmentt's publication the panel portraying St. Augustine, now in Munich, and the eight scenes from the life of the saint at Novacella are parts of a single work dating from about 1450–55; the panel depicting the Holy Family is dated to 1455–8, the Uttenheim panel to before 1470, the Moulins panel to 1475–80. We find, in short, a slight flexibility which not does however dispense with the problem. The difficulty is clearly revealed when Kmentt, speaking of the connections between the Moulins panels and those of St. Lawrence, concludes, in partial contradiction of what she has stated elsewhere in her study, that both were executed at Brunico by their respective artists at the same time—between 1464 and 1470—and in the same workshop. In this way she evades the problem of having to decide which of the two artists was the originator and which the copier. But the workshop relationship was then clear: either the workshop was Michael's, in which case it was he who signed contracts and directed and assumed responsibility for the work, or else it was the workshop of the anonymous artist. It cannot have been headed by both artists at the same time. It is now known that Pacher had a workshop at Brunico from about 1460 onwards; there are no documents that mention any other one in the same town. Later on, in 1474, the tax records speak quite plainly of two artists at Brunico, each of whom had a house of his own—Michael Pacher and Friedrich Pacher. No other artists are mentioned. The rest of the study consists entirely of learned digressions of no particular interest in the history of art.

Naturally, therefore, these misleading theories have not played a part in our reconstruction of Pacher's life, nor will they be considered in the present attempt to provide a clearer picture of the Uttenheim Master by the examination of his works and the material from archives which helps to date them. It has been considered appropriate, however, to discuss the problem at some length and to present ample evidence in support of my own position. The opinion of a scholar of such eminence as Pächt, professor of the History of Art at the University of Vienna, must be accorded some regard; he is an excellent theoretician of *Kunstwissenschaft* and an accomplished exponent of his own theories. He is, however, perhaps a little removed from the object of his researches—the work of art itself—whereas the present writer, for professional reasons, is in daily contact with it.

First let us consider the problem of the so-called "St. Anne panel", starting with the relevant documentary evidence, made available to the author by the courtesy of the Rev. Dr. Schrott, the archivist of the convent of Novacella, to whom I here express my gratitude. As we shall see, this is the only work by the Uttenheim Master which can be dated with any certainty and around which the chronology of his other works can be constructed. It is also the work which is of most assistance in establishing precisely the nature of the connection between the artist and Michael Pacher and so in finally unravelling the knot which has hitherto prevented agreement on some fundamental points. In 1453, as one of a number of alterations to the interior of the church at Novacella, an altar in the choir dedicated to St. Anne was consecrated by Provost Aigner. His successor, Leonhard Pacher, (provost from 1467 to 1482) was not content with these minor alterations and entered upon an ambitious scheme involving the reconstruction of the entire church in Gothic style. He had already completed the new choir and the sacristy when the imminent peril of the Turks forced him to interrupt the work in order to construct fortifications around the convent. Precise information concerning the construction of the choir is to be found in the chronicles of the convent, although its exact date is not given: "Hic ecclesiae nostrae chorum construxit novum una cum sacristia nova optimis quadratis bene formatis ut hodie cernitur lapidibus." The date can, however, be deduced from a different source (Codex 27 b of 1698) in which it is related that in 1601 the parchment commemorating its construction was discovered in the roof of the choir, where it had been placed in 1478. We are told that "in dem steinernen creiz ausser den chor und ober den gemalnen St. Mariae bildt, ain altes pergamentenes zötele ligent auf welchem auf der ainen seiten St. Johannes Evangelium geschrieben und auf der andern seiten stehet wie folgt: 1478 Leonardus praepositus, Hieronymus decanus und 23 fratres..." Provost Leonhard next installed the marble table of the high altar and had two painted panels made for the Fathers of the Church and the St. Catharine altars: "Tabulas duas depictas in ecclesia unam videlicet ad sanctos quatuor doctores, aliam ad sanctam Catharinam fieri fecit. Summi altaris lapidem pulchre politum magnis de Tridento adochi fecit sumptibus." Finally on 3 November 1482 he crowned his work of restoration by consecrating the altars in the choir (Document WW 37): "Tria altaria sita in novo choro dicti monasterii primo summum altare sanctae et individuae Trinitatis in honore et intemeratae Virginis genetricis Dei Mariae, S. Augustini et S. Agnetis, alius altare in dextra parte dicti chori in hon. S. Jacobi Apostoli et S. Stephani, tertium vero altare in sinistra parte dicti chori in hon. S. Johannis apostoli et Evangelistae sanctique Achatii cum sociis." But the altars had no altarpieces as yet, or else were temporarily furnished with those from the old church. The altarpieces for the side altars were not made until about 1506, while that of the high altar was installed by Pacher's successor, Lucas Härber, who became provost on 10 Jannary 1483. On 13 November 1485 Härber consecrated two new side altars in the presbytery, one dedicated to St. Anne (evidently its predecessor had been removed during the construction of the choir) and the other to St. John the Baptist. In addition he had a carved altarpiece made for the *mensa* of the high altar which his predecessor had installed and consecrated, and the new tabernacle, which must have been placed against the wall of the choir, as was then the normal practice. We are told (Koler, p. 574). "Primam igitur abbatialis sui directorii lineam recta ducturus eam cum studio ac pietate divino numini consecravit, erigens in maiori collegii basilica per praedecessorem suum fabrefacta novum pro principe altare opera sculptili per quam artificiose confectum nec non S. S. Synaxeos tabernaculum cum voldistorio in summis praelatorum festivitatibus ceremonialiter occupando."

From the sources quoted above we learn that an altar dedicated to St. Anne was consecrated in 1453, that it was destroyed during the construction of the new choir, and that a replacement was made and consecrated in 1485. We have no evidence, however, that the new altar originally possessed an altarpiece, nor as to when this was finally provided or replaced. On the other hand, we know that the *mensa* of the high altar, made in Trent marble, was installed some time towards the end of 1482 and that a carved altarpiece was added, probably on the occasion of the consecration of the other altars in 1485 and in any case during Provost Härber's tenure of office. The greater part of the Gothic redecoration of the church was destroyed in the course of the construction of the present church, and much of the remainder, which had been preserved in the treasury or in the corridors of the convent, was taken away by the Bavarians in 1812. Among the Gothic panels still in existence was (No. 305 in Colleselli's catalogue) "a genealogical tree of the Virgin Mary, a large piece in Gothic style", which can be identified as the panel still preserved at Novacella today, depicting the Holy Family on the inside and Joachim driven from the Temple on the outside. There remained also another panel painted on both sides, depicting the Visitation and Zacharias conversing which the angels (Colleselli, Nos. 277 and 278); this was sent to Innsbruck, and its ultimate fate is unknown. As we have seen, Pächt (in 1929) identified the panel which remains in the Novacella convent as belonging to the altar of St. Anne consecrated in 1453; he considers it to have been painted around that year and consequently assigns to an earlier period the whole of the artistic production which he associates with this panel and attributes to the Uttenheim Master. But if this were indeed the panel of the St. Anne altar, it is most unlikely that the Holy Family would be depicted on the front of it, for this subject, at least in German art, is generally to be found at the beginning of a series depicting the life of the Virgin. Nor can one be convinced by any suggestion that the scene of Joachim driven from the Temple, one of the many episodes from the cycle of the Virgin, would be found on the back of the panel. It would also be completely contrary to accepted practice to paint the reverse side of the panel—generally summarily painted with simple ornamentations or compositions using thin tempera and without priming (see the Gries and St. Wolfgang altars, the Uttenheim and the Munich panels, etc.)—with the technique usually employed for the exterior decoration of altar wings. We therefore have no grounds for identifying this work as the central panel of the St. Anne altar. There is, however, every reason to suppose that it is a wing-panel of an altar dedicated to the Virgin, which, in view of the dimensions of this work (1.68 by 1.68 metres), must have had a shrine measuring roughly 4 by 4 metres, which could only be the high altar of the church; it must also belong to the new church, for it would have been difficult to accommodate it in the Romanesque church. It has been objected that both the paintings on the panel are presented frontally and that therefore they cannot be parts of a wing but must constitute the central painting of an altar. In reply one need only point to an altar by Leonhard of Bressanone depicting a similar scene, which was installed only a little earlier, probably in the choir of the cathedral of Bressanone. The eight wing-panels of this altar have survived and are shared between galleries in Budapest and Vienna. The scenes revealed with the altar wings closed were the Holy Family, the Birth of Mary, the Presentation in the Temple, and the Betrothal of the Virgin. Opened out the wings showed the Annunciation, the Nativity, the Presentation of Jesus in the Temple, and the Adoration of the Magi. At least four of these scenes are arranged with the architectural elements in the centre, as in the two scenes at Novacella. As far as we can judge from the surviving fragments and from documentary evidence, the scenes visible when the altar was closed were as follows: above, Joachim driven from the Temple (preserved) on the left, and the Annunciation to Joachim (erroneously said to be Zacharias) on the right; below, the Meeting of Joachim and Anne on the left, and the Birth of Mary (?) on the right. The altar opened to reveal the shrine containing a carved group, the Trinity crowing the Virgin (?); the panels showed: above, the Holy Family (preserved) on the left, and the Visitation (documented) on the right; below, the Nativity (?) on the left, and the Adoration of the Magi (?) on the right. The basic difference between the two altars, in my view, lies in the position of the painting of the Holy Family: in Leonhard's altar it is placed on the outside of the wings, but in the Novacella altar on the inside.

Enough has been said, I think, to show conclusively that the panel which depicts the Holy Family is not the centre painting of an altar dedicated to St. Anne, but one of a series of episodes on the wing paintings of an altar, illustrating the life of the Virgin. Furthermore, the altar can only be the high altar which was consecrated in the church at Novacella in 1482 and was provided with an altarpiece soon afterwards, probably in 1485, by Provost Härber.

There are a number of other works by the same artist which probably date from the same period, namely eight wing-panels, four inner and four outer, depicting scenes from the life of St. Augustine, and a panel in which the central figures are St. Augustine and St. Monica. The former are still at Novacella while the latter is now in Munich, where it was taken in 1812. Pächt held that this panel was the predella of the St. Augustine altar, a hypothesis difficult to maintain, while Kmentt suggests that it is the centre panel, from which the lower half has been removed, of the altar itself. In the first place, however, the characteristics of the gilded backgrounds are obviously different, and secondly the panel is only 1.14 metres wide

Perspective plans of a panel of the Fathers of the Church Altar (the Saint in Ecstasy, Plate 62) and a panel for the St. Augustine Altar at Novacella by the Master of Uttenheim (the Mass of St. Augustine, Fig. 146). A comparison of the two reveals the clumsy borrowing of the second from the first which establishes a clear link between them. The author of the first composition is without doubt Michael Pacher who uses the same motif later on in the St. Wolfgang Altar (see the plan on p. 141)

and is far too small to belong to the St. Augustine altar, the centre panel of which must certainly have exceeded 1.5 metres in breadth (each of the wing-panels measures 0.74 metres without the frame). Lastly, the stylistic features of the work suggest that it dates from a slightly later period than the St. Augustine altar. A point of some interest which has generally escaped attention in the past is that two panel fragments which have now disappeared but were formerly preserved in the convent at Novacella were described by Semper, who regarded them as being by the same artist: "Two fragments from the painted architectural frame of an altar panel, each with two saints facing one another and standing upon Gothic corbels decorated with foliage motifs, surrounded by ornamental tracery and separated by a stone pillar; the saints are depicted in the act of blessing and hold scrolls of parchment in their hands (0.34 metres high and 0.25 metres across)." If we mentally take away the middle pillar from Michael Pacher's Fathers of the Church panel leaving the figures of St. Peter and St. Paul on one side and those of St. Andrew and St. Simon on the other, together with their respective bases and canopies, I think we can form a clear picture of the appearance of the two missing parts. A rough idea of what the centre panel of the St. Augustine altar looked like can be gained by studying the panel of Friedrich Pacher's altar to St. Peter and St. Paul at Innsbruck, where we again find two saints separated by a pillar, with statuettes obviously derived from the Fathers of the Church altar. Also relevant in this connection is Marx Reichlich's panel for the altar of St. Stephen and St. James, painted in 1506 and formerly in Novacella, now in Munich. In the St. Augustine panel we should probably have seen the figures of St. Augustine and St. Monica in a painted architectural setting with two canopies borne by pillars decorated with small statues of saints or prophets. The centre pillar, to which the two lost fragments must have belonged, would have been a double one such as we find in the other works just cited, and thus, when it was decided to preserve the figures or busts of the two saints, they were cut out of the panel which was no longer in use; they are now lost, but the two centre fragments with the two pairs of saints, which were also cut out, were rescued and have survived.

This theory would imply that the unknown artist had already seen Pacher's altar before he planned the St. Augustine altar, and it is very likely that he sought to create an altar which would be its equal or at any rate worthy of comparison with it. There are many instances of his borrowing of formal motifs and compositional ideas from Pacher, as we can see in the individual panels. A good example is the Vision of St. Augustine (Fig. 146); indeed, the setting in which the Trinity appears to the celebrant would remain incomprehensible without the aid afforded by the Saint in Ecstasy panel (Plate 63) of Pacher's altar. On the left are two altars which stand against the rood-screen of a monastic church, on either side of the doorway leading into the choir. They have projecting stone canopies above them with rib-vaulting, and the altar-tables are covered with embroidered white altar-cloths. The south wall of the church, which closes the background of the painting, contains an open door through which some sky and landscape are visible. But this is not all: we find Pacher's figure of an angel descending head first from the sky, although weakened by the unskilful foreshortening of the fluttering stoles, clearly an echo of those of Pacher's angel. Similarities of this kind can only be interpreted in one way: the painter took Pacher's composition as his model; the reverse of this cannot possibly be the case. This proves conclusively, if any doubt remain after what has already been said, that the scenes from the life of St. Augustine are later in date than the Fathers of the Church altar. With that point established, the lectern shown in perspective is explicable as another derivation from Pacher's magnificent examples, as is the characteristic attitude of the figure on the left who looks over the saint's shoulder from behind, a recurring element in Pacher's compositions (the first figure on the left in the St. Wolfgang Circumcision, for example) and one which ultimately derives, as we have shown earlier, from Filippo Lippi.

The background of the painting of the Mother consoled by the Bishop reflects a motif of Pacher's which achieves its fullest and most advanced development in the Flagellation of the Salzburg altar, but which can already be found in the Marriage at Cana at St. Wolfgang. One of the most interesting compositions of the whole altar, the picture of the Baptism of the Saint, contains several features which are typical of Pacher: the usual marble floor, derived from Lippi, the fine perspective of the font, and the figures surrounding it which emphasize the spatial depth of the composition, and above all the foreshortened figure of the catechumen who kneels in the foreground as he takes off his shirt. The Saint in Disputation, a poorly composed scene, is set in a room with a coffered ceiling which recalls the painting of the Miraculous Cure of the Fathers of the Church altar; it also has the perspective marble floor set at an angle, a rather uncommon feature which Pacher might have taken from Mantegna (see his St. Sebastian, now in Vienna). Where he is not helped by Pacher's ideas, this artist clearly displays his failings: the foreshortened ship of the Embarkation scene, which is crammed with people, is more suggestive of sardines in a barrel than of spatial depth. The contrast between the artist's manifest desire to convey spatial recession and his inability to achieve his aim reaches its extreme limit in the Conversion scene. Here the foreshortened figure of the saint lies stretched out towards us on the ground, with the apparent intention of filling the whole space with his body and outstretched arms, his cap thrown down in front of him. The result is very laboured. Also suggested by a precedent in Pacher is the attempt in the Sermon picture to set the figures in the resonant cavity of a church interior, but the attempt fails because the architectural perspective is not adequately defined.

The larger dimensions of the panel depicting the Holy Family—and probably its greater importance—result in a more careful execution abounding in admirable details. The composition, however, betrays the same weakness: in the painting of Joachim driven from the Temple, the apse, which is viewed frontally, obviously reflects a model by Pacher, but it is too crowded with short, stocky figures. The placing of two pinnacles on top of the two buttresses which adorn the outer arch framing the scene reveals the artist's ignorance of architectural matters.

Quite different in quality is the panel of St. Augustine and St. Monica, now in Munich, which may date from the same period as the high altar, or a few years later. It was executed with great care and the most striking effects are attempted, from the imperfectly shaved beard of the saint to the embroidery on his cope, the crystal shaft of his crozier in which the metal core is visible, the delicate veil hanging from the knot, and the half-open book which one almost feels could be read. The whole painting displays a remarkable skill in the careful analysis and accurate reproduction from life. Where the composition does not involve complex scenes requiring the arrangement of figures and objects in an architectural or natural setting, we gain a most favourable impression of this unknown artist's ability.

It is only a short step from the magnificent panel described above which, moreover, is in such a good state of preservation that we are able to enjoy its every detail to the full, to the Uttenheim panel, so-called because it was formerly the altarpiece of the high altar of the church at Uttenheim in Pusteria, from whence it was taken to Vienna. The wings of the altar, if it ever had any, have disappeared, but otherwise it is preserved in its entirety. It depicts the Virgin Enthroned, with St. Margaret and St. Barbara on either side, set within a Gothic frame in the form of a triptych, whose dividing pillars are supported by Gothic flying buttresses. The light falls across from the right, producing an effective chiaroscuro emphasizing those parts in relief which—with the exception of the buttresses—constitute a framework rather than an architectural construction. In other words, they are conceived as simple relief rather than as spatial recession. Between the background and the buttresses three figures are set on a floor of marble squares, raised by a step in the centre, which is shown in perspective. The two angels holding a draped curtain behind the Virgin are the only elements which give the impression that the spatial depth of the scene itself is greater than that of the framework. The latter includes the usual curved arches decorated not with multifoil tracery, as it appears to be at first glance, but with the lacework often found in the Veneto. The motifs of the curtain repeat those of the gold background of one of the Novacella panels depicting St. Augustine enthroned, or of the altar in Joachim driven from the Temple. We do not find here the grim facial expressions of the Novacella panels, with their swollen eyelids and wide open eyes; the faces are much closer to those of the Munich panel. The elements of simulated architecture are similar to those found in the Joachim panel, but are handled with superior skill. The central group of figures is reminiscent of the St. Lawrence Virgin, but it may be an adaptation of a prototype, indirectly derived through Michael Pacher, by Antonello da Messina, similar to the Virgin of his triptych. We know, in fact, that Pacher saw works by Antonello while he was in Venice, and that he adopted some motifs from them which are used for the first time in the Church Fathers altar. Round the neck of the Infant hangs a piece of coral which is also found in the Novacella panel of the Holy Family; at that time coral was regarded as a precious stone and was believed in Italy to possess curative and prophylactic powers, and this motif occurs in the panel by Antonello and in other Venetian paintings of the period. There is a certain stiffness, never quite absent in the works of this painter, in the short rigid fingers of St. Margaret, and also in the figure of St. Monica in the Munich panel. All indications are that this is a work of slightly later date than the paintings at Novacella already discussed, and can therefore be dated to around 1490.

The reverse side of the panel is decorated with floral motifs which, although somewhat roughly painted in thin tempera without priming, are definitely of the same period. Among these decorative elements stands the figure of the Redeemer, who presses the wound in his side, causing drops of blood to spurt out—a devotional image then widely used both in Venice and in the region under discussion. This painting would be of little interest were it not for the fact that it appears again and by the same hand, as Kmentt rightly observes, on the back of the panel in Munich depicting the Coronation of the Virgin (Plates 125–127). Formerly at Novacella, the painting was seized by the Bavarians in 1812, at which time, as the description of it shows, it was already in its present condition, that is, with the sides of the panel sawn off, resulting in the loss of the two figures contained in niches which undoubtedly flanked the central group as in the Gries altar shrine and the London panel. Attributed by Braune (in 1911) to Michael Pacher, the painting has continued to be regarded as his up to the present day despite the doubt voiced by the present writer in 1950, and although some of its characteristics, nowhere to be found in other works by Pacher, have frequently troubled scholars. Leaving aside de Stange's attempt in 1960 to show that the work dates from about 1460—even earlier than the St. Lawrence altar—the most illuminating suggestion was made by Hempel in 1931. Hempel noted the similarities of the composition to that of the Gries altar, but then went on to establish the presence of formal elements which could only have been developed in Pacher's work at a later stage; he therefore dated the panel to sometime after 1475. However, in spite of its extremely careful execution the panel cannot be included among Pacher's *oeuvre*, nor can it be considered as the work of other artists working from his drawings under his direct supervision.

The low horizon of the picture brings us to the period of the Fathers of the Church altar. Several details support this dating, particularly the device whereby the figures are placed on a flight of steps in order to compensate for the low viewing point. Another is the shape of the canopies, with their curved arches and trefoil decoration, which in the Church Fathers panel successfully conveys the solidity of stonework, whereas in the Coronation it is so thin it seems to have been carved in wood. The setting consists of an octagonal pavilion open on all sides, an insubstantial structure unusual with Pacher and found only in the London panel, the attribution of which is open to question. Furthermore, the gold background deprives the figures of substance and prevents any of the subtle effects of light, colour and atmosphere which are characteristic of Pacher. The impoverished simplicity of construction in the tracery of the canopy certainly bears no connection with the style of the Fathers of the Church period, nor yet with that of the Gries altar, which is far more accomplished and inventive.

Let us now look at the figures. Christ and God the Father, seen at an angle so as to accentuate the receding lines of the octagon, are crowning the Virgin who kneels in the foreground. The light falls on the group from the right, as usual, but it is not used by the artist to create depths of shadow from which the hands could reach out with the crown, and the few effects of light employed are too timid to make any impression. The hands are drawn with great care and accuracy, and are perhaps superior to Pacher's but they lack expression. In the Gries altar the blessing hand of God the Father stands out in strong light, and its impressiveness heralds the wonderful energy of the hand of Christ raised in benediction in the St. Wolfgang altar. Let us next compare the dove, or rather the fat pigeon with its tail caught in the Virgin's crown, with the doves in the Church Fathers altar. In the Coronation panel the dove has wings like cardboard, solid claws and appears to be hatching an oval stone. The doves of the Church Fathers altar, on the other hand, are soft, downy and shining with light. Although conjured out of nothing they are incredibly realistic and perfectly made. This comparison alone is sufficient to show that the Coronation panel is not by Pacher. The heads of the figures, again, are painted with meticulous care: we can count each separate hair of the eyelashes and eyebrows, measure the folds and wrinkles in the skin, lose ourselves in the undulating hair and beards, yet we are still forced to conclude that these heads, though painted with unsurpassable skill, have no life, no character, no expression. It is clear that the artist has thinned the point of his brush and given of his best, but the results are these round heads, with their stubbly chins, fat, flabby ears, and prominent lower lids, the lower lips swollen and drawn downwards with a fine brushstroke in white, the eyelashes and eyebrows clearly and diligently indicated with tiny parallel strokes—each feature contributing to the frigid convention of the whole. This work is, however, of high quality and is undoubtedly by some artist who lived within Pacher's sphere of inuflence and was in close contact with his works. The problem of attribution is not easy to solve. Having rejected the possibility that it is by one of Pacher's immediate pupils and collaborators, known from various other works, we are left with the anonymous and mysterious Uttenheim Master. We have already been guided to this conclusion by the floral decorations on the back of the painting, so similar to that of the Uttenheim panel. The Munich panel can also be attributed to him, if we can prove he was capable of the degree of formal refinement found here. Certainly the quality of his superb panel of St. Augustine and St. Monica is impressive and it must have been a commission of particular importance, executed some considerable while after his other works. In the interval he was undoubtedly influenced by the style of Michael Pacher's last period as exemplified in the Salzburg altar.

The present author has also (in 1968) pointed out the similarity between works known to be by the Uttenheim Master and a series of wing-panels with scenes from the life of the Virgin on the inner sides and scenes from the Passion on the outer, suggesting that these panels are in fact the wing-panels of this altarpiece. The two upper panels on the inside represent the Birth of Mary (now at Nuremberg) and the Annunciation (now in Munich) and have an elegant frame with multifoil tracery ornamentation, identical in form with the multifoil work of the Munich panel, which in turn is derived from the Church Fathers altar. In that altar, however, the tracery ornamentation was "painted" whereas in the Nuremberg wing-panel and the Munich altarpiece it is "drawn" in outline with the point of the brush. This difference, although barely perceptible, is in fact substantial, and establishes a connection between the Munich panel and the wing-panels. Generally considered to be the last works of the unknown painter the wing-panels are of uneven quality, but in parts executed with great care display-ing the features which we have already seen to be characteristic of his work. His lack of skill in perspective results in some incongruities in the composition of complex settings and the placing of figures within them, but the accurate rendering of detail is particularly evident in the delightful Nativity scene at Nuremberg, the closest to the Munich Coronation panel in facial features and technique of execution. Once again we find traces here of ideas adopted much earlier—during the formative years of the unknown artist—from works by Pacher, such as the St. Lawrence altar; the composition of the latter is copied in the Munich Annuncia-tion panel, perhaps indirectly through another version made a decade after the original. The panel depicting Christ in the Garden is compiled from various sources, perhaps again derived at second hand through Pacher: the guards jumping the fence are obviously taken from the Vipiteno altar, while the first apostle on the left appears to have been inspired by a figure in the famous painting by Mantegna in London. The composition of the Death of the Virgin is derived from Vipiteno but more immediately from a version by Pacher as shown by the detail, already seen in the St. Lawrence altar, of St. Peter taking holy water from a bucket offered him by another apostle. Two other details, the apostle blowing on the censer, and the candle, both appear at St. Wolfgang. As in the St. Lawrence altar, the head- and footboards of the bed, absent in the bed at Vipiteno, are shown in perspective to add depth to the scene. The kneeling figure with his back turned and his head buried in his hands would seem to be an adaptation of the Saint in Ecstasy of the Fathers of the Church altar. In the Crowning of Thorns scene (discovered by Rasmo in 1968) the setting with its coffered barrel-vaulting is undoubtedly taken from Paduan models, such as the *tondi* by Nicolò Pizzolo in the Ovetari Chapel (the *tondo* of St. Augustine). Derived from many different sources and uneven in quality, these works must be fairly late in date, although they are not necessarily contemporary with the Munich panel.

Other works by the same master can easily be included in this brief catalogue. The Moulins and the Graz panels, however, do raise serious problems of attribution. Frey invented a new and quite different artist, and more recently Kmentt had done the same, to account for the Graz panels. It seems necessary, however, to tackle the problem as it is presented, even though the conclusions reached may be difficult to accept. In the Moulins altarpiece the artist clearly reveals himself as an imitator of Michael Pacher, but seems to be acquainted only with those works dating from the period before 1471, and in particular with the St. Lawrence altar. From this it would seem that the panels were executed around 1470. It is interesting to note, however, that the artist imitates perspective without knowing its principles or those of the spatial disposition of figures in perspective, for he gives us the usual ascending line of vision with high vanishing points which sometimes end up above the top of the picture, the figures piled up one on top of the other. We may conclude that the artist never entered Pacher's studio but saw the works it produced and imitated them as best he could.

The Graz panels are of mediocre quality and may be regarded as being somewhat later in date, since we have shown their chronological connection with the consecration of the tower chapel (1465) at Novacella to be unfounded. Some of the details have certain affinities with Pacher's style of around 1480, and the Moulins panels too, are thus to be regarded as dating from this later period.

The Novacella group differs from the Moulins and Graz series in that it reveals a greater familiarity with the laws of perspective and can be considered to be later in date. Certain of its stylistic features, particularly the heaviness of form and the exaggerated, wide-eyed expressions, are absent in the later Uttenheim panel and the scenes from the life of the Virgin. These latter works again have the same features that are found in the Moulins panels but reveal a more advanced knowledge of perspective and a greater facility in its use.

It has already been suggested that Michael Pacher did not come into contact with the convent at Novacella until Leonhard Pacher, parish priest at Falzes, had been elected provost. His work, attested for that period by the frescoes in the sacristy and also by the Church Fathers altar, in my view was more extensive than is apparent from the few surviving works there. These formed part of the ambitious scheme for the enlargement and rearrangement of the church, abruptly halted on the retirement of his patron at the end of 1482 on the eve of the commission for the high altar. The succeeding provost, Lucas Härber, a stranger to the region, was chosen, despite unanimous opposition from the canons, because he enjoyed the favour of Sigismund of Austria. Härber evidently selected another artist who had no connection with the previous one, but shared his own personal taste, which inclined towards the artistic tradition of southern Germany. It comes as no surprise that he bestowed his favour on the Uttenheim Master, who during this period achieved a kind of compromise between local taste—which in the Novacella convent had been guided by the work of the two Pachers—and the taste of the new provost. The artist did not prove himself incapable of the task and he must have stayed on to work, mainly at Novacella, concentrating on the production of works of art for the convent and its dependent parishes.

Finally it remains to examine the problem of the identity of this artist, a considerable figure who was nevertheless eclipsed by the overpowering presence of Michael Pacher. Since none of his works is linked with the name of any artist, the problem admits of no easy solution. However, as there are still many sources in local archives which relate to this period it is most unlikely that they would contain no record of the name of an artist of such prominence, who certainly must have had his own workshop. We can exclude artists from the locality of Pusteria, all of whom are quite familiar, and concentrate instead on the Bressanone area. From this part of the world we can disregard Leonhard of Bressanone (documented for the years 1441–74, d. 1475), whose style and works are known to us, and Hans, a Bressanone painter for whom documentary evidence exists for the period 1477–98 (Scheffler), who can be identified without any doubt as Hans Klocker. We are then left with Georg von Nuremberg, who was in Brunico in 1474, Hans Reinhardt, a citizen of that town (1475), Konrad Haselpack, also a citizen (1469) and lastly Marx Scherhauff. Scherhauff was the eldest son of the painter Leonhard of Bressanone and brother of Jerome, canon of Novacella; we have no evidence that he was a citizen of Brunico, nor that he had a workshop there, but we do possess information, part of which is connected with the Novacella convent, relating to the years 1474 to 1484. The *Liber anniversariorum Novae Cellae* tells us that Leonhard of Bressanone bequeathed 20 marks, and his son Marx 10 marks, to the convent: "Item a Leonardo pictore de Brixina, patre domini Jeronimi, nostri confratris, provenerunt monasterio nostro marce 20, similiter a Marco pictore, dicti confratris germano, marce 10 in remedium animarum suarum, impense pro cultu divino." Unfortunately this note, certainly written after 1475, the year of Leonhard's death, bears no date and can only be dated very approximately. Certain assets which Marx and his brothers had inherited from their father passed into other hands in 1484, from which it can be deduced that Marx did not die until after that year. The two legacies suggest the existence of much closer ties between the convent and the donors than that created merely by the admission of Jerome, Leonhard's son and Marx's brother, as a canon of Novacella. Almost all the works of the Uttenheim Master (the Graz panels, the high altar in the convent church, the St. Augustine altar, the panel of St. Augustine and St. Monica, the Coronation of the Virgin altar and the panels associated with it) were executed for the Novacella convent. It seems not improbable that this artist, because of the connections of his brother and particularly his father, who was the artist responsible for the St. Mary Magdalene altar and the frescoes in the tower chapel, enjoyed the goodwill of the convent and was entrusted with the execution of certain works of art for it. He may therefore be tentatively identified as the unknown Uttenheim Master. Now that his connection with the art of Michael Pacher has been clarified there is no need to dwell on the problem further.

CONCLUSION

This attempt to reconstruct Michael Pacher's artistic personality by carefully sifting through all that was previously known or believed to be known about him, has led me to realize that the conclusions I have reached were in some cases quite unexpected, even to myself. The chronological order of Pacher's works outlined here differs from the traditionally accepted one; certain works hitherto attributed to Pacher have been excluded from his *oeuvre* and his art has been placed in a new context, with the result that a different picture has emerged of the relative importance of the artists with whom he came into contact. I am convinced, however, that we have gained a clearer idea of Pacher and a better understanding of his art. The Munich Coronation, to take a typical example, has always presented problems: in spite of its careful execution it seems impossible to include it in the list of Pacher's works, for the painting lacks the clarity of theme and composition that prevails in the artist's other works. Again, the Fathers of the Church panel when assigned to the period between the St. Wolfgang and the Salzburg altars was justifiably a puzzle to scholars; placed in the context of the stage of development reached by Pacher prior to the St. Wolfgang altar, however, the panel assumes its full significance as a key work of fundamental importance in the stylistic and conceptual development of his art.

We still have no clear picture of the Uttenheim Master as an individual artist, but his true significance and worth emerges when he is seen as a later artist. He was an intelligent and able follower of Pacher and has been regarded as the leader of the new artistic movement in the Adige region, although he lacked the personality to assume a guiding role. To date the St. Augustine panels to the middle of the fifteenth century, that is before the beginning of Michael Pacher's career, is, as we have seen, unfeasible and shows how little understanding there has really been of Pacher's influence as an artist.

The St. Thomas and the St. Lawrence panels, when included within the body of Pacher's painting as his earliest works, clarify the importance of his Paduan influences; to reduce these experiences in Padua, as has been the tendency in the past, merely to an acquaintance with the early works of Mantegna is an oversimplification. By presenting and comparing several of his compositional schemes we have indicated the successive stages both of Pacher's knowledge of perspective and also of the Gothic influences that he underwent through his contact with the Paduan painters, influences which he adapted to the needs of his own personal creativity, finally and fully achieved in the Salzburg altar.

We have followed the artist's conception of colour and atmosphere from its first manifestations up to its final developments, showing how it was closely connected with prevailing tendencies in the art of the Veneto and how it led, in the great wooden altars, to a pictorial and dynamic interpretation of architecture. He freed his architectural features from the severe construction of the earlier stone altars and conceived them in terms of pure spatial composition.

Pacher's skill in reducing his narrative to essential elements and in characterizing his figures by means of concrete outlines so that they are more than simple portraits or psychological studies, and his ability to suggest the harmonious and moderate expression of emotions, have all been emphasized. We have frequently pointed out the singular reserve and restraint with which the artist conveys aggression and cruelty and, in contrast, the touches of tremulous admiration in his representation of the tenderness of infancy and the glory of youth.

The whole of Pacher's work is pervaded by a serene and balanced observation. From attention to detail he progresses to the visualization of the composition as a whole and to the arrangement within it of what he wished to express. Nothing illustrates more clearly Pacher's isolated position in the context of Austrian art of the time than the comparison of his works with those of Frueauf, unintentionally shown side by side in the Vienna Museum. But when compared with the Italian artists of his time, Michael Pacher is still a figure apart. Like certain plants that grow among the stones marking the boundary between two properties, he is a frontier dweller, belonging to all and to none. The roots absorb the vital water from the depths of both fields, but the fruit has a sharpness and a flavour all its own. Born and raised between two different cultures, Pacher unconsciously separated and isolated himself in his desire to convey his deepest feelings sincerely and lucidly. The melancholy which Dürer saw in objects and in men and which he expressed in his famous engraving, is the basic sentiment emanating from Pacher's work, a melancholy that defies analysis and discussion not because of any arrogance but because of its awareness of inevitability.

Michael Pacher is perhaps the greatest representative of that section of humanity which has for thousands of years lived in the valleys which descend from the massifs of the Dolomites to the plains of the Veneto and the Danube. These are the Illyro-Venetians, over whom Celts, Romans, Slavs and Bavarians have imposed themselves down through the ages, bequeathing their languages and their cultures but unable to change the fundamental characteristics. Early on these were revealed in a tendency towards humane and peaceful cohesion, which produced the highest known examples of the organization of communal liberty up to the time of the Roman conquest. They desired to live artistically or, better, to represent in art their feelings rather than their actions, and the relief decoration of their *situlae*, free of any narrative or didactic intention, already expresses a pantheistic feeling towards life and nature. With the passing of time, the vocabulary of expression perhaps became more precise, but the subject-matter remains substantially unchanged. It shows a serene vision of the world, the gift of a few rare moments of happiness to be preserved in thought and image, and tinged with the melancholy of those who know from thousands of years of human experience the difficulty of attaining it.

Seen in this environment Pacher can be understood and his art explained. His work can be placed alongside that of the greatest artists of the ancient region of Veneto-Illyria—Mantegna, Giovanni Bellini, Giorgione, Titian, Hans von Judenburg, Morlaiter and Troger.

112, 113 Virgin from the former high altar, and detail. Salzburg, Franciscan Church

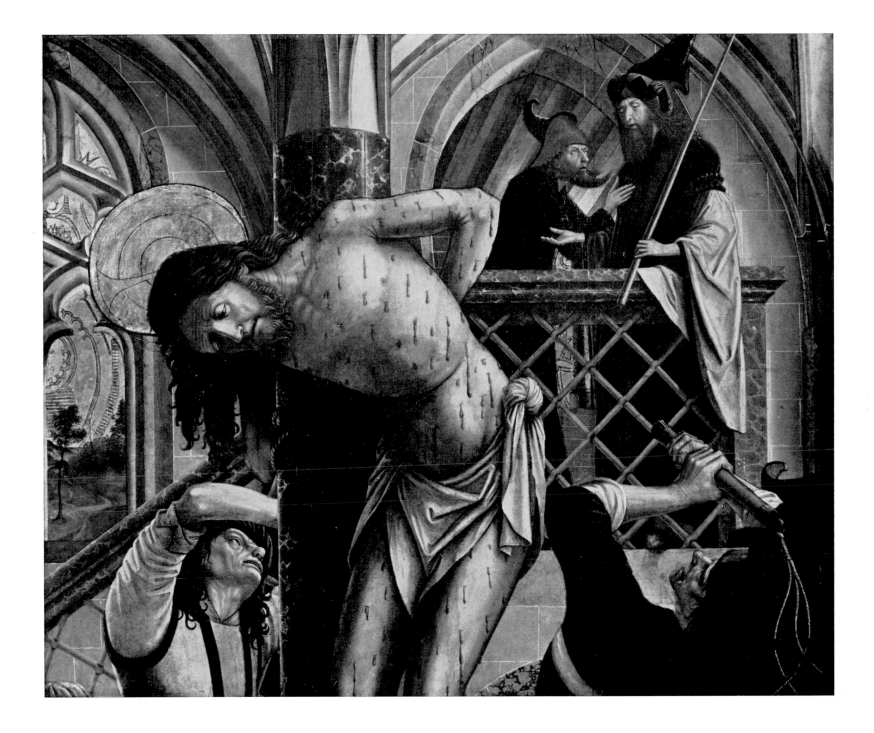

114 *Fragment of the Flagellation from the Salzburg Altar. Vienna, Österreichische Galerie*

115 *Fragment of the Flagellation (detail of Plate 114)*

116 *Fragment of the Marriage of the Virgin from the Salzburg Altar (Michael Pacher and workshop). Vienna, Österreichische Galerie*

117, 118 Fragment of the Marriage of the Virgin (details of Plate 116)

119 *Fragment of the Birth of the Virgin from the Salzburg Altar. Vienna, Kieslinger Collection*

*120 Fragment of the Flight into Egypt from the Salzburg Altar (Michael Pacher and workshop).
Basle, Öffentliche Kunstsammlung*

121 Joseph being lowered into the well, fragment of the Salzburg Altar (Michael Pacher and workshop).
Vienna, Österreichische Galerie

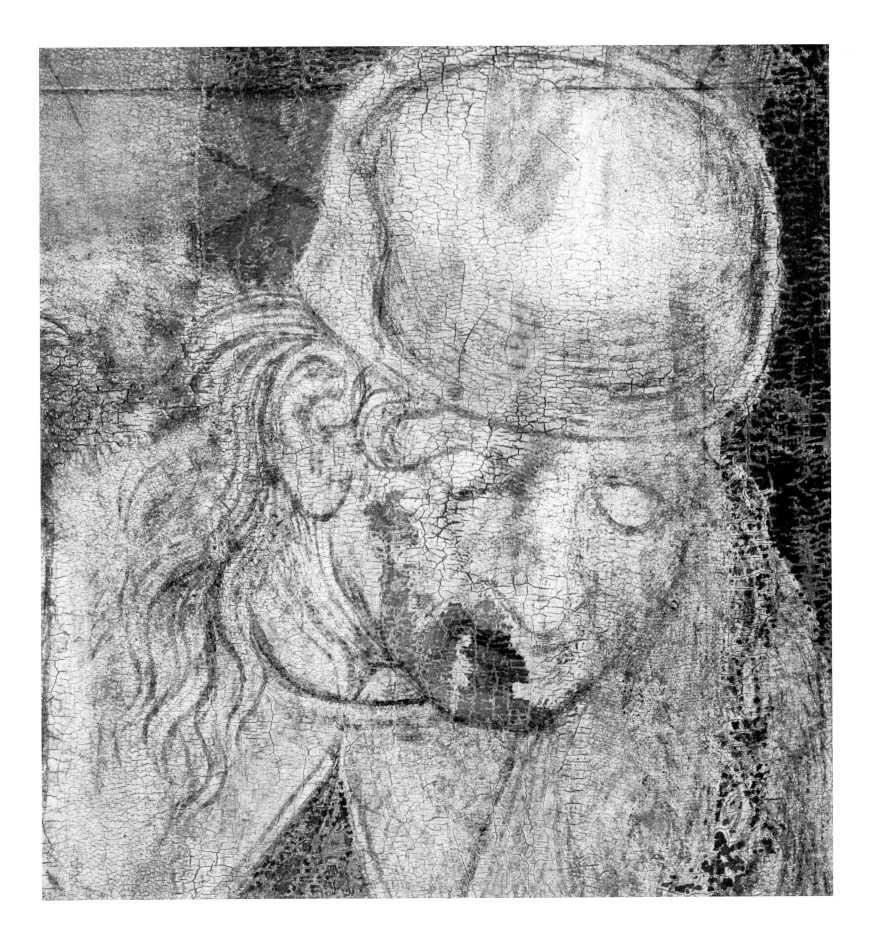

122 Joseph being lowered into the well (detail of Plate 121)

123 Mystical Marriage of St. Catharine (Hans Pacher).
Castagnola, Thyssen-Bornemisza Collection

124 *Mystical Marriage of St. Catharine (detail of Plate 123)*

125 Coronation of the Virgin (Uttenheim Master). Munich, Alte Pinakothek

126, 127 Coronation of the Virgin (details of Plate 125)

WORKS ATTRIBUTABLE TO MICHAEL PACHER

Graz, Joanneum Museum. St. Thomas Becket Altar: Plates I, II, 1-5.

Two wing-panels from an altar in pearwood (44×44 cm.). On the inner side are the symbols of the Evangelists St. Mark and St. Luke on a gold background, and on the outer side the Murder of St. Thomas Becket, and his Burial.

These panels were in the convent at Novacella when they were selected by Dillis on 29 July 1808 to be taken to Germany. They were stolen during the night of 9-10 January 1809 (cf. Colleselli, 1954, pp. 45-47: "Martyrdom of a Bishop, on the back a lion, and a bishop lying on a bier and surrounded by priests, in wood"). In 1861 they were the property of a Count Ignaz Attems who bequeathed them to the Joanneum Museum, Graz. Atrtibuted to Michael Pacher by Stiassny (1895, p. 26). M. Schrott proposed (1918) that they were originally intended for the tower chapel at Novacella which was apparently reconsecrated and decorated in 1465. Hempel (1931, p. 68), following Pächt (1929, pp. 79 ff.), attributed them to Pacher's workshop, suggesting a date towards the end of the century rather than that proposed by Pächt of 1475, observing that the same painter had worked previously on the S. Lorenzo panels. Winkler (1941, p. 237) supported the attribution to Pacher of the symbols of the Evangelists, pointing out their derivation from Donatello, and assigning the rest to the workshop. Rasmo (1948, p. 6) assigned all four paintings to Michael Pacher, suggesting they all derived from Lippi and Donatello, with a dating to circa 1460-65. This attribution was accepted by Oberhammer (1950) and recently confirmed by Rasmo (1950, pp. 144 ff.) and dated to *c.* 1460. Hempel's re-examination (1952, p. 29) accepted the attribution to Pacher but proposed a date of *c.* 1465, while Lutterotti (1950, p. 365) rejected it and urged a dating to the end of the fifteenth century, in which he was followed by Stange (1960, p. 179) who, however, accepted the two symbols of the Evangelists as the work of Pacher, as proposed by Winkler.

An examination of documents in the locality has revealed that in 1218 an altar dedicated to Christ, St. Thomas Becket and St. Augustine, was in fact consecrated in the tower and in the niche above the altar were then frescoes of the Crucifixion with the Virgin and St. John, with God the Father and the Holy Ghost above them and the two patron saints on either side. The Romanesque fresco was largely destroyed and replaced in about 1465 by a fresco of Christ crucified between Mary and John by Master Leonhard. The relative passage in the chronicle (*Annales*, fol. 613-614, years 1218 and 1465) should perhaps be given a different interpretation to that hitherto accepted following Schrott; it may well mean that the decoration was not of the tower altar but rather of the new altar of the Fathers of the Church, as appears from the account cited here in full: "Haec deinde [capella] anno 1362 ab Henrico Ziegler Clusinensi cive 120 marcis argenteis dotata quotidiana missa et lumine condecorata fuit uti Johannis Librarii libellus fol. 4 clarius meminit et demum anno 1465 postquam ob incommoditatem loci profanata fuisset, cum onere suo quotidiani sacri ad aram 4 Doctorum translata ibidemque pluribus indulgentiis a Gaspara suffraganeo aucta et exornata quemadmodum suis in locis et annis fusius ex Chronographia nostra lectori exhibebitur." Moreover, an altar structure such as the St. Thomas altar could not have stood on the altar table at that time, as it would have hidden the niche fresco which had just been repainted; furthermore it does not emerge explicitly that in 1465 the chapel was either decorated or consecrated.

S. Lorenzo in Pusteria, Parish Church. Statue of the Virgin on the high altar: Plates 6, 7.

Statue in pinewood, repainted and with some carving restored (the crown and part of the throne). Overall height 1.32 m.

From the central part of the shrine made by Michael Pacher between 1460 and 1465. When the altar was dismantled the statue was placed in a side chapel. In the 1880s it was sold, apparently for 7 florins, to an antique-dealer, but immediately repurchased for a sum contributed by all the women of the village, and then passed to the sculptor Trenkwalder for restoration and repainting. Formerly attributed to Pacher's workshop by Atz, who described this episode (1892, p. 39); Weingartner (1923, p. 263) ascribed it to Pacher himself. Considered by Hempel (1931) a relatively late work after the discovery of the document relating to the execution of the altar it was dated by Rasmo (1949, p. 32) to *c.* 1460-65, but Lutterotti oddly maintains it to be of *c.* 1481-5.

Wing-panels from S. Lorenzo: Plates III, IV, 10-20.

1-2 Munich, Pinakothek: inner side showing the Annunciation, outer side the Distribution of Alms to the poor.
3-4 Munich, Pinakothek: inner side, the Death of the Virgin, outer side the Martyrdom of St. Lawrence.
5-6 Vienna, Österreichische Galerie: The Capture of Pope Sixtus and St. Lawrence before the Prefect (outer sides).
Nos. 1-5 were chosen by Dillis from the treasures of the convent of Novacella on 29 July 1808, removed to Innsbruck in 1809 and finally to Munich (Nos. 310-311 of the Colleselli list).
Nos. 5-6 were identified (Hammer, 1912) in the Dieteneck house at Dietenheim, the property of Eckert and acquired for the museum at Vienna in 1913.
Hammer considered the paintings were parts of a single complex work (1912, pp. 537 ff.) which he attributed to Michael Pacher's workshop and suggested was originally intended for the cathedral of Bressanone (the St. Lawrence altar commissioned by Canon Wolfgang Neundlinger, *c.* 1486-91), and he was followed in this opinion by Pächt (1929, p. 79) and Hempel (1931, p. 63), the latter however rejected the provenance from Bressanone and dated the panels to *c.* 1480-85, postulating that they came from the high altar of S. Lorenzo in Pusteria. After the discovery of the S. Lorenzo document (Huter, 1946) they were assigned to Pacher and dated 1460-65 (Rasmo, 1949), and influences of Donatello and Lippi were noted (Rasmo, 1950, p. 147); Hempel (1952, pp. 29 ff.) suggested a date of *c.* 1470 and accepted the attribution to Pacher but with a reservation in favour of workshop participation. D. Frey on the other hand (1952, pp. 46 ff.) proposed a dating to *c.* 1475, rejecting as too late Lutterotti's suggestion (1950, p. 365) of 1480-95, which was accepted by Stange (1960, p. 174).

Innsbruck, Ferdinandeum Museum. Statue of St. Lawrence: Figs. 140, 144.

Statue in pinewood, 1.33 m. high, representing St. Lawrence, the gridiron (held in one hand) and the book (held in the other) are missing; repainted in Baroque style. Probably from Pusteria, acquired for the Ferdinandeum in 1869. It was shown in the Innsbruck Exhibition (1950, p. 55) dated 1480-90 but "not credited to any definite artist or workshop style". Considered by Ringler to be by the hand of Pacher and to have formed part of the St. Lawrence altar (1953, p. 355); the provenance was denied by Rasmo (1950, p. 144) who however admitted the possibility that it might be an early work by Michael Pacher. Baldass (1950, p. 217) considers it the work of another artist, and Frey does not exclude the possibility of workshop participation (1952, p. 52).

Munich, Bayerisches Nationalmuseum. Statue of St. Michael: Plates 8, 9.

In pinewood, 1.47 m. high, hands missing, original colouring. Apparently found in 1875 in the Bressanone valley (North Tyrol) and with considerable restoration transformed into St. George with the Dragon and placed in the castle at Matzen. In 1939 the nineteenth-century additions were removed and replaced by others more in keeping with the original character of the statue; in the same year it was acquired by the Schnütgen Museum, Cologne. It was recently removed to the Bayerisches Nationalmuseum and there in 1962 the arbitrary additions and repainting were removed. Identified as a work of Pacher by Stiassny (1895, pp. 26 ff.). The suggestion that it is the central figure of the St. Michael altar of Bolzano made by Pacher between 1482 and 1484 (Doering, 1913, p. 95) has been generally accepted except by Benesch (1956, pp. 196 ff.) who preferred to identify another statue as that belonging to the Bolzano altar and attributed this one to the workshop.

Formerly Wilten (Innsbruck), Convent. Four panels with heads of saints: Plates 21-24; fig. 142.

Two panels painted on both sides and formerly wing-panels of a predella; later sawn through and separated. Pinewood, 51×49.5 cm.
The inner paintings show St. Peter and St. Paul on a gold background, the outer ones St. Barbara and St. Catharine. Attributed to Pacher by Braune (1915, pp. 249 ff.). and confirmed by Hempel (1931, p. 33) who included them among the early works, before the Gries altar. In 1937 the first two paintings were acquired by the Kunsthistorisches Museum, Vienna, St. Catharine by the Innsbruck Museum, and St. Barbara passed into private ownership. The first three were cleaned of their repaintings and were shown at the Innsbruck Exhibition (1950, p. 38) with a date shortly before that of the Gries altar.

Gries (Bolzano), former Parish Church. Altar of the Coronation of the Virgin: Plates V-VII, 25-54.

Shrine 3.70×3.02 m. high; Virgin 1.15 m. high, Christ 1.47 m., God the Father 1.54 m., St. Michael 1.40 m. (excluding the arm raised above the head), St. Erasmus 1.65 m., angels at the feet of the Virgin 0.65 and 0.68 m., angel with viol 0.56 m., angel with lute 0.62 m., angels with trumpets 0.52 and 0.57 m. Reliefs, excluding frames, 1.72×1.38 m. high.
The altar for which Michael Pacher was commissioned in 1471 and which was completed presum-

128 *Relief of the Adoration of the Magi. Brunico, Ursuline Church* | 129 *Relief of the Death of the Virgin (detail). Brunico, Ursuline Church* | 130 *Christ Carrying the Cross (detail). Brunico, Parish Church* | 131 *Detail of head from the former high altar of Bolzano Parish Church, by Hans von Judenburg. Nuremberg, Germanisches Museum* | 132 *Statue of St. Valentine. Falzes, St. Valentine's Church* | 133 *Statue of the Virgin and Child by Hans Multscher, from Val Pusteria or the neighbouring Ladino area. Munich, Bayerisches Nationalmuseum*

134 *Prophet by Donatello, from the campanile (detail). Florence, Museo dell'Opera del Duomo* | 135 *Plaster cast of the head of St. Wolfgang from the St. Wolfgang Altar* | 136 *Plaster cast of the head of St. Benedict from the St. Wolfgang Altar* | 137 *Detail of the Burial of St. Jerome by Filippo Lippi. Prato, Cathedral* | 138 *Detail of the Trivulzio altarpiece by Filippo Lippi. Milan, Museo del Castello Sforzesco* | 139 *Detail of one of the frescoes by Nicolò Pizzolo, now destroyed. Formerly Padua, Ovetari Chapel in the Eremitani Church*

ably in 1475 was moved from the main apse in 1736 and replaced by the present altar in stucco lustre. When it was rediscovered the surviving shrine was preserved in the former chapel of St. Bartholomew in the parish church itself. It was restored towards the middle of the last century and then repainted. In about 1950 the extraneous additions were removed and the altar moved to the centre of the chapel, so that the painted back could be seen, and provided with a predella and wings to which were attached the remaining fragments of the wing reliefs. The restorations were made at the expense of the Soprintendenza di Belle Arti under the direction of N. Rasmo. In 1846 Koch published the first report on the Gries altar and the contract for its execution. In the following year Ladurner published the entire contract. In 1853 Förster by error dated it 1481, which was corrected in 1854 by Koch, who confirmed 1471 as the date of the contract. In 1857 Messner made the first detailed description of the altar which had in the meantime been restored, deploring this tampering with the work ("... Moreover it is unfortunately not possible to say that the repainting has preserved the delicacy of the individual expressions and features; indeed, some of the heads now seem rather insignificant"); similar regrets were expressed by others, including Atz (1862). In 1864 Ladurner republished a revised and corrected edition of the text of the contract for the altar, which later disappeared.

Messner (1857) was the first to suggest the former high altar of Bressanone parish church—commissioned from Hans von Judenburg in 1421 and later lost—as the model for the Gries altar, although Semper adhered to the earlier opinion of Förster (1853) that it derived from the St. Michael altar in the same church, but Messmer's thesis persisted (Hempel, 1931) and was confirmed by the identification of the remains of Hans von Judenburg's altar (Rasmo, 1947) of which the centre group, now in Nuremburg, and the lateral statues, now in Cologne, were shown together at the Innsbruck exhibition, and could easily be studied. The dimensions are as follows: Virgin 1.05 m., God the Father 1.20 m., St. John 1.73 m., St. Vigilius 1.80 m. and these correspond approximately to those of the Gries statues.

Gries, former Parish Church. Statue of the Virgin and Child: Figs. 141, 145.

Pinewood, 1.24 m. high, at present in a Gothic edicule in the church. According to Schwabik (1933) it is the work of Michael Pacher and can be identified as the statue belonging to the cymatium of the high altar. This suggestion remains unsupported.

Munich, Pinakothek. Altar of the Fathers of the Church: Plates VIII-XI, 56-69.

Pinewood, centre section 2.16 m. high × 1.96 m. including the frame; wings 2.16 × 0.91 m.; outer sections of the wings 1.03 × 0.91 m.
The *mensa* of the Fathers of the Church altar was consecrated in the church of Novacella on 4 February 1465; in the same year the benefice of a daily Mass with various indulgences were transferred to this altar from the chapel of St. Augustine and St. Thomas Becket in the Tower. Under Provost Leonhard (1467-82) the altarpiece painted by Michael Pacher was placed here ("Tabulas duas de-

pictas in ecclesia unam videlicet ad sanctos quatuor doctores, aliam...fieri fecit"). Removed and stored in the monastery treasury in about 1735, it was seen and admired there by Roschmann in c. 1735. On 29 July 1808 Dillis (Colleselli, nos. 315-318) decreed that it should be transferred to Innsbruck, the move taking place in 1809, and ultimately it was transferred to Munich. It was shown in the Schleissheim Gallery and after 1872 in the Augusta Gallery, part of it being removed to the Alte Pinakothek in 1890, where the whole work has now been reassembled.
Attributed to Michael Pacher by Semper (1887, p. 275), in 1895 Strompen interpreted the episodes on the wing-panels as scenes from the life of St. Wolfgang, attributing the execution of the work to the patronage of Canon Wolfgang Neundlinger of Bressanone (d. 1486) and concluding that it had come from the cathedral of Bressanone. Pächt (1929, p. 79) accepted this provenance and the dating of 1486-91, but considered that the scenes of the saint's life were workshop productions. Hempel (1931) proposed Novacella as the altar's place of origin and placed it in the last years of the life of Provost Leonhard, c. 1480-83. He followed Pächt in considering the outer panels to be workshop production, and also observed that two of the stories thought to relate to St. Wolfgang did not correspond with the known tradition (the episodes of the thief and of the devil). Rasmo (1949) used Roschmann's evidence to prove definitively the provenance of the altar from Novacella. The dating to 1482-3 was generally accepted (Oberhammer, 1950) but doubts were raised by Frey (1953, p. 47).

Monguelfo, Tabernacle: Plates XII, 70-71; figs. 150-152.

Erected in the apse of the parish church and destroyed in the floods of 1882, the remaining fragments of the frescoes were reassembled in a new tabernacle (1893) completely repainted by Melicher (1895) with the help of drawings made by Blachfelner. The frescoes were identified as Michael Pacher's by Förster in 1853, and the attribution confirmed by Dahlke (1885) and by Semper (1891). Stiassny (1900) suggested the collaboration of Master Nicholas, the presumed artist of the frescoes in the parish church of Bolzano, and of Marx Reichlich. Röttinger (1901) suggested the collaboration of the artist responsible for the paintings on the outer wings of the St. Wolfang altar, (later identified as Friedrich Pacher). Pächt (1929, p. 79) dated them to c. 1470, following Semper, and considered only the Crucifixion, the Virgin and Sts. Peter and Paul to be by Pacher himself, and the rest, including the Fathers of the Church, to be workshop production. Hempel (1931) considered them all original. Rasmo (1950, p. 147) assigned two sides to Michael and two to Friedrich Pacher on the basis of photographs which he had discovered, taken before the destruction by flooding.

Novacella, Sacristy. Frescoes on the vaulting: Plate 72; figs. 147-149.

Attributed to Pacher by Semper (1891) who considered that the frescoes had been partially repainted and only recently inserted in the quadrifoil settings, dating them to between 1469 and 1470. Pächt (1929, p. 79) assigned then all to the workshop; Hempel (1931, p. 34) accepted the dating to 1467 proposed by Mannowsky (1910, p. 60), correctly

indicated that the quadrifolis were original and ascribed them all to Michael with the exception of the Virgin on the keystone, which he correctly assigned to Friedrich Pacher. Rasmo (1950, p. 147) discussed the collaboration of Michael and Friedrich Pacher. Stange (1960, p. 169) considered the whole to be work of Friedrich Pacher from drawings by Michael.

S. Candido, Collegiate Church. Frescoes above the south door: Figs. 153-158.

Attributed to Michael Pacher by Dahlke in 1885, confirmed by Semper (1892); Pächt (1929, p. 79) assigns them to the workshop and dates them to c. 1480; Hempel (1931, p. 37) considers them authentic work of Michael and earlier than the St. Wolfgang altar; Stange (1960, p. 170) also considers them authentic and datable to the period between the Gries and the St. Wolfgang altars.

St. Wolfgang, Parish Church. High altar: Plates XIII-XVIII, 73-111; figs. 135, 136, 159-166, 168, 169.

The shrine contains the Blessing of the Virgin flanked by St. Wolfgang and St. Benedict; in the predella, the Adoration of the Magi; at the sides of the shrine St. George and St. Florian and in the pinnacles above the shrine, St. Catharine and St. Margaret; on the cymatium in the centre Christ on the cross, with the Virgin and St. John, and on either side St. Michael and St. John the Baptist; in the pinnacles above the central group, God the Father blessing the Angel of the Annunciation and the Virgin of the Annunciation. Above the side pinnacles are St. Ottilia and St. Scholastica (?). On the frame of the shrine, the Tree of Jesse, on that of the predella, according to Hempel, Abishai, Benaiah and Sabothai taking water to David or possibly the Queen of Sheba with two attendants bringing gifts to Solomon. The paintings on gold backgrounds of the open first wings represent: top left, the Nativity; top right, the Presentation in the Temple; bottom left, the Circumcision; bottom right, the Death of the Virgin. The paintings on the first wings closed and the second wings open show: above, the Baptism of Christ, the Temptation of Christ, the Marriage at Cana, the Miracle of the Loaves and Fishes; below, the Attempted Stoning of Christ, Christ cleansing the Temple, Christ and the woman taken in adultery, the Resurrection of Lazarus. The paintings on the second wings closed show: top left, St. Wolfgang preaching and top right, giving alms; bottom left, St. Wolfgang building a church and, bottom right, curing a woman possessed by the devil. Those of the predella wings show: inside, on gold grounds, the Visitation and the Flight into Egypt; outside, the four Church Fathers with their respective symbols; on the back of the predella, the four Evangelists with their symbols.
Painted on the back of the shrine are: in the centre, St. Christopher; in the lower row on the left, St. Erasmus and St. Ulrich; on the right, St. Clare and St. Elizabeth (the latter with the date 1479); in the upper row on the left, St. Otmar and St. Francis of Assisi; on the right, St. Hubert and St. Egidius. On the bottom of the outside frame of the two wings is the following inscription: "Benedictus abbas in mansee hoc opus fecit fieri ac complevit per magistrum Michaelem pacher de Prawnegk anno dni MCCCCLXXXI."

Mainly in pinewood. Shrine 3.90 m. high, 3.29 m. wide, 0.72.5 m. deep; predella 1.19 m. high, 2.92.2 m. wide at base, 2.42.5 m. at centre. Cymatium 4.75 m. high. Overall height 11.10 m. Statues of the shrine: Christ, excluding crown, 1.29 m. (crown 0.45 m.); Virgin, with crown, 1.16 m.; St. Wolfgang, 1.81 m.; St. Benedict, 1.70 m.; statues of St. George and St. Florian, 1.74 m.; statues of the predella: St. Joseph, 0.64 m., Virgin, with base, 0.62 m.

Wings of the shrine, with frames, 3.84+1.64 m, the single paintings, 1.73 × 1.40.5 m.; wings of the predella, with frames, 0.86.5 × 0.74.5 m.; the single paintings 0.71.8 × 0.59.5 m.

The measurements were checked by Hempel who corrected Stiassny's previous calculations.

The contract for the altar was signed on 13 December 1471, but work was delayed for several years. The paintings on the back of the shrine bear the date 1479 whereas the inscription on the outer wings records its completion in 1481. It was decided in 1675 to replace the altar with another, but nothing came of this. A radical restoration was undertaken in 1861, many broken and missing pieces were repaired and replaced, including the hands of the Virgin, under the direction of the sculptor Hans Rint of Linz, while the paintings were cleaned in Vienna by Erasmus Enger.

The altar was described for the first time by Primisser (1822, p. 476) who gave a detailed account of it, including the inscription with the name of the artist. Weidmann (1834) however maintained that Pacher was responsible only for the carved parts and attributed the paintings to Wohlgemut, whereas the *Bote für Tirol* shortly afterwards (1838) claimed the paintings as well as the carving for Pacher. Schnaase (1868) supported this claim, and to him we owe an early account of Pacher's work and the recognition of his contact with the art of Mantegna. Stiassny however allowed Pacher only the painted parts of the altar (1897, 1903), and Dehio considered that he was merely the entrepreneur for the work. In 1912 Zibermayr discovered and published the contract for the altar. Mannowsky (1910) maintained that Pacher was the artist responsible for most of the panels, assigning to the workshop, or to "an artist closely linked with Michael Pacher but relatively independent in his conceptions", the Temptation of Christ, Christ cleansing the Temple, the Marriage at Cana, Christ and the woman taken in adultery and the Church Fathers; and he attributed to Friedrich Pacher the Baptism of Christ, the Attempted Stoning, the Loaves and Fishes, the Resurrection of Lazarus and the four stories of St. Wolfgang. In 1919 Stiassny inclined to the idea that Pacher was the creator of the carvings as well as of the paintings. Hempel (1931, pp. 49 ff.) analysed the problem of the contributions by other hands, reaching conclusions which are still generally acceptable. He did not agree with Pächt's attribution (1929) of the paintings on the back of the shrine to a painter from Braunau (Meister des Bäckeraltars). Hempel (1929), revising his previous conclusions, indicated as works by Pacher's hand, in addition to the four stories of the Virgin on the shrine and the two on the predella, the four stories of Christ on the first wings and St. Erasmus and St. Ulrich, St. Clare and St. Elizabeth, on the rear wall. Finally, he indicated as workshop production most of the figures of the cymatium and considered late studio work the group of the Adoration of the Magi in the predella. Stange (1960, pp. 170 ff.) ascribed to Georg Stäber the paintings on the back of the shrine.

Salzburg, Franciscan Church (formerly Parish Church). High altar.

The contract for the altar was signed at Salzburg in 1484; in 1495 Michael Pacher moved to Salzburg with his assistants to complete what still remained to be done and to erect the altar. Save for some minor details of the predella the work was finished when Pacher died in 1498, probably between the end of July and early August (Wolfsgruber, 1969). The settlement of his estate was completed on 6 December 1502 and probate granted to Caspar Neuhauser, the husband of a daughter of Pacher, and from this it appears that the total cost of the altar was 3,500 Rhenish florins.

The altar was dismantled in 1709 and largely destroyed in order to extract the gold and silver. Only the statue of the Virgin was kept in the church, set on a contemporary altar in Baroque style and dressed in cloth garments. The documents concerning the erection of the altar were published in 1869 by Fr. P. Haberleiter O.S.F. In 1918 F. M. Haberditzl announced the acquisition of the double panel showing the Flagellation and the Betrothal by the Österreichische Galerie, Vienna. This had previously been in private hands at Baden, near Vienna. He later (1919) attributed it to Michael Pacher and suggested that it had come from the St. Michael altar at Bolzano (1481-4). The Salzburg provenance was proposed first by Benesch (1928), then with reservations by Pächt (1929) and Hempel (1931), Baldass (1934) and Frey (1953). The discovery of fragments of a panel of the altar in the Franciscan convent at Salzburg (Hoppe, 1954) removed any lingering doubt as to the provenance of the Vienna panels from this altar. The problem of the original arrangement of the altar was tackled by Demus (1954) whose conclusions must still be considered the most probable. He suggested that a fragment of the Flight into Egypt now in the Basle Museum must come from one of the predella wings. Stange (1960, p. 177) ignored this suggestion, proposing a heterogeneous collection of panels of different provenance and by different hands as wing-panels.

Salzbug, Franciscan Church. Statue of the Virgin: Plates 112, 113; fig. 176.

Limewood, 1.46 m. high.
The only part of the altar to remain in the church. Mutilated in order to accommodate the cloth garments at the end of the sixteenth century, it was placed in the Baroque high altar in 1709-10. In 1864-5 the garments were removed and the statue restored, but the figure of the Infant was considered too badly damaged and it was removed and probably destroyed, and replaced by another figure which in turn was removed and replaced by the present statue. Finally the later painting was removed and the original colouring, in so far as it had survived, was revealed.

Vienna, Österreichische Galerie. Panel with the Betrothal of the Virgin and the Flagellation of Christ: Plates XIX, XX, 114-118.

Pinewood, 1.51 high × 1.395 m.
Formerly in a private collection at Baden (Vienna), purchased by the Gallery in 1918 and divided into two parts.

Vienna, Österreichische Galerie. Part of a panel with Joseph being lowered into the well: Plates 121, 122.

Pinewood, 2.61 × 0.85 m.
Discovered in 1854 (Hoppe) when an old cupboard in the Franciscan convent at Salzburg was demolished and identified as part of the former high altar.
According to Demus it is partially workshop production of a design by Michael Pacher.

Basle, Öffentliche Kunstsammlung. Panel with the Flight into Egypt: Plate 120.

Oak, 0.51.6 high × 0.45.6 m.
A bequest by the Bachofen-Burckhardt Foundation from a private collection in Vienna. Published as a work of Pacher's by Suida in 1922, this attribution was accepted by Pächt (1929) and Hempel (1931), who assigned it to the period of the St. Wolfgang altar and suggested that it was the predella panel of an altar of modest dimensions. Demus (1954, p. 90) proposed the provenance of the Salzburg altar and dated it to the Salzburg period, maintaining that it was by the hand of the master. Stange (1960, p. 169) however returns to the old theory, dating it to c. 1470.

Vienna, Private collection (Dr. F. Kieslinger). Fragment with the head of St. Anne: Plate 119.

Pinewood, 51 × 37 cm.
Published by Öttinger (1942, p. 28) as a fragment of a panel of the Birth of the Virgin from the Salzburg altar. The suggestion was accepted by both Oberhammer (1950) and Demus (1954).

LOST WORKS BY MICHAEL PACHER

Formerly at Bolzano, Castel Novale. Votive altar.

In 1862 Karl Atz published anonymously a description of the principal works of religious art in the deanery of Bolzano, and recorded for the first time (p. 24) an altar in the chapel of Castel Novale, whose centre panel showed a Pietà executed in 1465 but which had been restored in about 1676 ("In the chapel . . . there is a medieval altar in bad condition whose centre panel shows a Pietà, a work of 1465 which was restored in 1676"). Later Woltmann-Wörmann (1882, p. 127) described the same altar, affirming that it was a winged altar on which were painted Christ with the symbols of the Passion, two saints and the donor with the inscription "Micha.. Pa.er 1465". Atz (1885, p. 334) mentioned it again in the first edition of his History of Art in the Tyrol. The altar was later sold to the antiquarian dealer Überbacher of Bolzano who resold it to a Professor Klein of Vienna (Semper, 1911, p. 311) but in spite of the researches of Mannowsky and others it has never come to light. The altar has thus disappeared leaving no indication of its fate, as Atz explains (1903, p. 79); he also names the donor as a parish priest of Caldaro, according to an inscription. In 1465 the parish priest was one Lupi, chaplain to Duke Sigismund; he was installed in 1447 and died shortly after 1467. All attempts to identify the altar have so far proved fruitless (Hempel, 1931, p. 81).

140, 144 Statue of St. Lawrence, and detail, attributed to Michael Pacher. Innsbruck, Ferdinandeum Museum | 141, 145 Statue of the Virgin and Child, and detail. Gries (Bolzano), former Parish Church | 142 Panel with St. Barbara. Formerly Wilten (Innsbruck) | 143 Fresco on the keystone. Tesido, Welsberg Chapel | 146 Panel with the Mass of St. Augustine by the Uttenheim Master. Novacella, Convent

147, 148, 149 Vault frescoes with the Fathers of the Church. Novacella, Sacristy | 150, 151 Frescoes on the south and west sides by Friedrich Pacher, before destruction. Monguelfo, Tabernacle | 152 Detail of the frescoes on the east side. Monguelfo, Tabernacle.

153, 156 Figure of St. Candidus over the south door, and detail. S. Candido, Collegiate Church | 154, 157 Figure of the Emperor Otto over the south door, and detail. S. Candido, Collegiate Church | 155, 158 Figure of St. Corbinian over the south door, and detail. S. Candido, Collegiate Church

159, 160, 161 Baptism of Christ; Miracle of the Loaves and Fishes; and the Raising of Lazarus. Paintings from the middle wings of the high altar. St. Wolfgang, Parish Church | 162, 163, 164 St. Wolfgang giving alms; St. Wolfgang preaching; and St. Wolfgang building a church. Scenes from the outside wings of the high altar. St. Wolfgang, Parish Church

Novacella, Altar of St. Thomas Becket.

Two small panels 0.44 × 0.44 m. with the symbols of the Evangelists John (an eagle) and Matthew (an angel) on a gold background on one side, and episodes from the life of St. Thomas Becket on the other. Also a centre panel of unknown subject of about 1 × 1 m.

S. Lorenzo in Pusteria, Parish Church. Former high altar.

Two paintings of the life of the Virgin, about 1.04 × 1 m., probably depicting the Visitation and the Nativity of Christ; with statues of St. Lawrence and St. Michael (?) on the shrine, other statues from the cymatium and unidentified fragments on the predella.

Gries (Bolzano), former Parish Church. Former high altar.

The following statues in the round are missing at present from the altar: St. Sebastian and St. Florian (about 1.50 m.); Christ Crucified mourned by Mary and John; the Virgin (identified by Schwabik as the existing statue, but considered too large by Hempel). Statues in high relief: heads of St. Blaise, St. Leonard, St. John the Baptist, St. Vigilius. Low reliefs: Nativity of Christ (1.72 × 1.38 m.) and Death of the Virgin (same dimensions); St. Wolfgang and St. George (from the predella wings). Paintings: Christ in the Garden, the Flagellation, Crucifixion, Resurrection, all 1.72 high × 1.38 m. St. Barbara and St. Catharine (predella wings).

Bolzano, Parish Church. St. Michael altar.

The contract for the altar was drawn up on 14 November 1481, the last payment made in November 1484. The altar was removed and disappeared in 1687. A description of it is found in the Visitors Records of 1674: "Visitatum fuit altare Sancti Michaelis existens in cornu Epistolae in medio ecclesiae, quod altare habet icones ligneas sculptas et inauratas, videlicet in medio Beatissimae Virginis, ex partibus vero Sancti Michaelis et Sancti Martini. Pala facta more antiquo ad formam armarii, quae clauditur duobus portis." (Arch. Curia Vesc. Trento).
Koch first mentioned the altar in 1846 after an examination of the accounts of the church; Spornberger (1894, p. 28) traced its history. The documents were published in their entirety by Hoeniger (*Schlern*, 1936, pp. 7 ff.). Doering suggested (1913, p. 95) that the statue of St. Michael now in the Bayerisches Nationalmuseum was a surviving part of the altar, he was supported by Fülner (1939 pp. 357 ff.), Hempel (1940, pp. 48 ff.) and others. Benesch (1956, pp. 196 ff.) denied this possibility on stylistic grounds and proposed instead that a small statue of St. Michael in the Museo di Palazzo Venezia, Rome, might be a portion of the Bolzano altar, arguing that the altar had cost only 26 marks in all and could thus comprise only a single statue of modest dimensions. The 1674 document cited above leads one to reject Benesch's hypothesis, especially since the St. Michael statue in Rome would not be suitable for the altar described above as the shrine is in the round and thus designed to be viewed from all sides.

Formerly at Salzburg, altar of St. Michael am Aschhof.

On 23 November 1496 the Abbot of St. Peter's, Salzburg, paid a sum of 15 pounds for a panel of St. Michael am Aschhof, and another 5 pounds shortly after and finally on 24 August 1498, the artist having died in the meantime, another 20 pounds to his son-in-law, Caspar Neuhauser. Since we have only this evidence to go on, certainly insufficient to solve the problem, it is not known whether it concerns the altarpiece for the high altar or for one of the side altars. For the same reason the attempts to identify the work with the St. Catharine panel, which in fact comes from St. Peter's, Salzburg, and is now in the Fondazione Rohoncz in Castagnola, have no foundation and can neither be accepted nor rejected. We have tried to show the work is not by Michael Pacher but by his son Hans.

Salzburg, Franciscan Church. Former high altar.

Three panels depicting episodes from the Passion, three from the life of the Virgin, one fragment of which shows the Nativity of the Virgin, and three biblical stories. The sculptures and reliefs were destroyed so as to extract the gold.

WORKS BY MEMBERS OF HIS CIRCLE FORMERLY ATTRIBUTED TO MICHAEL PACHER

WORKS BY HANS PACHER

London, National Gallery. Small panel with the Virgin and two saints: Plate 55.

A panel (41 × 40 cm.) purchased apparently in Bressanone in about 1880 and bequeathed to the National Gallery in 1947, published by Gould (1951) as possibly by the Master of Uttenheim, and by Ringler (1951) with an attribution to Michael Pacher confirmed by Hempel (1952, p. 28), and acknowledged as possible by Frey (1953, pp. 56 ff.). Demus pointed out analogies with the Virgin of the Ursulines at Salzburg (1957). Rejected by Stange (1960, p. 178) who assigns it to the workshop and dates it to the 1480s. If, as is possible, it is by Michael Pacher, it should be assigned to the early years between the St. Thomas and the St. Lawrence altars. But it could be a particularly successful work by Hans Pacher of c. 1480.

Vienna, Österreichische Galerie. Panel with St. Barbara: Fig. 175.

A panel in pinewood according to Hempel, in beechwood, according to others, 54 × 41 cm. depicting St. Barbara in half-length with her tower and a sword. Said to come from Salzburg where it was purchased by the antiquarian Annegg, it was sold by him to Klotz at Merano and by the latter to Colli at Innsbruck, whence it was acquired in 1933 by the Österreichische Galerie where it is now exhibited. Published by Hempel (1931, p. 76) as the work of Michael Pacher during his stay in Salzburg, it was dated by Baldass (1934, pp. 12, 29) to c. 1470. Kuhn (1935, p. 175) identifies it as one of a pair of wing paintings, the other being a St. Catharine, which is however by Friedrick Pacher.

Suida (1936, p. 303) confirmed Kuhn's suggestion but with a change of location, maintaining that the outer part of the panel should be identified as a St. Florian on beechwood which has the same grain as the Vienna panel; but he sets the date at 1470, while Stange (1960, p. 177) prefers a dating to c. 1490, considering it part of the predella of the Salzburg altar. Ascribed to Michael Pacher by Oberhammer (1950) and, with some hesitation, by Baldass (1950). Demus (1957, p. 5) sees "a lack of precision and clarity which is quite alien to Pacher's art", and attributes it to "a younger assistant following the late style of Pacher but giving a pictorial interpretation which heralds future tendencies of the Danubian style". Rasmo (1959, p. 131) denies the prevailing attribution to Michael Pacher, proposing a dating to about 1500.
Hans Pacher, c. 1495-1500.

Rome, Museo di Palazzo Venezia. Statue of St. Michael: Fig. 170.

Statue in Styrian fir, 90 cm. high, worked in the round. Presented to the Museum by E. Wurts and formerly considered the work of an unidentified Alsatian sculptor of the mid-fifteenth century. Attributed to Michael Pacher by Benesch (1956, pp. 205 ff.) and thought, without any evidence, to be part of the St. Michael altar made by Pacher for the Bolzano parish church between 1481 and 1484.
Hans Pacher, c. 1480-90.

Glasenbach (Salzburg), Ursuline Convent. Statue of the Virgin and Child: Fig. 167.

55 cm. high. Formerly in the convent at Salzburg. Part of the right arm of the Child has been renovated; early colouring but not original; crown missing; otherwise in good condition. Demus, who first published the work in 1956, denies that it could come from the predella of the Salzburg altar, as it is a statue for devotional purposes worked in the round. He sees facial resemblances to the Virgin in the Betrothal panel formerly in Salzburg and now in Vienna (which I consider a collaborative work of the Pacher workshop), to the St. Barbara in Vienna and the St. Sebastian in Innsbruck, which I have attributed to Hans Pacher. He does not exclude the participation of Michael Pacher, but leaves the verdict open.
Hans Pacher, c. 1495-1500.

Castagnola (Lugano), Thyssen-Bornemisza Collection. Panel with the Betrothal of St. Catharine, formerly in St. Peter's, Salzburg: Plates 123, 124.

Panel in beechwood, 1.67 × 0.77 m. It depicts the Virgin enthroned with the Child, crowned by angels and worshipped by St. Margaret (with a cross in her hand and a demon at her feet) and St. Catharine (portrayed receiving the ring from Christ with the broken wheel at her feet). Exhibited for the first time in 1888 in the Künstlerhaus, Salzburg, it was attributed by Semper (1891, p. 62) to Michael Pacher and thought to be part of the high altar of the old parish church. Stiassny rejected this part of the hypothesis, but considered it a late work of the master. Doering (1913, pp. 69 ff.) considered it a work of c. 1480. Hempel (1931, p. 69) retained the attribution to Pacher with some collaboration from the workshop, and dated the panel to about 1485, while Allesch (1931, pp. 191 ff.) rejected the

participation of the master and thought it a work-shop piece of the Salzburg period. In 1949 the panel joined the Thyssen collection at Lugano, from which it passed to the Fondazione Rohoncz at Castagnola, where it remains at the present time. Exhibited at Innsbruck in 1950, it was considered by Oberhammer and others a collaborative work or by pupils (Stange, 1960, p. 177, with a dating to c. 1490). Lutterotti thought it a late work begun by Michael Pacher and completed by the work-shop (1950, p. 365).
Hans Pacher, c. 1500.

Novara, Private collection. Panel with St. Margaret.

The panel depicting the head of St. Margaret, now in private hands at Novara, is 55 × 41 cm. and was first published by Rosci (1959, pp. 128 ff.), but it appears to have been known to Stange (1960, p. 177 and confirmed by letter of 8 January 1962). The work was heavily restored at some period and the background, the crown and the cross comple-tely regilded. Described by Rosci as the work of "an individual working in the footsteps of Pacher who collaborated on the St. Wolfgang altar (the predella) and then, in more personal work, em-phasizes the 'Flemish' aspect of the master's char-acter, without departing from the style of the St. Wolfgang altar, which can be found, Hempel observes, in the Lugano panel formerly in St. Pe-ter's, Salzburg". Rosci adds a useful comparison with the Basle fragment of the Flight into Egypt. Stange's view that the panel should be considered part of a predella together with the St. Barbara panel formerly in Colli's possession and now in Vienna, and two other panels in private collections representing St. George and St. Florian, was rejected by Rasmo (1959, p. 130), and is now discarded. Stange's assertion that this heterogeneous collec-tion constituted the predella of the Salzburg altar has also been rejected. The breadth of the Casta-gnola panel (77 cm.), moreover, makes it unlikely that it was connected with a predella whose wings alone, without the frame, being each 41 cm. wide, would be far larger than 82 cm. Furthermore, the Castagnola altarpiece presupposes predella wings at least as long as the centre panel. The artist who worked in Michael Pacher's footsteps and who emphasized his Flemish aspects was, in my opinion, his son Hans, to whom this panel should accor-dingly be assigned.

Location unknown. Two panels with St. Andrew and St. Catharine, St. Benedict and St. Scolastica, formerly in St. Peter's, Salzburg.

In beechwood, 56.5 × 50 cm., formerly in St. Pe-ter's, Salzburg (cf. Österr. Kunsttop. xii, p. 110). Pächt (1929, p. 79) believed then to be from Mi-chael Pacher's workshop and the work of the artist of the St. Thomas Becket panels; they were assigned by Hammer (Thieme-Becker, XXVIII, 1934, p. 107) to Marx Reichlich. Later sold pri-vately. The first was exhibited at Innsbruck in 1950 with the attribution to Pacher (Oberhammer, 1950, p. 38, Pl. 146; Baldass, 1950, p. 217; Lutterotti, 1950, p. 365) and dated to about 1470, in close association with the Munich Coronation. Stange (1960) linked it with the other panel and assigned both to Pacher's workshop, suggesting as prov-enance the predella of the St. Michael am Aschhof altar. Stange correctly considers then to be by the same hand as the Innsbruck St. Sebastian.

The panel with St. Benedict and St. Scolastica was auctioned at Christie's in 1964 with an attribution to Reichlich (cf. *Burlington Magazine*, March 1964, p. XIV).
Hans Pacher, c. 1500.

Innsbruck, Ferdinandeum Museum. Two panels with St. Sebastian and St. Barbara: Figs. 172, 173.

Two larchwood panels, 44.5 × 34.8 cm. from the inner and outer sides of two sawn off predella wings. Formerly the property of Gottfried Vor-hauser of Brunico, whose name is on the back, they passed into the collection of Bernhard Höfel at Innsbruck and in 1943 were bequeathed to the Ferdinandeum Museum, Innsbruck. The St. Se-bastian panel was exhibited in 1950 after repainting had been removed, and judged to be a work of Michael Pacher by Oberhammer (1950, p. 40), Baldass (1950, p. 217) and Lutterotti (1950, p. 365). Demus expressed doubts (1957, p. 5) and Stange (X, 1960, p. 178) rejected the attribution assigning the work to the artist of the St. Andrew and St. Catharine panel formerly in St. Peter's, Salzburg. The outer panel of St. Barbara cannot have been cut from the St. Sebastian panel, as has been thought, because the wood has different characteristics and because the figure would then be looking outwards from the centre of the predella. It must be the outer side of the left wing of the same predella. The attribution to Michael Pacher cannot be justi-fied for either panel. The St. Sebastian panel is certainly by Hans Pacher, datable to 1505-07, among his last works, and later than the Castagnola panel. I suggest it was painted at Brunico after the artist's final return to his country and shortly before his death.
Hans Pacher, 1505-07.

Vienna, Academy of Fine Arts. Two fresco fragments.

A fragment with the head of the Virgin of the Annunciation (56 × 49 cm.) and another with the head of the Angel of the Annunciation (85 × 52 cm.). Apparently originating in the Alto Adige, they were acquired in 1952 and restored in 1956. Linked to Pacher by Münz (1956, no. 11) and by Rasmo, they were assigned to Michael Pacher by Stange (1960) and thought to be contemporary with the fresco on the parish church at Bolzano (now held to be by Friedrich Pacher) and the Lonodn panel. Perhaps by Hans Pacher. Most recently published by Poch-Kalous with an attribution to an artist of Pacher's circle (1960, pp. 15 ff.).

WORKS BY FRIEDRICH PACHER

Spanheim, Abbey of St. Paul in Lavant. Ceiling frescoes.

Considered by Benesch (1929) to be by Friedrich Pacher after drawings by Michael Pacher. Similar conclusions were reached by Hempel (1931, pp. 52 ff.) who suggested a date between 1470 and 1476. Frodl (1944, p. 108) attributed the heads of Sts. Michael, Peter, Paul, Egidius, Benedict, and Wolf-gang, to Michael and the others to Friedrich Pacher.

Bolzano, Parish Church. Fresco of the Virgin ("Plapper-mutter"): Figs. 171, 174.

Fresco showing the Virgin enthroned and Child against a landscape background, with an inscrip-tion beneath, which is now illegible. Badly restored and painted over in oils by Hintner in 1886 (*Kunst-freund*, 1886, pp. 15, 68; 1887, pp. 2167) in spite of the objections of the Vienna authorities, it de-teriorated rapidly through the disintegration of the colour. Damaged during the last war, it was re-cleaned and restored in about 1950. Stiassny arbi-trarily applied to this work a document which led him to attribute it to Master Nicolaus, executed in about 1486-7; Weingartner (*Kunstdenkm. d. Etschl.*, III, p. 103) associated it with Pacher and made a penetrating stylistic analysis (*Die gotische Wand-malerei in Südtirol*, 1948, p. 58). Rasmo showed (*Cult. Ates.*, 1948, pp. 52 ff. and 1950, p. 147) that the fresco had nothing to do with the document of 1486-7; he confirmed its close connection with Pacher and proposed a date of c. 1470.
Friedrich Pacher, c. 1475.

Novacella, Cloister. Fresco with episodes of the Rich Man and Lazarus.

Discovered in 1931 above an earlier fresco on the same subject commissioned from Paul Geltinger (d. 1367), it was unfortunately split in two by a memorial tablet fixed into the wall. On the surface of the vault is the figure of Lazarus in Abraham's bosom, on the wall a rich architectural frame with prophets, saints and angels in niches, and between them the rich man among the flames of hell; on the left, the scene of the feast, of which only fragments remain, in the centre, and the right, a street in perspective, probably the background to a scene showing Lazarus begging. Attributed by Schrott (1931, pp. 424 ff.) and Salvini (*Le arti*, 1949, p. 191) to Michael Pacher with the collab-oration of Friedrich; by Theil (1946, pp. 32 ff.), who wrongly believed he could distinguish the artist's signature, to Michael alone. The frag-mentary inscription, however, probably refers to the donor ("Maria hatt dises..."). Attributed by Weingartner (1948, pp. 58 ff.) to Michael Pacher; by Rasmo (1950, p. 153) to Friedrich.
Friedrich Pacher, c. 1480-85.

Anterselva, St. Walpurga. Fresco of St. Christopher.

Prince Clement of Bavaria showed it to Hempel who published it with an attribution to Michael Pacher (1931, p. 76).
Friedrich Pacher, c. 1490.

New York, Private collection. Panel with St. Catharine.

Painted on beechwood (44 × 41 cm.) showing a half-length of St. Catharine with the sword and wheel. From the Hugo Perl collection, Berlin, it passed to H. Schniewind in New York; it was exhibited at Chicago in 1934 and published by Ch. L. Kuhn in 1935 (pp. 174 ff.) as a work by Michael Pacher, dated c. 1485. Kuhn considered it part of a single larger work including the Colli St. Barbara now in Vienna, and surmised that the difference in height was due to the way they had been sawn apart.
Suida (1936, p. 303) accepted the attribution, but not the view that the St. Catharine of New York

165, 166 The Fathers of the Church, on the predella wings of the high altar. St. Wolfgang, Parish Church | 167 Statue of the Virgin and Child. Glasenbach (Salzburg), Ursuline Convent | 168, 169 The Evangelists, on the back of the predella of the high altar. St. Wolfgang, Parish Church | 170 Statue of St. Michael. Rome, Museo di Palazzo Venezia

171, 174 Fresco with the Virgin Enthroned, and detail. Bolzano, Parish Church | 172 Panel with St. Barbara. Innsbruck, Ferdinandeum Museum | 173 Panel with St. Sebastian. Innsbruck, Ferdinandeum Museum | 175 St. Barbara Panel. Vienna, Österreichisches Galerie | 176 Virgin and Child, from the former high altar (before nineteenth-century restoration). Salzburg, Franciscan Church

was the corresponding panel to the Vienna St. Barbara, because the former had a blue ground (it had however been restored) and the latter a gold ground; he announced that the real companion painting was a half-figure of St. Florian in a private collection in Austria, which he claimed was the separated outer side of the St. Barbara panel as the grain of the wood coincided. He altered the dating to c. 1470. Hempel (1952, p. 33) considers the St. Catharine panel is closer to the circle of Friedrich. Stange (1960, p. 177) accepted Suida's views, assigning the panels, with the exception of the St. Barbara of Vienna, to Pacher's workshop and proposing as provenance the predella of the Salzburg altar, together with a St. George in a private collection, already identified by Oberhammer. Rasmo (1950, p. 130) rejected these proposals and attributed the panel to Friedrich Pacher.
Friedrich Pacher.

WORKS BY MARX REICHLICH

Hall, Parish Church. Statue of the Virgin in the Waldauf Altar.

Attributed by Sommer (1927, pp. 226 ff.) to Michael Pacher, rejected by Hempel (1931, pp. 83 ff.) though with some hesitation. Ascribed by Rasmo (1950, p. 155) to Reichlich after Oberhammer (1950, pp. 50 ff.) had attempted to justify the earlier attribution assuming that the altar was commissioned from Pacher after 1492 and begun by him but finished by others.
Marx Reichlich, c. 1500-05.

Innsbruck, Wilten Convent. Frescoes in the Chapter-House.

Discovered in 1948 and over-restored (cf. Kmentt, 1967), they were attributed to Michael Pacher (Gritsch, 1948) with the collaboration of others and dated to about 1480 by the identification of a view of Novacella with the fortifications of 1476 (rejected by the present writer). Kmentt (1967, pp. 67 ff.) assigns them to the Uttenheim Master, with the date already suggested. The frescoes are certainly not by Pacher, and probably not by the Uttenheim Master, but can be dated to c. 1500-10 and tentatively assigned to Marx Reichlich, with whose work they have various characteristics in common.
Marx Reichlich, c. 1500-05.

WORKS BY THE UTTENHEIM MASTER

Munich, Pinakothek. Coronation of the Virgin: Plates 125-127.

Painted on pinewood, 1.44 × 0.92 m., sawn along all four sides; probably there were two figures of saints in niches at the sides, as in the Gries shrine. The Gothic tracery suggests by analogy that a group of other wing-panels may be associated with it: the Nativity of the Virgin (Nuremburg), the Death of the Virgin (Munich), the Annunciation (Munich), Christ in the Garden (Vienna), and Christ crowned with thorns (Bressanone). Removed from Novacella in 1812, it was taken to the Augusta Gallery and from there to the Munich Pinakothek in 1910. Attributed by Braune in 1911 to Michael Pacher and dated to 1460-70; the attribution was generally accepted (Stiassny, Pächt, Hempel, Oberhammer); Hempel however dated the altar as later than that of Gries. Rasmo (1950) questions this and assigns it to the last decades of the fifteenth century as a possible work by the Uttenheim Master executed to designs by Michael Pacher. The wing-panels brought together with the Munich centre panel on the occasion of the Innsbruck exhibition should all be assigned to the Uttenheim Master. The studies of Colleselli (1955) showed that the panel did not come, as previously believed, from the castle at Ambras, but from the Novacella convent, together with two wing-panels. After Stange (1960) had revived the old attribution with a date of c. 1460, Rasmo (1968) renewed the suggestion that the work was by the Uttenheim Master when another panel from the wings of the same altar was discovered.
The Uttenheim Master (Marx Scherhauff?) c. 1490-95.

OTHER WORKS FORMERLY ATTRIBUTED TO MICHAEL PACHER

Vipiteno, Wildenburg Collection. Statue of the Virgin and Child.

Formerly in a roadside tabernacle near the church of St. Margaret at Vipiteno; published by Weingartner (1922, p. 108); Hempel (1931, p. 64) assigned it to the Pacher circle; dated first by Rasmo (1950, p. 144) to c. 1455 or shortly after, not excluding the possibility that it was an early work by Pacher; Later on (1963, pp. 55, 65) he attributed it to Hans Harder and dated it c. 1460-70.

Vipiteno, St. Peter's. Fresco of the Virgin with St. Peter and St. Paul.

The fresco, wich depicts the Virgin enthroned between St. Peter and St. Paul within a richly decorated frame, is above the entrance to the church where it was broken up by the insertion of a marble doorway (late Gothic). It is probably contemporary with the building of the church (1464). Attributed by Mannowsky (1910, p. 64) to Michael Pacher, it was dated by Weingartner to about 1480 and assigned by him (1923, p. 99) to the Pacher workshop. Stylistically akin to the Wildenburg Virgin, the fresco reflects artistic taste in Vipiteno around 1470-75, strongly impregnated by motifs from beyond the Alps, perhaps from south-west Swabia. It has good qualities but is in very bad condition, so a precise opinion is difficult to reach.

Erlangen, University Library. Two sheets of drawings.

Two sheets with drawings in pen and watercolour wash on both sides: on the first a bishop's mitre, front- and side-views, with the sketched head of a bishop; on the second, the back of a mitre and the curved top of a crozier, with the inscription St. Zeno. Bock linked them with Reichenhall. The sketches, possibly intended as models for a goldsmith or an embroiderer, were perhaps made from old episcopal accoutrements, and were attributed by Bock to Michael Pacher, accepted by Hempel (1931, pp. 86 ff.), rejected decisively by Demus (1954, pp. 116 ff.).

Hanover, Polytechnic Library. Drawing.

A sketch depicting a bishop with a forged Dürer monogram, attributed to Pacher by Tietze (1929), Hempel (1931, p. 87) and Baumeister (1949), rejected and identified as by Burgkmair (cf. Demus, 1954, pp. 117 ff.).

Innsbruck, Ferdinandeum Museum. Head of John the Baptist.

Limewood, 0.27 m. This fine carving, bought in Hall in 1884 by the antiquarian Colli, was attributed to Pacher by Langhans (1912), accepted with some reservation by Hempel (1931, p. 8); considered by Oberhammer (1950, p. 40) to be influenced by Pacher but not by his hand. It has no connection with the Pacher circle.

Munich, Pinakothek. Portrait of Archduke Sigismund.

Formerly attributed to an anonymous painter from Munich (Buchner) and to Ulrich Fuetrer (Dworschak); assigned to Michael Pacher by Stange and dated to about 1465.

Location unknown. Portrait of Alexander Mornauer.

Formerly attributed by Buchner to an anonymous Munich painter, it was recently ascribed to Michael Pacher by Stange (1960, p. 179) and dated to c. 1480. The attribution seems to be without foundation.

Rychnov (Czechoslovakia) Castle, Gallery. Panel with the Birth of the Virgin.

Probably identifiable as the panel depicting a similar subject attributed by Pächt to the Pacher school in about 1475, and incorrectly assigned to the Rudolfinum, Prague (Pächt, 1929, p. 79). Published by Pcsina (1956, pp. 42 ff.) as a work of Pacher's circle of c. 1480. Ascribed by Stange (1960, p. 175) to Michael Pacher himself and dated to the final decade of the fifteenth century.

Bressanone, Diocesan Museum. Four wooden busts of saints.

Busts representing Sts. Ingenuinus, Albuinus, Cassianus and Armannus: the first two are late Gothic, restored in the eighteenth century, the other two probably date from the eighteenth century. Attributed by Morassi (1928, pp. 93 ff.) to Michael Pacher, rejected by Hempel (1931, p. 84) on information from Müller (1929, p. 66) who attributed them to Hans Klocker, which was confirmed by Scheffler (1967, p. 34) with a date of 1490-95.
Hans Klocker, c. 1495.

Bressanone, Diocesan Museum. Fresco in the old Chapter-House.

The fresco was discovered in 1926 and badly restored. It is divided into three parts by Gothic frames and the central Crucifixion has been partly destroyed by a window opening; on the left is the Sacrifice of Isaac, on the right the episode of the Brazen Serpent. Hempel (1931, p. 77) assigned it to Michael Pacher dating it to the last decade of the fifteenth century, followed by Stange, who however (1960, p. 175) suggests the collaboration of Friedrich. It is certainly not by Pacher, but a late work, datable to the first decade of the sixteenth century if not later, by a painter who had Pacher's work in mind. The present condition of the fresco does not permit a close examination.

Location unknown. Panel of St. Florian.

Painted on beechwood, (54.5 × 41 cm.) formerly in a private collection in Austria, it was published by Suida (1936, p. 303) with an attribution to Michael Pacher and a dating to about 1470. He also asserted that the matching of the grain of the wood permitted the assumption that this was the outer side sawn from the St. Barbara panel in the Österreichische Galerie, Vienna; he associated the two panels with the St. Catharine panel published in 1935 by Kuhn, which he considers the outside of the left wing of the same predella. These views were accepted by Stange (1960, p. 177), but he attributed the work to the Pacher workshop, assigning it to the predella of the Salzburg altar. Rasmo (1959, p. 130) was unwilling to form a judgement on the link with the Salzburg altar but rejected the attribution to Michael Pacher and his followers, proposing as artist a painter of the studio of Hans Klocker. This suggestion is a tentative one, and brings the date to the end of the fifteenth century if not later. The panel is not, however, by the St. Barbara artist, nor can it be ascribed to Pacher's immediate circle.

Tesido, Parish Church. Keystone of the Welsberg chapel: Fig. 143.

Fresco of the head of a Virgin and Child, first attributed to Pacher by Semper in 1891, rejected by Pächt (1929, p. 79), accepted by Hempel (1931, p. 35) who dates it *c.* 1471-2, and in any case prior to the Gries altar.

1462-3. Works on the altar of S. Lorenzo in Pusteria.

1465. Signs the Castel Novale (Bolzano) altar.

1467. In Brunico.

1468. Named as proprietor of property near Brunico, acquired from his deceased brother-in-law.

1469, 8 March. Present at the drawing up of the accounts for the parish church of Brunico.

1471, 27 May. Draws up the contract for the Gries altar at Bolzano.

1471, 13 December. Draws up the contract for the St. Wolfgang altar (at St. Wolfgang?).

1471. Witnesses the drawing up of a document concerning Sigismund Peuntner of Brunico; later becomes guardian of Peuntner's daughter.

1472, 23 January. Witnesses the drawing up of the accounts for the parish church of Brunico.

1475, 15 May. Present at the drawing up of the accounts for the parish church of Brunico.

1479. Date inscribed on the paintings on the back of the shrine of St. Wolfgang.

1480, 21 August. Present at the drawing up of the accounts for the parish church of Brunico.

1481. Inscription celebrating the completion, by his hand, of the St. Wolfgang altar.

1481, 12 July. Invests the sum of 78 marks with Sigismund Mor of Brunico.

1481, 14 November. In Bolzano to draw up the contract for the altar of St. Michael in the parish church.

1481, 25 November. Invests another 20 marks with Sigismund Mor.

1482, 25 December. Receives 15 marks on account for the altar of St. Michael at Bolzano.

1483, 22 February. Becomes the guardian of the daughter of Sigismund Peuntner of Brunico.

1483, 24 August. Writes a letter to the episcopal chancellery of Bressanone in the capacity of guardian to Peuntner's daughter.

1484, 10 January. Receives a payment of 10 marks for the altar of St. Michael at Bolzano.

1484, 26 August. The Civic Council of Salzburg write to ask him to deliver the design for the high altar for the parish church.

1484, 19 October. The episcopal chancellery writes to him about the same matter.

1484, 18 November. Reminder from the Salzburg Civic Council.

1487, 28 August. Invests the sum of 20 marks with Sigismund Mor of Brunico.

1488, 8 December. Signs the final receipt for the Gries altar.

1491. Appears as creditor of Jacob Pinter of Chiusa.

1491. Invests the sum of 10 marks with a certain Puchfeldner.

1492, 11 December. Mentioned in the accounts of the parish church of Brunico.

1495. His visit to Salzburg documented.

1496. Witnesses the drawing up of the accounts for the parish church of Brunico.

1496, 1 May. Receives a payment of 54 pounds for work on the high altar of the parish church of Salzburg.

1496. His visit to Salzburg documented.

1496, 23 November. Receives from the Abbot of St. Peter's, Salzburg, a payment of 15 pounds for the altar of St. Michael am Aschhof (Salzburg).

1497, 1 May. Receives 25 pounds for work on the Salzburg altar.

1497, 18 June. Receives 7 pounds to buy gold for the Salzburg altar.

1497, 27 September. Receives another 12 pounds for work on the Salzburg altar.

1497. The episcopal administration at Brunico settles a debt on his behalf with 26 bushels of rye.

1498, 7 July. Receives 30 pounds for work on the Salzburg altar.

1498, 24 August. His son-in-law Caspar Neuhauser receives a payment of 20 pounds for the altar of St. Michael am Aschhof.

1498, 9 September. The episcopal chancellery of Bressanone asks the judge at Brunico to fix the date of the debate on the hereditary dispute between Michael Pacher's widow and his son-in-law Caspar Neuhauser.

1498, 17 November. Caspar Neuhauser on behalf of the heirs of Michael Pacher receives 300 Rhenish florins for the Salzburg altar.

1500. From a notarial protocol of the Innsbruck government it appears that Michael Pacher has bequeathed to his daughter Margaret, wife of Caspar Neuhauser, two tithes, a house and other property at Brunico, sold by Neuhauser in 1500 to Andrea Söll and others.

1502, 10 December. Caspar Neuhauser issues the final receipt for 3,300 Rhenish florins for the Salzburg altar.

1512. The deceased Hans Pacher, painter from Brunico, is documented as the son of Michael Pacher.

GENEALOGICAL NOTES ON MICHAEL PACHER AND FRIEDRICH PACHER

Elsewhere, I have pointed out that the name Pacher was, and still is, a common one in the Alto Adige during the Middle Ages. It was then the practice to translate not only the first name but also the family name; thus, the name Pacher was applied to all those whose names had the same meaning in Italian, particularly in the Ladino area.

By a strange combination of circumstances, Michael Pacher was destined to meet a pupil and collaborator with the same name, Friedrich Pacher, or Lebenpacher (Pacher of the Lion), and at Novacella another namesake, the provost Leonhard Pacher, who was to become his patron. It is not surprising therefore that some have concluded that

all three were related, perhaps even brothers. However, such a view is difficult to prove. The Rev. Dr. Max Schrott, archivist at the convent of Novacella, undertook the task, but although he has applied himself diligently the results so far have not been definitive. Nevertheless, his researches have borne fruit in other respects.

These three individuals, belonging to the same period of history and bearing the same name, knew each other and were often in close contact, but the only links between them appear to be ones of common interests and mutual esteem. Documents discovered by Schrott have enabled us to ascertain that Friedrich Pacher was of Novacella origin, the descendant of Friedrich Putznager of Elvas, who was called Pacher after he had acquired the lease of a small-holding of that name in Novacella. Later the holding passed to a certain Leonhard Pacher and from him to the painter Friedrich Pacher and his sisters. From this I would deduce that Leonhard was the son of Friedrich Putznager and the father of Friedrich Pacher, the painter. Schrott, however, suggests that he was their elder brother; Schrott was trying to reconcile these facts with the accepted chronology of the painter which at that time placed his birth date between 1430 and 1440, about the same time as Michael's. In my opinion we should conclude that Friedrich Pacher was the first-born child of Leonhard and that, having preferred to dedicate himself to art, he gave up his rights to the holding, as we learn from the documents, in favour of his

sister's husband, so as to take up residency in Brunico where for the remainder of his life he was to own a workshop.

The hypothesis that Provost Leonhard Nafner (1400/2-1484), called Pacher in late documents, was the brother of Leonhard and Friedrich Pacher, is without firm foundation. And the theory that the painter Friedrich was the brother of a certain Michael who died a little before 1501, son of a Leonhard who was in turn son of Hans Pacher—that he was in fact the brother of the Michael who Schrott would like to identify as our painter Michael, is contradicted by information which Schrott himself has given us. According to this, Friedrich Pacher is the son of Friedrich Putznager, called Pacher; or, since my interpretation is somewhat different, the son of Leonhard who is the son of Friedrich. In neither case does the painter Friedrich, a native of Elvas, belong to the immediate family of that Michael Pacher of Rasa stock who has been indentified as the painter. We cannot exclude the possibility of a family relationship between the painter Friedrich and the provost Leonhard Pacher, who probably came from Elvas, but the evidence for this is not reliable and for our

purposes only of secondary importance.

To conclude, we must admit that the problem of the relationship between the painters Friedrich and Michael, and the question of the former's provenance from Novacella, are still unsettled. The documents concerning the respective families imply that they are not brothers. The fact that Friedrich on moving to Brunico had to distinguish himself from Michael, or other local branches, by adopting the name Lebenpacher (from the lion on his coat of arms), while Michael Pacher and the members of his family always kept the same name, reinforces the hypothesis that the two men belonged to different families. Michael's was from Pusteria and native of Brunico, or the neighbourhood; while Friedrich's was from Bressanone and had moved to Brunico with Friedrich in about 1470, or sometime before 1474. I have already indicated that numerous families bearing this name were drawn to the area around Brunico from the surrounding valleys, and above all to the Ladino area.

Below are the family trees of Michael and Friedrich Pacher, based on existing documents, together with the family tree suggested by Schrott where the two families are shown united.

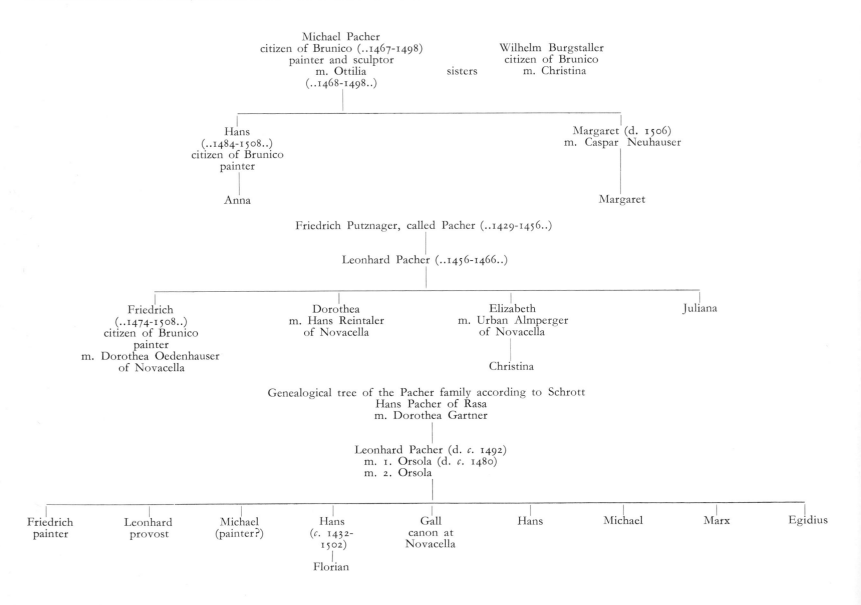

Genealogical tree of the Pacher family according to Schrott

1467, *Deed of gift from Jörg to Pamgarten.*

...und des sind gezewgen die erbnn Fritz Görle der zeit bürgermeister zu Brawnekh vnd meister Michel der maler vnd Christian Kranegker, beide purger zu Brawnegk.

(Formerly at Brunico, Archivio comunale, now lost. Extract published in *Bothe für Tirol*, 1838, p. 168, and by E. Förster in *Deutsches Kunstblatt*, 1853, p. 131)

1468, *Deed of purchase of real estate at Brunico by the painter Michael.*

Ich Cristina weylentt Willhalmen Purgkstalers seligen eliche witibe bechenn offenlichen mit dem brieff und tun chundt allermänigklichen als dann der obgenante mein lieber elicher gemachel seliger, Otilian meiner lieben elichen swester sculdig worden ist ain summa gelts nämliches vierundfunfftzig marckh perner nach innhaltung ains versigelten geltschuldbrieffs so die obgenante Otilia darumben von im hat und also hat der obgenante Wilham mein lieber hawswirt saliger, maister Michelen maler der obgenannten Otilia elichen hawswirt zu khauffen geben ainen stadell, hoffstatt und gartten gelegen under der statt Brawnegkhen zwischen des Jörgen Impawmgartten und Matheysen Kursners städeln um ain summa gelts benantlichen funffzechennthalbe marckh perner meraner müntz und tzalung und dieselben jetzgenanten summa gelts funfftzechennthalb marckh perner hat der ogemelt Wilham seliger dem egenannten Michel maler abgezogen und abgerautt an den vierundfunffzig marckh perner die er der benanten Otilian schuldig ist worden von wegen irs vaterlichen und mueterlichen erbentails und sind pey demselben kauff gewesen die fürsichtigen erbern und weysen Jacob Kirchmair, Peter Hofsteter und Cristian Kranegkher alle drey purger zu Brawnegk und ander erber leut mer, und also hat sich gefuegt das der obgenante Wilham mein lieber gemachel inn kranckhait kommen und mit tod abgangen ist und dem obgenanten Michelen den chauffbrieff umb den obgenanten stadel hoffstatt und gartten nit gevertigt hat und im doch die funffzehenhalbe marckh perner an den vier und funffzig marckhen abgeraitt und abgezogen hatt. Das alles wie oben geschriben stet ist mir obgenantten Cristina dem obgenanten maister Michelen diesen kuntschafft brieff versigelten mit des fursichtigen weysen Petern Hoffsteter zw Brawnegkhen anhangenden insigl das er umb meiner vleissigen pett willen dar angehangen hat im und sein erben an schade. Des

sind getzeugen umb pett des insigels die erbern Lienhart Verchell, Martein Peham bede purger zu Brawnegkh und Augustin Senfftt inwoner daselbs und mer erber leutt gnug und das ist beschechen nach Cristi gepurdt als man zalte viertzehenhundert und im achtundsechtzigisten jaren am nachsten montag nach sand Lucastag des heiligen ewangelisten.

(Novacella Archive, HA 42. Max Schrott, "Michael Pachers Verwandtschaft" in *Cultura Atesina*, XX, 1966)

1469, 8 March. *Accounts of the Parish Church, Brunico.*

...Bey der vorgenantten raytung so Caspar Mentlberger getan von peiden Jaren sein gewessen, Stoffl an der Luchen an stat dez purgermeister, Jacob Kirchmair, Peter Hofsteter, Sigmundt Sell, Fridreich Gerlin, Jorg Im pamgarten, Leonhart Wolff, Matheis Chürschner, Chonrat Pidinger, Hainreich Kürschner, Michel maler, Toman Hamerl, Vlrich Poltz, Hanns Füchsl, Hanns Väsl, Steffan Cantzler kirchbrapst, all purger ze Brawnekg. Geschehen an dem vorgenantten mitichen vor letare In der fasten anno Domini 1469.

(Brunico, Archivio comunale. Accounts of the Parish Church, 1445-1508, p. 75 verso)

1471, 27 May. *Contract for the Gries Altar.*

Wir die hernachgeschriben mit namen Ludwig Gandl, Afist Zaslarer, Symon mesner, Symon Abracham, Staffler am Rawt, Jeronimus Puchler, Lorenz am Haimgarten die alle sesshafft zu Gries in gegenwärtigkchait der fürsichtigen und weisen Chunradten Lerhueber dieczeit burgermaister ze Boczen und Maister Thoman Hafner Burger daselbs Hab wir ain abred vnd tading getroffen Mit dem Erberen und weisen Maister Michln Pacher Maler von Brawnegk von wegen aines werchs einer Tavel In vnser liebn frawenpharrkirchen ze Gries die da gemacht soll werden Nuczperlich werperlich vnd gancz veruanckhlich Im verdingt vmb ain Sum gelts vierthalb Hundert Marsh perner guter Meraner muncz, Jtem wann das werch volbracht vnd an die stat gemacht wirdt, als oben bestimbt ist vnd ob sach wär vnd es sich begab das die obgenannten von Gries und Maister Michl ettwas schrittig wurden und des mit einander vber ains nicht machten werden, so sol jettweder tail zwen piderman Nemen die sich dann auf solch

arbeit versten vnd des fünften vber ain werden, vnd die selben versuchen sullen, wes sy sthriittig waren Sy des mit gutigkchait entschaiden vnd was dann dieselben erkennen dabey es hinfür an alle weitre waigerung besten vnd beleiben sol Jtem Mer ist beredt worden, das die Maister das Werch in vier Jaren machen beraiten und aufsetzen sol ungeuarlich Jtem Mer ist beredt wann der Maister das werch auf seczt vnd vergalt sullen Im die von Griess die speiss tuen als einem solchen man zugehort, Mer ist beredt vnd betadingt worden das die Kirchprubst von Griess Maister Micheln geben sullen Auf nachstkunftig Mitteuasten funfzig markch vnd darnach alle Jar auf Mitteuasten Zway vnd dreyssig markch biss auf volle werung der obgenannten Sum yedeszyl zu bezallen als geschieden vnd gesprochen gelt an allen schade. Jtem von Erst undten Im Sarch vier geschniten prustpild sannd Blasy Sannd Lienhart Sannd Johannes gotstauffer vnd Sannd Vigily vnd an die flugl des Sarchs Inwendig geschniten pild Sannd Wolffgang vnd Sannd Jorg vnd ausn an der flug Sannd Barbara vnd Sannd Katherina Item oben In der Tavel vnnser lieben Frawen Kronung In aller der massen als In vnnser lieben frawen pharkirchen In der Tavel ze Boczen stet vnd an die seiten Sannd Michl vnd sannd Erasm Item Inwendig In die flug geschniten pild als unser lieben frawen geburdt als zu weinachten vnd die Heilig deri Kunigen. In die ander flug vnnser frawen gruss vnd vnnser frawen schidung Item Ausen an die ain flug den olperg vnd die gaislung vnnsers lieben Heren vnd an die ander seiten das Crucifix vnd die Vrstend vnnsers Heren gemalt Item Inwendig der Tauel die Ruckwendt hinten pannyr golt Item die Ruckwendt In flugern mit plaber farb Item an orten der Tauel an ainer saitn sannd Sewastian vnd sannd Florian Item oben Im Tabernackl ain Crucifix mit vnnser frawen vnd Sannd Johanns vnd ze obrist In dem Tabernackl ob dem Crucifix ain Maria pild mit dem Kind Item was von Eysenwerch der maister debarff zu dem werch sullen die Kirchprubst bezalen. An solchem werch so Im verdingt ist zu machen ist Im zur Aarr gegeben zechen Reinisch gulden vnd zu einer Merern sicherheit So hab ich benanter Michl Pacher maler fleissigklichen gebeten den fursichtigen vnd weisen Conrad Lerhueber dieczeit Burgermaister ze Boczen das der sein aign petschafft hiefür gedruckcht hat doch Im vnd sein Erben an schaden. Beschechen ze Boczen am Montag nach Vrbani anno domini MCCCCLXXI.

(Formerly at Gries, Archivio comunale, the original now lost. Revised text published by L. Spatzenegger in *Mitt. d. Gesellsch. f. Salzburger Landeskunde*, IX, 1869, p. 26)

1471, 13 December. *Contract for the St. Wolfgang Altar.*

Vermerchkt dy abred und das geding der tafel gen sannd Wolfgang ze machen, so beschehen ist zwischen des erwirding und geistlichen heren Benedicten abbt zw Mannsee und seines convents daselbs und maister Micheln maler von Prawnegk an sand Lucientag im LXXI iare.

Item von erst ist zw merken, das dy tafel sol gemacht werden nach dem ausczug und visierung, als er uns dy hat zwbracht gen Mannsee als vil das gesein mag hoch halben.

Item der sarich sol innen vergolt sein darzw dy pildung Marie mit dem chindlein siczund, Joseph und dy drey kunig mit dem opfer, und ob dy den sarich nicht fulten, so sol er mer pild oder wappner machen alles vergolt.

Item das corpus sol sein dy chronung Marie mit engeln und gulden tuechern nach dem chostlichem und pesten, so er das gemachen mag.

Item zw ainer seyten sand Wolfgang mit innfel, stab, kirichen und hacken, zw der andern sand Benedict in aim birret mit stab und mit ainem glas, gancz vergolt und versilbert nach notturft.

Item aussen zw den seyten der tafel sullen steen sand Florian und sand Jorig, guet wappner versilbert und vergolt nach notturft.

Item dy innern flug der tafel sullen sein guet gemall, dy veldung vergult und mit wintpergen und vial, yede mit vier materien.

Item dy andern auch vergolt und guet gemal als vor.

Item die ausern flug, so dy tafel zw ist, sullen sein guet gemal von varben und dy illuminirung vergolt, dy materi von sand Wolfgang.

Item dy pild oberhalb des corpus schullen sein nach der aufzaichnung des auszugs, gevast mit vergolter illuminirung.

Item so dy tafel berait wirt, sol er uns dy antwurten gen Oberhall auf sein zerung und darnach mit seinen leib auf unser zerung und wagnuss gen Prawnaw, von dann sullen wir im dy antwurten gen sand Wolfgang auf unser chost und zerung, was aber auf dem weg zebrochen wurd, sol er widerumb gancz machen.

Item zw sand Wolfgang, so er dy tafel ausweraitt und aufseszt, sullen wir im pfrundt und eysenzeug zw aufseczung der tafel geben und raiche, auch laden, ob er der durftig wurd.

Item das geding ist gemacht auf zwelif hundert ungrisch gulden oder ducaten oder dafur munss, wie dan der gulden gilt.

Item ob dy tafel des gelts nicht werd oder etwas hinüber pesser wurd und wir uns unteinander nicht vertragen möchten, so sullen payd tail darzw geleich werichlewt geben, dy sach zw entschaiden.

Item es ist nämlich geredt worden, das dy tafel nicht scholl höher gemacht werden dann auf dy XII hundert hungrisch gulden getreulich und angevär.

Item daran haben wir im geben fünczig hungarisch gulden und ducaten.

Item so er gelts bedarf, sol er uns schiken alberg ain quittung.

Item es sol auch maister Michel uns versorgnuss thun mit gueten letwen umb das gelt, so wir im an der bemelten tafel raichen, dy weil er dy ausberaitten ist, des geleichen so dy tafel berait und geantburt ist, ob wir im dy benannt sum gelts nicht berait zalen, sol er von uns auch versägt werden nach notturft mit geschriftlicher kuntschafft.

(Linz, State Archive. Published by Ignaz Zibermayr, "Michael Pachers Vertrag über die Anfertigung des Altars in der Kirche zu St. Wolfgang" in *Mitteilungen des Inst. f. Österr. Geschichtsforschung*, XXXIII, 1912, pp. 481 ff.)

1471, *Deed of purchase of property at Brunico by Provost Leonhard of Novacella.*

Littera pro area et stabulo in Brawnegk a Johanne Wynkler ibidem empta.

Ich Hanns Wynkler gesessen ze Brawnegken bekenn mit disem offen für mich und alle mein erben und tun khund allermennigklich das ich mit gunst, wort, willen und wissen meiner lieben ehrlichen wirtin Magdalen und mit gutem eignen willen und mit wohlbedachtem mutt recht und redlich durch schlechts und ewigklichen so du hinfür nach dem landsrechten der graffschaft Tirol am allerbesten chraft und macht wohl gehaben chan oder mag verkaufft und hingeben han wissentlich in craft dits brieff nemlichen meine paurecht des stadls und gartens beieinander zw Brawnegk gelegen. Des ich auch vormals von dem benannten stadel ein drittail dem Sigismund Pewnter verhaufft hab, und stösst oben an des benannten Sigmund Painters stadl und gartten unden an des Franz Händleins sun stadl und garten, voran die gemein strass, hinden an die Wüer, und verzinst und verdient man dass dem erbaren und weisen Lienharten Öder gesessen ze Värn im gericht Salern mit vier pfuntt perner und acht kreutzer, dem hochwirdigen gottshaws Brichssen von der hofstat. Desgleichen von der draitil so der benant Sigmund kawfft hat, auch dem benannten Öder zw zins zwai phundt perner und dem benannten gottshaws Brichsen vier krewtzer von der hofstat; desselben Öders aygenschaft, dienst, zins, und recht altzeit unverzigen und ausgenommen.

Dyeselben obgenant pawrecht des benannten stadls und gärtleins mit aller seiner zwgehörung, besucht und unbesucht, erpawen und unerpawen mit infart, ausfart, mit weg und steg und mit allen den ernehaften rechten nutzen, pesserungen und gesuchen die jtzund daran sindt dazu daringehören oder noch mit pesserung daran bescheen mwgen wie das alles genannt ist nicht ausgenommen. Also hab ich die verkawft und hingeben in form und mass als dann oben geschrieben ist, dem erwirdigen und andächtigen herrn Leonhardten, probst des würdigen gots hauses Newnstift und allen seinen nachkomen oder wem sie es verner verchauffen schaffnd oder gebent...

...So haben wir obgenannte wirtslewt Hanns und Magdalena für uns und all unsere erben fleyssigklich gebeten den erbern und weisen Carspern Mäntlwerger burger zw Brawnegken, dass er sein insigl an diesen brieff gehengt hat, doch im und seinen erben an schaden. Umb pett des insigls seind gezwgen die erbaren und beschaiden Maister Michel maler, Erhart Zott, Wolfgang Scheider, Stephan Kantzler. Asem Seld, alle burger ze Brawnegken, und ander erber leut genug. Bescheen am sambstag nach sand augustins tag als man zalt nach Cristi gebird tausend vierhundert und in dem einundsybntzisten jahre.

(Novacella Archive, Cod. 5 B, fol. 261. Copy made by N. Rasmo; cf. Max Schrott, "Michael Pachers Verwandtschaft" in *Cultura Atesina*, XX, 1966)

1472, 23 January. *Accounts of the Parish Church, Brunico.*

Item an phinztag nach Sand Vinzez tag im lxxij Jar hat Andre Vilde als kirchprast ein Gantze volkömmne raytung von dem Nutz vnser lieben frawen kirchen vnd des spitals zw Brawnekg von dem siebenzigsten Jar nutz Getan...

...Bey der raytung sind gewessen Hans Bössel die zeyt Statrichter, Caspar Mentlberger purgermaister Kristof an der lucken Sigmund Scll Sigmund König Sigmund... Sigmund Nech Fritz Gerlin Stephan Kanzler Vlrich Böckl Tomas Handlin Michl Maler vnd Matheis Kurschner.

(Brunico, Archivio comunale. Accounts of the Parish Church, 1445-1508, pp. 84, 85)

1475, 15 May. *Accounts of the Parish Church, Brunico.*

Item am montag in phingstveyrtagen im lxxv. Jar hat Sigmund Sell als kirchpräst ain Ganze volkomne raytung getan von dem Kirchprästambt von dem Nuzen des lxxiij. Jares jnnemen vnd ausgeben als hir nach stet...

...Bey der raytung sind gewesen Sigmund König purgermaister Jobst... kirchpräst Andre Velder Caspar Mentlberger Hans Sell Jacob Handel Kristof an der lucken Tomas Hämerlin maister Michel Pacher Niclas Steber vnd Paul Plur.

(Brunico, Archivio comunale. Accounts of the Parish Church, 1445-1508, pp. 91, 92)

1480, 21 August. *Accounts of the Parish Church, Brunico.*

Item an montag Nach vnser frawen tag schidung im lxxx Jar hat Jacob Sell ain Ganze volkomne raytung getan von des kirchpräst ambt wegen von dem lxxvij Jar Nutz wegen alen jnnemen vnd ausgeben als hernacht stet...

...Bey der raytung Sind gewesen Vlrich Gewestorffer Die Zeyt richter Caspar Mentelberger purgermaister Stephan Kantzler kirchpräst Sigmund Sell Jobst... Jacob Händel Michel maler Georg im paumgarten Sigmund Kramer vnd Hans Serber Beschehen als vor geschriben stet.

(Brunico, Archivio comunale. Accounts of the Parish Church, 1445-1508, pp. 98, 99 verso)

1481, 12 July. *Master Michael Pacher, citizen of Brunico, purchases for 78 marks from Sigismund Mor, citizen of Brunico, two annual dues each of 13 Verona pounds.*

(Formerly in the Novacella Archive, HA 45. Report by the Rev. Dr. Max Schrott)

1481, 21 September. *Master Michael Pacher presents himself before the Episcopal Chancellery, Bressanone, as guardian of the daughter of Sigismund Peuntner.*

(Bressanone, Episcopal Archive. Court Registry, III, 593. Noted by Karl Wolfsgruber, "Beiträge zur Pacher-Forschung" in *Der Schlern*, XLIII, 1969, p. 128)

1481, 25 November. *Master Michael Pacher, citizen of Brunico, purchases for 20 marks from Sigismund Mor, citizen of Brunico, an annual due of 15 bushels of rye.*

(Formerly in the Novacella Archive, HA 45. Report by the Rev. Dr. Max Schrott)

1481-4, *Accounts of the Parish Church, Bolzano. Documents concerning the St. Michael Altar.*

1481, 14 November

Item am Mittich nach Martinj als man die tafel die auff Sand Michels altar sol sten angedingt hat ist Maister Michel von Brawneck Vber nacht hie gewesen mit ainem ross hat verzert 1 lb.

Item eodem die des Leonharde des Lantramers schreiber die spannzedel abgeschrieben VI gr.
(Bolzano, Archivio comunale. MS. no. 645, p. 30)

1482, 25 December

Item mayster Michel von Brawneck hab Ich an dem geding der raffel auff santt Michels altar so er machen sol bey Sigmundt Gerstll enttricht Inn den weyhenachtn vergangenen des lxxxiij Jars benentlichen XV mrk.
(Bolzano, Archivio comunale. MS. no. 646, p. 35)

1482-3

Item von Erhardt Hucken als gerhaben der Kindt weylent Vlrich Huckem hab Ich empfangen an dem gelt so die alt Ganznerin zw der Tafflen auff Sant Michells Altar geben hatt des xxvj mrk iij lb. perner ist vnd der benannten gerhaben an statt der Kindt seindt schuldig gewessen hab Ich empfangen viij mrk.
(Bolzano, Archivio comunale. MS. no. 646 p. 15 verso)

1483, 22 February. *Letter from the Episcopal Chancellery, Bressanone, to the Captain and Civic Council of Brunico.*

An Haubtman, Bürgermaister und Räte der Stat Brawnegk.
Edler lieber getreuer und getreue lieben. Alsdan unsere getreue Michel Maler als Gerhab weylanndt Sigmunden Pewntners tochter an ainem vnd Sebastian Pragk unser Burger ze Braunegk am andern Tail der scheden ains kaufs halben so sy geneneynander im rechten gestanden auf ew gentzlichen gangen und chomen, Sy darumb zu verainen als wir bericht sein. Nu ist vns solhs alweg genam, wo Spänn vnd zwitracht gütlichen hingelegt werden. Und darauf begern wir an ew und emphelhen ewr jedem, das ir allen vleis ankern wellet damit die beruert zwitracht geleichlichen hingelegt und das kind mit der billikait von ew fürgesehen und dawider nit beswärt werdet des welln wir uns zu ew versehen. Ir all und yeder jn, sunders tuet uns dannoch daran guet gevallen und unser ernstliche maynung. Geben zu Brichsen an sand Peterstag der Stuelfeyr. Anno 83.
(Bressanone, Episcopal Archive, Court Registry, IV, 131. Transcribed by Karl Wolfsgruber; cf. "Beiträge zur Pacher-Forschung" in *Der Schlern*, XLIII, 1969, p. 129)

1483, 8 December

Item am Montag Nach conceptionis Marie hat mir Erhart Huck vnd Hanns Gantzner enttricht an dem gelt so die Alt Gantznerin zu der Tafel geben hat benentlichen x mark.
(Bolzano, Archivio comunale. MS. no. 647, p. 15 verso)

1484, 10 January

Am freytag Nach Erhardi hat Gerstl von meine wegen maister Michelln von Brawneck geben auff sein quittumb vnd an der Tafel auff Sand Michels Altar benentlichen x mrk.
(Bolzano, Archivio comunale. MS. no. 647, p. 30 verso)

1484, 28 March

Item Im marckt Mitervasten hat Erhart Huck mir durch den Swaiger enttricht an dem gelt zu der Tafell von der Gantznerin geschaffen viij mark.

1484, undated

Item Erhart Huck als gerhab seins Brueders khinder am Eysack ist noch schuldig zw der Taffel auff Sand Michelsaltar als die Gantznerin geschaffen hat x mark. iij lb.
vnd der Gantzner Im gardavn x mark.
(Bolzano, Archivio comunale. MS. no. 647, pp. 15 verso, 42)

1484, *Documents relating to the high altar of the Parish Church, Salzburg, 18 May (according to Spatzenegger 11 May). Letter from the Civic Council of Salzburg to the painter Rueland Frueauf.*

Vnsern Dienst. lieber Rueland. Wir sein im Willen ain tafl in vnserer lieben Frawn pfarrkirchen hic machen zulassen, die wir nach ewrm Rat antzefahen vermainen. Begern wir an Ew Ir wellet Ew Inner acht tagen auf unser kostung her zu vns gein Saltzburg fuegen wellen wir daraus verer mit Ew reden. Datum Saltzburg am Erichtag nach Bangratii 84. Burgermaister vnd Rat der Stat Saltzburg. Dem erbern weisen Rueland Frueauf Maler burger zu Passaw.
(Salzburg, Communal Archive. Letter no 58, published by L. Spatzenegger, op. cit., pp. 23 ff.)

1484, 16 August. *Letter from the Civic Council of Salzburg to Virgil Hofer.*

Dem Erbern vnd Weisen Virgilien Hover ytz zu Rotennberg. Vnnser dinst bevor. Als Ir in kurtzvergangenen tägen Hannssn Eisennhaimer bey Micheln Pacher Maler von Brawnegk geschriben vnd Im denselben für ainen guten Werchman gepreist, Ine auch Zu dem furgenomen Werch der Tavel hie Zutueglich geschetzt vnd begeert an Im auch gevallen ze haben So wellet Ir mit ewren tawsent gulden anfahen vnd die von erst ausgeben. Und so das bescheen ist darnach mit vnnsrm teil auch nit sewmig ze sein. Solch ewr schreiben hat vnns der genannt Ellsennhaimer fuergehalten das wir vernomen, vnd haben vnns auf ewr schreiben mit dem bemelten Maister Michelln des berurten Werchs halben vertragen vnd ain abred gemacht Innhalt Zwayer Spanzetl der abschrift wir ew hie Innbeslossen Zusenden, has haben wir ew als billich ist nit wellen verhalten, ew darnach Wissen zerichten. Geben zu Saltzburg an phinztag vor sannd Augustinstag Anno 84. Burgermaister vnd Rate zu Saltzburg.
(Salzburg, Communal Archive. Letter no. 18, published by L. Spatzenegger, op. cit., pp. 24 ff.)

1484, 26 August. *Letter from the Civic Council of Salzburg to Michael Pacher.*

Vnnser Dinst bevor. Nachdem Ir Ew des Werchs der Tafel in vnser Frawen pharrkirchen hie aufzerichtenn verfangen habt, So wellet vns die Visierung derselben ytz zu sannd Gilign Markts zu Potzen bey Hannsen Puhler vnnsrem Ratsfrundt oder aim andern vnsrem mitburger hersennden. Dann die meynung so Ir mit vns Burgermeister vnd Hannsen Elsennhaimer geredt vnd gebeten die an vnser Rats-

frundt Ze bringen, das wir also getan vnd Ew stewr vnd wacht frey zelassen erlanngt haben. Geben zu Salzburg an phinztag vor Augustini Anno 84. Burgermeister und Räte der Stat zu Salzburg.
(Salzburg, Communal Archive. Letter no. 82, published by L. Spatzenegger, op. cit., p. 27)

1484, 9 September. *Letter from Virgil Hofer to the Civic Council of Salzburg.*

Den firsichtigen Ersamen weisenn Burgermeister vnd dem Rat der Stat Zu Saltzburg meinen besondern lieben Herrn.
Mein gar willig Dinst. Wist zuvoran besonder lieb Herren Ewr schreiben vnd den Vertrag so Ir than habt mit Maister Micheln hab Ich vernomen, vnd hab daran ain gut wolgeaullen, vnd Maister Michel hat mir den selber auch also gesagt, vnd hab Im auch dieweil daran geben hundert gulden vnd In gepeten damit Er auf das allerfurderlichist zu dem Werch greiff. Ich woll zu nit lassen mit gelt solang vnd souil bis Ich tawsennt gulden ausgeben hab, die Ich mich dann erpoten hab zegeben. Er hat mir auch gesagt wie Er mitsambt Ew red gehalten hab mit Maister Leonhartn Zimmerman auch mit Vlreichen Tisschler Holtz halbem slahen zulassen ain genuegen. Da seyt ob, damit das furderlich geschech, desgleichen mit allen sachenn. Ich wil auch zu nichte sparn damit schafft vnd gepiett mir. Geben zu kopfstain an phinztag nach vnnser Frawn gepurd im lxxxiiij. Virgili Hofer.
(Salzburg, Communal Archive. Letter no. 100, published by L. Spatzenegger, op. cit., p. 28)

1484, 19 October. *Letter from the Chancellery, Bressanone, to Michael Pacher.*

Michelen Pacher Burger zu Braunegkh.
Getreuer. Als dir die jrrung halben zweischen dein und Sebastian Pracken auch vnserm Burger zu Braunegk, das wir uns die hinzulegen angenomen haben, hierumb baiden tailen zu guet, ist unser maynung, willen und erclärung, das dem Pracken der losbrief hinaus geben werde und ain jar zynns vom haus vervolge und nit mer, damit so seyt nachtperlich und freuntlich. Und welcher tail vermaint damit beswärt sein, wo wir des bericht wurden, wolten wir mit gnaden dem so beswärt wäre, genaigt sein zu gevallen und halten es dafür, das jr nun sult dadurch aller unainigkait entladen sein und ainer dem andern zu willen werden, als gueten freundten zu tue zuesteet. Das kumbt uns von ew zu guetem gevallen. Geben ze Brichsen an Erichtag nach Galli. Anno dñi 84.
(Bressanone, Episcopal Chancellery, Court Registry, IV, 166'. Transcribed by Karl Wolfsgruber; cf. "Beiträge zur Pacher-Forschung" in *Der Schlern*, XLIII, 1969, p. 129)

1484, 2 November. *Deed of gift by Hans Ramsperger at Salzburg.*

Ich Hanns Ramsperger des Rats Zu Salczburg. Bekenn fur mich mein hawsfrawn vnd all vnnser Erben offennlich mit dem brief vnd thun kunnd menigklich Daz Ich Zu lob vnd Ere vnnser lieben Frawen auch Zu hillff vnd trost meiner Hawsfraun vnser voruordern vnd aller gelaubigen Seelen Zu Hillffe vnd furdrung des Werchs vnd grossen Tauel so In der bemelten vnnser lieben Frauen pharrkirchen Zu Salczburg gemacht vnd aufgericht sol werden aus veraintem gutem willenn gegeben geaigent vnd verschriben habe. Gib aigen vnd verschreib auch wissenlich In vnd mit kraft dits briefs mein burkrecht Haws vnd Hofstat mit sambt dem garttn aller vnd yegklicher seiner Zugehorung gelegen daselben Im Nunntal gegen weylennd Hannsen Topler haws vber mit allen den Eeren rechten nutzen vnd gesuechen die Zu recht vnd von aller dar Zu gehorn als Ich dasselbs Inngehabt genutzt genossen vnd mein voruordern mitsambt mir herbracht haben ongeuer In der beschaiden daz ain yegklicher der bemelten vnnser Frawen pharrkirchen Zechrobst so ytz ist vnd konnftigklich sein wirdet nu furan ewigklich mit demselben Haus vnd gartten hanndln, thun vnd lassen mugen mit versetzen verkumern verkauffen Zinnss vnd gullt dauon Einnemen die nutzen vnd der geniessen vnd sich aller der gerechtigkait geprauchen als Ich oder mein Erbenn dasselb hieten thun mugen vnd damit hanndeln als mit annderem des gedachten gotshaws freyen ledigen vnd aigen gut. Doch daz Sy von dem gemelten haws vnd gartten Jerlich vnd ewigklich die Burkrecht phennig vnd gullt ainer Abbtessin vnd sannd Ernndraut gotshaws auf dem Nunnberg Zwelf Burkrecht phennig vnd den Siechen Zu Salczburg viervndzwainzig phennig dienen raichen vnd geben sullen Vnd sol also dasselb burkrecht haus vnd gartten mitsambt der allten brieflichen Vrkundt daruber lauttund auf vnd vbergeben aus mein meiner Hausfrawen vnd aller vnser Erbenn nutz vnd gewer In des bemelten gotshavs vnd Zechrobsten vnd aller Ihrer nachkomen hannden nutz gwalt vnd geprauch alsdann solher vbergab vnd der stat Salczburg recht ist ongeuer. Ich bemelter Hanns Ramsperger verzeich mich auch darauf des berurten Hawss vnd Gartten mit aller Zugehorung für mich vnd all mein Erbenn wissenlich In Grafft des briefs Zu ganntzer durchslechter vnd ewiger Zicht Also daz Ich vnd all mein Erben Zu dem vermelten Gotshaws vnd Zechprobsten deshalben khainerlay Zuspruch gerechtigkait noch anuordrung nicht mer haben sollen wellen suechen oder gewynnen sullen noch mugen In khainerlay gstalt weg noch weise. Wir sollen vnd wellen auch des offt bestimbten hawss vnd gartten Ir recht gewern vnd furstandt sein für all Infall krieg vnd anspruch Sy sein geistlich oder weltlich vnd Sy gegen menigklich schermen vnd veranntworten als offt In des not beschicht. Alsdann solher gewerschaft fürstanndts vnd der gemelten stat Salczburg recht ist ongeuer. Tetenn wir aber oder ettwer von vnnsern wegen wider dise gegenwurtige verschreibung In aim oder mer was schaden des des vermelts gotshaws vnd Zechrobst nemen klain oder gros dhainen besonndert noch ausgezogen des mugen Sy habhaft werden vnd bekomen auf aller hab vnd gut so wir haben oder gewynnen Inner oder ausser lannds gelegen vnntz auf Ir volligs genuegen Alles getrewlich vnd vngeuerlich Vnd des Zu warem Vrkunnd vnd ewiger gedechtnuss hab Ich In disenn offenn brief daruber gegeben Besigeltenn mit des fursichtigen Ersamen vnd weisenn Oswalden Ellsennhaimer Statrichter Zu Salczburg aigem anhanngundem Innsigl den Ich mit vleiss darumb gepetenn hab doch Im seinen Erbenn vnd Innsigl on schaden Darunnder Ich mich für mich mein hawsfrawn vnd all vnnser Erbenn mit meinen treuen verpinnde alles abgeschriben war vnd stat Zu halltenn Vnd sind Zeugen meiner gepett vmb das Innsigl die Edln vnd Ersamen weisen Lucas Lamprechtshawser vnd Rubrecht Morawer baid des Rats Zu Salczburg. Bescheen an Eritag aller Seelentag nach Christi gepurde Vierzehenhundertn vnd Im Vierundachzigstem Jaren.

(Salzburg, Archiepiscopal Consistorial Archive. Published by L. Spatzenegger, op. cit., pp. 50 ff.)

1484, 18 November. *Letter from the Civic Council of Salzburg to Michael Pacher.*

Dem Erberen weisen Maister Micheln Pacher.
Vnser Dinst bevor. Als Ir ew auf die abred Zwischen vnser vnd ewr der Tafel halben hie ze machen beslossen vnd auf ewr Zusagen in dem abschid bescheen, daz Ir vnns die fisierung derselben Tafelen kurtzlich Zuzesenden vnd ew darnach her zefuegen das wir dann vntzher warttund gewest sein vnd noch erbeten habt. Dem nach begern wir mit Vleis ze wellet ew mit solcher Fisierung aufs furderlichist herfuegen auf das den sachen nachgannen mug werden. Dann wir mit dem holtz das nun geslagen ist, ausser ewrem Beiwesen nichts mer ze hanndeln wissen. So mag auch Maister Wolfhart der Goldsmid hie on ewr Fisierung an dem Werch kainerlai arbait furnemen daran thuet Ir vnnser guet geualln. Geben zu Saltzburg an phinztag nach Sand Marteinstag Anno domini 84.
Burgermeister vnd Rate der Stat Saltzburg.

(Salzburg, Communal Archive. Letter no. 104, published by L. Spatzenegger, op. cit., pp. 28 ff.)

1484, 18 November. *Letter from the Civic Council of Salzburg to Virgil Hofer.*

Dem Ersamen weisen Virgilien Hofer.
Vnser Dinst mit guetem Willen bevor. Wir schreiben hiemit Maister Micheln Pacher auf meynung als Ir an der abschrift hie innbeslossen Vernemen werdet. Bitten wir mit vleis Ir wellet demselben Maister Micheln auch schreiben vnd In anhallden daz Er sich mit der Fisierung aufs furderlichist herfuege, auf das den sachen laut der abred nachgannen mug werden. Daran ertzaigt Ir vnns guet geuallen.
Geben Zu Saltzburg am phinztag nach Sannd Marteinstag Anno Domini lxxxiiik.
Burgermeister vnd Rate der Stat Saltzburg.

(Salzburg, Communal Archive. Letter no. 105, published by L. Spatzenegger, op. cit.)

1486, 6 April. *Letter from the Civic Council of Salzburg to the Archpriest Ulrich, Provost of Berchtesgaden.*

Dem Groszwirdigen in got Hern. Hrn. Vlrichen Ertzbriester vnnd Brobst Zu Berchtersgadem vnnsrem gönnstigen Hern.
Groswirdiger Lieber Herr. Vnser willig dinst allzeit bevor. Wir haben got Zu Lob vnd seiner gepererin der Junckfrawn Marie in vnnser frawen pharrkirchen Zu Saltzburg ain werch auf den höchsten altar aufzurichten fuergenomen. Deshalben wir etlichs Zewgs gebrechen haben. Schicken hierauf Zu ewer groswirdigkeit vnnseren Ratsfrund gegenburtigen Cristoffel Werder zeiger dits Briefs, Beuelhen selb männlich Zuendeckhen mit vleys bittend, Ewer groswirden welle denselben vnnsern Ratsfrund Cristoff Werder in seinem anbringen vnser bete hören vnd auf dasmal, wie vns gänntzlich glawben genediclich abferttigen; dabey wir abnemen mugen solcher vnserer Bete empfinden genossen haben. Das wellen wir vmb ewrer groswirden in ainem solhen oder meresem ewer gotshaws vnd die ewren gern vnd willig verdienen.
Datum Saltzburg am pfinztag vor Clauorum Anno domini lxxxvj
Richter Burgermeister vnd Rat der Stat Salzburg.
(Salzburg, Communal Archive. Letter no. 162, published by L. Spatzenegger, op. cit., pp. 30 ff.)

1487, 28 August. *Master Michael Pacher purchases for 20 marks from Sigismund Mor, citizen of Brunico, an*

annual due of 16 bushels of rye and some of barley.
(Formerly in the Novacella Archive, HA 45. Report by the Rev. Dr. Max Schrott)

1488, 8 December. *Final receipt by Michael Pacher for the Gries Altar.*

Ich Michael Pacher maler purger zw Brauneck wekenn mit diser offen quittumb für mich und all mein erben, nach dem und mir verdingt ist worden von dem erwirdigem und geistlichem herren brobst des wirdigen goczhawss ze Griess und den kirchbräbsten und gmain der ganczen nachtpaurschafft der pfarr unser lieben frauen zw Griess ain tafel ze machen in ainer summa gelt, benantlich neun hundert und fünfczig reinisch gulden, welcher obgeschribner summa gelcz bekenn ich mich gancz gewert und bezalt durch den ersamen und weisen Jeronimus Püchler die zeit kirchbräbst der obgeschribnen pfarrkirchen zw Griess. Des zw ainer urkundt gib ich obgeschribner maister Michel dem bemelten kirchbräbst und der pfarmenig ze Griess dise quittumb versecretiert mit dem secret des erwirdigen geistlichen herren her Jürgen brobst ze Griess, der das durch meiner fleissigen gepet willen zu endt der geschrifft gedruckt hat. Der aller obgeschribner sachen sind zewgen die erwirdigen und geistlichen her Hainrich pfarrer ze Märling, her Hanns Gwin pfarrer ze Mayss, Simon mesner von Griess, maister Jobst peck zw Poczen und ander erberg leut genueg. Geschehen an unser lieben frauen tag der entphauung im acht und achtzigsten jar.

(Gries, Convent Archive. Published by K. Th. Hoeniger, "Eine Quittung Michael Pachers" in *Der Schlern*, XVII, 1936, fasc. 1, pp. 2 ff.)

1491, *Letter from Jacob Pinter of Chiusa to the Episcopal Chancellery, Bressanone, concerning a debt he owed to Michael Pacher.*

H.F.G.H. - E.F.G. fueg ich undtertanigklichen zuvernemen, das ich Maister Micheln Maler han versetzt aus meinem aigen stuckh genant Pirchegkh, darin wisen und ägker ist und dhein weingarten fünfzehen phundt gelts jerigen zynns umb 40 mark perner aus zwinglicher not. Darauf er mir losung geben hat zehen jar, doch also beschaidenlichen, dieweil solh losung ich nit tät in der gemelten zeit all jar, für die 15 lb gelts jm zu synnsen drey yrn wein und nach ausgeender gemelter zeit sol der zynns der 15 lb perner ewigklich an losung, das alles zwischen unser also geredt ist jnnhalt der brief darob aufgericht. G.H. nun bin ich zwen zynns hinderstellig worden für disen sein aidem E.G. Zollner zu Clausen ausgelegt han berait 30 lb perner, daran er nit benngen sonder vermaint den wein zu haben oder für yede yrn 10 lb perner, brächt 6 mark. Also das mich etwas swer bedünckhet, das zollner sein und mein Seel also beswern wolt, angesehen, daz das ainem kauff nit gleich ist. Also E.F.G. versteet, wie wol mich die not darin bracht hat. Bitt darauf E.F.G. mit aller Undtertänigkait, die geruhen gleich dem Zollner zu schreiben und daran zu weisen, damit er sich mit den 30 lb perner von den vorgenanten zwain jarn benügen lassen mechte, mich sein und mein Seel darwider nit beswär mit ainer anvorderung. Wan ich solhs zu seiner zeyt inhalt der losbrief tun muss mit verkaufung des meins guets und bevelch mich hiemit E.F. Gn. gnediglich zu bedenkhen. Datum Freitag vor Alexi 1491.

(Bressanone, Episcopal Archive, Court Registry, V, 64'. Transcribed by Karl Wolfsgruber; op. cit., p. 129).

1491, *Master Michael Pacher, citizen of Brunico, purchases for 10 marks from Puchfeldner of Laion a due of an urn of wine.*

(Formerly in Novacella Archive, HA 45. Report by the Rev. Dr. Max Schrott)

1492, 11 December. *Accounts of the Parish Church, Brunico.*

Item von zehent so In das Spital ist kommen vnd der Michel Pacher nitt ingenomen hat
Rogken xviij
Gersten vj
Haber viij
Bey der Raytung Sind gebesen Vlraich Gebestorffer Richter, Jacob Sell Primus Sellen Sun Burgermaister, Georg Pidinger kirchpräbst, Sigmund Sell, Sigmund Heger, Andre Velder, Jacob Schreyner, Lienhart Vnterpad, Gilg Tischler, Sigmund Rech, Auch Dem Besluss Michel Pacher Beschehen an dem tag vor Im Anfang Berürt.
(Brunico, Archivio comunale. Accounts of the Parish Church, 1445-1508, p. 127)

1495, *Accounts of the Parish Church, Salzburg. Payment for lodging Michael Pacher.*

Item dem Gabriel seydnater zyns fur Michel maler des 95 Jars 11 lb. d.
(Salzburg, Communal Archive. Accounts of the Parish Church, 1495, p. 37 verso. Published by L. Spatzenegger, op. cit.)

1496, 3 March. *Accounts of the Parish Church, Brunico.* Mathes Kirsner als kirchpräbst angefangen in Michahelis Im 95 Jar huntz auf Michahelis Im 96 jar hat ein volkomne Raitung getan vmb alles sein einnemen vnd ausgeben.
Item die Berürt Raitung Ist Geschehen am Sambstag vor oculi In der Vasten des 96 Jar In pejwesen richter Purgermaister Kirchprabst Jacobs Sell der Junger, Jorg Pidinger, Jacob Schreiner, Asam Sell, Michel Pacher, Johannes Sell der Jünger, Hanns Prenner, Tomas Kirchperger, Jacob Kesler, Hanns Kronegkler, Primus Sockler.
(Brunico, Archivio comunale. Accounts of the Parish Church, 1445-1508, p. 134)

1496, *Accounts of the Parish Church, Salzburg. Payments for the construction of the high altar.*

Item an mitichen vor ycari da ich die stöck aufgetan hab darnach an sand Philipps vnd Jacobstag hab ich maister Michel maler an der arbait geben 54 lb. d.

1496, undated.

Item dem Gabriel seydenater fur maister Micheln maler zyns zalt von sein gmachen 11 lb. d.
(Salzburg, Communal Archive. Accounts of the Parish Church, 1496, pp. 39, 43. Published by L. Spatzenegger, op. cit.)

1496, 23 November. *Account book of Virgil Puchler, Abbot of St. Peter's, Salzburg. Payments for the altar of St. Michael am Aschhof.*

Item mgr. Michael pictor de Prawnegk habet ex me dn. lb. 15 in labore tabule ad S. Michaelem am Aschhof die Clementis a. 96...

...Item habet iterum dn. lb. 5 vel circa in pnte. Heinr. pictoris Petri aurifabri et prioris nostri.
(Salzburg, Archive of St. Peter's Abbey. Published by O. Fischer in *Mitt. d. Gesellsch. f. Salzburger Landeskunde*, 1907, p. 122)

1497, *Accounts of the Parish Church, Salzburg. Payments for the construction of the high altar.*

Item An sand Philpfs vnd Jacobs tag geben maister Michel Pacher maler von dem gelt aus den stokhen 25 lg. d.

1497, 6 May

Item an Sand Johanstag Sunibenten dem Hödlmoser sloszer vmb smidberch Zw der tafel zalt 8 lb. d.

1497, 18 June

Item mer zalt dem Maler hat eingenomen Asm Puchler vmb geslagen golt an sambstag nach Viti Anno 97 7 lb. d.
Dem Kremitzer goltsmid von den gressern 12 tobln zuuersetzen In kupfren kasten zw pilden In dy tafel 1 lb. d.
Dem Partolmee goltsmid von 12 kleinern tobln zw der tafel 5 1/2 lb. d.

1497, 23 July

Item Suntag Nach Marie Magdalene dem Veit Maurer zalt bey der tafel gearbait 6 tag zw 26 d. ft. 5 lb. 10 d.
Vnd Oswalten zymerman auch dabey gearbait 1/2 tag ist 12 d.

1497, 23-29 July

Item in der bochen Jacobi dem Veit maurer aber bey der tafel 5 tag ist 5 lb. 10 d.
Dem Rueprecht Zymerman 2 tag ist 52 d. padgelt 8 d. Vnd 9 knechtz taglon Zw 16 d. bringt mit fruestuck padgelt 5 lb. 2 d. vmb negl 10 d.

1497, 28 July

Item an freitag nach Jacobi An. 97. Maister Michel Pacher maler aber an der arbait der tafel Zalt lautt ainer quittunb 12 lb. d.

1497, 24 September

...Item Zw Sand Rueprechts tag darnach Im herbst an der arbait der tafel zalt 10 lb. d.
Item von der grossen plahen die vor der tafel gehanngen ist Zw waschen 14 d. vnd von 4 hanttuechern 2 d.
(Salzburg, Communal Archive. Accounts of the Parish Church, 1497, pp. 44 ff. Published by L. Spatzenegger, op. cit.)

1497, 27 September

Item mer denselben maister Michelen zalt in die Cosme et Damiani lautt ainer quittunb verhannden 24 lb. d.

1497, *Accounts of Oswald Staudinger, Episcopal Vicar at Brunico.*

« Ausgeben an Rocken und Abgang
Mer hat Michel Neuhauser Ambtmann empfangen von wegen Micheln maler 26 st. ».
(Bressanone, Episcopal Archive. General accounts, 1492-1509, fasc. 27333. Report by Adelaide Zallinger)

1498, *Accounts of the Parish Church, Salzburg. Information on the final work of the high altar.*

Item mer verkawft dem Vetz Stainmetz etlichew altew lindanew Holtz so von der tafel yber worden sein vmb Pfd. 1, lb. 0. d. 20.

1498, 26 April

Item an pfintztag nach sand Jörgen tag dem Hödelmoser schloszer auf arbait so er altens bei dem Hetzinger goldschmid Smidberch an der tafl awch bey mir vnd an dem leichter gemacht nach lawt seiner Zetl so Jacob Schonperger purgermaister mit ym abgerait vnd ich yem pezalt hab Innhalt ainer quittung Pfd. 11.

1498, 6 July. *Dispute between the painter Hans Pacher and Ulrich Walch of Villabassa. Notarial protocol of the Episcopal Judge of Bressanone.*

Als sich jrrung zwischen Hannsen Pacher Maler Bürger zu Brunegkhen aines und Hannsen weyland Hainrichen Kramers zu Niderndorff Sun anderstails aines kaufshalben ainer behausung und was daran berurt, gehalten hat in der gestalt. Nachdem Hanns Pacher von Ulrichen Walhen die behausung mit jrer zuegehörung gekauft und Hanns Kramer vermaint den kauff an sich als nagster freund ze nemen, haben wir bedig partheien auf heutigen tag heruber für uns deshalben in verhör ervordert und die dermassen erschinen und zwischen jne in der guttikait gehandlet und sy verait und betragen in massen dem ist also wie hernach volget: Am ersten sol benanter Hans Pacher des kauffs des haus und andert daran beruert, gedachten Hannsen Kramer als ainem nagst freund absteen und vervolgen lassen in form und mass wie er den gehabt hat von Ulrich Walhen. Derentgegen sol jm sein gelt so er auf bezalung solhs kauffs ausgeben mitsambt dem, so jm auf den kauff den zueververtigen umb brief und sigl und anders nach den landsrechten gangen ist, widerumb geben und bezalt werden. Nachdem aber Hanns Pacher über solhen ain geding hat in unser hofrechten ainer waigrung halben, die jm dort abgeslagen worden, daselbs ain urtail erlangt, mithin den schaden, wo er die nit ligen vermaint ze lassen, mugt er Hansen Kramer fürnemen wie recht ist, geredt das Hans Pacher solhe schäden weitter nit suchen sunder vallen lassen. Derentgegen sol jm Hans Kramer gebenvierzehen gulden Rhein. und sullen damit alle schäden so bede taile untz auf den heutigen tag geneinander genomen haben, ab sein und kain tail den andern ausserhalb geschribnen articlen nichts mer schuldig, sundern ain vakant und berichte sach sein. Vorbehalten Ulrich Walhen alle seine gerechtigkaiten so er vermaint gehabt ze haben gegen Hansen Pacher der losung oder widerkauffs halben. Sol und mag er in gleicher form und mass gegen Hannsen Kramer sein vettern haben und brauchen wie er vermaint, das billich sein und recht ze haben.
Solhen abschid haben uns bede partheien angelobt stat und vest ze halten und nachzekomen, dem wir

jeden tail, so der beredt worden ist, ainen ungleichen lawt verschaffen ze geben. Beschehen und geben zu Brichsen am Freitag nach Ulrici 98.

(Bressanone, Episcopal Archive, Court Registry, V, 555. Transcribed by Karl Wolfsgruber; op. cit., p. 131)

1498, 7 July

Item am Sambstag nach Vlrici Im 98 Jar maister Micheln Pacher maler auf das werch der tafel Innhalt ainer quittung geben Pfd. 30.

1498, 24 August. *Account book of Virgil Puchler, Abbot of St. Peter's, Salzburg. Payment for the altar of St. Michael am Aschhof.*

It. Gener suus ht. dn. lb. 20 circa festum Bartme. a. 98 dat. Caspar Neuhawser iudex an d. Klausen.

(Salzburg, Archive of St. Peter's Abbey. Published by O. Fischer, op. cit.)

1498, 5 September. *Letter from the Episcopal Chancellery, Bressanone, to the Judge at Brunico, Ulrich Gerbistorffer.*

Getreuer lieber. Wir senden dir hieryynen beslossen ain Suplication, uns durch unsern Richter zu Clausen Caspar Neunhauser fürbracht, die du vernemen werdest. Wo dem also, empfelhen wir dir, du wollest daran und ob sein, damit solhe hab und guet nach notdurfft untz zu anfrag der sachen beschriben und versorgt werden. Wo er auch solher brieflicher gerechtikait zu seinen hanndten notdurfft werden sein, wollest im die vor in legen lassen, dorch das die hernach wider zu ander hab und guet untz zu austrag des hanndels gelegt werden. Darin tust du unser willen und maynung.

(Bressanone, Episcopal Archive, Court Registry, V, 559'. Published by Karl Wolfsgruber, op. cit., p. 130)

1498, 9 September. *Letter from the Episcopal Chancellery, Bressanone, to the Judge at Brunico. Ulrich Gerbistorffer.*

Getreuer lieber. Wir sennden dir hiryynn beslossen ain Suplication, uns durch Caspern Neunhauser fürpracht, die du vernemen wirdest. Und empfelhen dir darauf, du wollest jm, auch weyland Micheln Pacher Verlassen wittiben ainen tag kurzlich benennen und beden taylen verkünden, sy irer span halben geneinander zuerledigen. Wo sy auf solhen tag erscheinen, wollest solh auf dermassen nachgeen. Wo das nicht, nichtsdestomynnder dennoch darjnen handlung wie sich nach geschrannen recht und gewonhait gebüren wirdet. Darob sich kain teil besweren moge. Daran tust du unsern willen und maynung. Datum Brichsen am Suntag nach (Nativitatis beate Marie Virg.).

(Bressanone, Episcopal Archive, Court Registry, V, 559'. Published by Karl Wolfsgruber, op. cit., p. 130)

1498, 17 November

Item an Sambstag vor Elisabet dem Caspar Newhawsser maister Michel Pacher malers ayden inhalt der spruchbrief vnd inhalt seiner quittung zallt fl. rh. 300.

(Salzburg, Communal Archive. Accounts of the Parish Church, 1498, pp. 10, 31 verso, 33 verso, 36 verso. Published by L. Spatzenegger, op. cit., p. 39)

1500, 7 July. *Letter from the Episcopal Chancellery to Jacob Schreiner, tax-collector at Brunico, and Hans Pacher, tithe-collector at Brunico.*

An Jacoben Schreiner Zollner zu Braunegkhen und Hansen Pacher Zehentambtmann im Pustertal. Getreuen lieben. Nachdem wir unsern Richter zu Braunegkhen Ulrichen Gerbistorffer bevolhen haben die Stair unsers ausgelihnen gelts halben in negstverschinen krieglaiffen bescheen anzelegen und anzebringen. Und so er aber solher anlegung jedem nach seinen stellen ze tun nit bericht ist, und uns angrueft, jm etliche hieryynn zuezugeben und zu verordnen jm solh Steur dermassen verholfen anzelegen. Daraf empfelhen wir ew beiden und jedem in sunders, wenn jr von jm ersucht werdet, wellet jm darin hilflich, rätig und beystendig sein. Daran tut ir und ewr jeder in sunderhait zu samt eur verpflicht unsern willen und maynung. Datum Brichsen an Eritag nach Ulrici Anno ut supra (1500).

(Bressanone, Episcopal Archive, Court Registry, VI, 77'. Transcribed by Karl Wolfsgruber; op. cit., p. 131)

1502, 10 December. *Final receipt from Caspar Neuhauser for the altar in the Parish Church, Salzburg.*

Ich Caspar Neunhauser Zu Claussen an stat vnd als vormuntt Margrethen meiner tochter so ich pey weylentt auch Margrethen meiner elichen hausfrauen maister Michel Pachers des malers etbo purger Zue Braunecken baider guter gedachtnus eleiblichen tochter elich erborben hab, der ich mich hernach pegrifner sachen gantz volmachticklich an Nim fur sy stee vnd versprich, Becken fur mich die selb mein tochter all vnnser erben vnd miterben offenlich mit dem prieff vnd thuen chuntt allen den er furchumbtt, als der obgemelt mein lieber schwecher saliger des viervndachzigisten iars der minderen Zale negst vershin ain taffel vnd berch Zu Saltzpurg in vnnser lieben frauen pfarkirchen laut ainer Spanzedel ze machen vnd auffzerichten angenomen vnd doch den sarch vnnden daran vor seinem absterben nicht gantz volpracht deshalben auch der Summe geltz vnd lons halben ich nach abgang des selben meins schwechers auff ain gebalt so ich deshalben von dem obgemelten meiner hausfrauen saligen gehapt vnd furpracht habe. In irrung vnd darumben mit meinen Herren, pfarrer, richter, purgermeister, rate vnd kirchprobst bemelter vnnser lieben frauen pfarkirchen auff vnnsers genadigisten herren von Saltzpurg etc. Rate Zu gutlichem entscheid vnd ausspruch verbilligt die vns dan peruerter irrungen halben gutlich miteinander vertragen haben, Wie dan die schrifften deshalben vnder seiner furstlichen gnaden Secrete ausgangen Solchs alles mit mer worten klarlichen in sich halten vnd ausbeisen An derselben taffel vnd Werch mir als trager peruerter meiner hausfrauen seliger durch vermeltz meins gnedigisten Herren Rate auff die vorpezalten summa so gedachter mein Schwecher an der arbait solcher taffel vnd Werchs in seinem leben selbs empfangen hatt noch darzue fur all sach spruch vnd vorderungen auff zeit vnd frist in demselben vertrag pegriffen gesprochen pis dreytaussentt vnd dreyhundert gulden Reinisch volliklich pezalt sein, also haben mich die obgemelten mein Herrn, pfarrer, richter, purgermaister, Rat, vnd kirchprobst der selben gesprochen summa gelts laut angeruerts vetrages zu meinen sicheren henden perait ausgericht vnd pezalt zu rechter beil vnd Zeitt on abgang vnd on allen schaden, daran ich an stat vnd als vormund peruerter meiner tochter, die selb mein tochter, al vnnser erben vnd miterben heutt vnd hinfur ebicklich ain gantz volligs genügen haben sollen vnd wellen, Sag auch darauff die obgemelten meine Herrn pfarrer, richter, purgermaister, Rate vnd kirchprobst peruerter statt Saltzpurg von pemelten gotzhaus vnd gemainer stat begen vnd all ir nachchomen der selbigen dreytausentt vnd dreyhundert Reinisch gulden vnd was wir deshalben pestimbter taffel vnd werchs aller Sachen halben von anfang bis auff dato diser quittung von gedachtes vnnserers Schwechers vnd vnnseren begen zu in vermelter pfarkirchen vnd gemainer statt zesprechen vnd Zu vordern gehapt oder gehaben heten mogen hierin genent oder jnn gantz nichts vorpehalten noch ausgeschlossen fur mich die pestimpt mein tochter all vnnser erben vnd miterben gantz frei quitledig vnd loes in crafft diser quittung Ich pemelter Caspar Neunhausser vnd all mein erben sollen vnd wellen auch peruerter sachen ir Recht geberen vnd furstentter fur all krieg infall vnd ansprach geistlich weltlich so offt in des noet peschicht auff vnnser costungen vnd darlegen vertretten vnd verantborten alles getreulich vnd vngeferlich. Vnd des Zu warem vrchunt so hab ich offtgemelten meinen Herren vnd gotzhausz diese quittung daruber gegeben vnd mein obgedachts Caspars Neunhausers aigen anhangenden Insigel vnd vor merer Sicherheit vnd gezeucknus wegen so hab ich mit fleis gepetten den fursichtigen beissen Hans von Aichach purgermaister Zu Claussen, das er sein aigen Insigel auch hieran gehengt hatt doch im, sein erben vnd insigel an schaden vnder die yetzgemelten Zwey Insigel ich mich vilgemelter Casper Neunhauser fur mich auch anstatt vnd als vormund mergedachter meiner tochter, all vnnser erben vnd miterben kreffticklich mit meinen treuen verpind Inhalt ditz prieffes war vnd stat zuhaltten Zeugen der pette vmb das Insigl Seind die erberen Jacob Portner purger Zu Claussen, maister Joest tischler purger Zu Prixen vnd Hans Pirchinger wonend Zu Claussen. Peschechen Zu Claussen an Sambstag nach sand Niclastag des heiligen pischoffes nach Cristi vnnsers lieben Heren gepurt tausentt funffhundertt vnd im andern iare.

(Salzburg, Communal Archive. Published by L. Spatzenegger, op. cit., pp. 31 ff.)

1503, 15 September. *Letter from the Episcopal Chancellery, Bressanone, to Caspar Neuhauser.*

An Casparn Newnhauser.
Getreuer lieber. Uns hat Hans Pacher Maler zu Braueggen diese Suplication fürbracht die du vernemen wirdest. Und empfelhen dir darauf, das du desshalben am Eritag nach Sand Katherinen tag negst vmb Mittentag vor unser in Verhör erscheinest, da er auch sein wirdet. So wollen wir ew geneinander verhorn oder verschaffen zu verhörn und darnach versuchen ew zu beder seit guetlich miteinander zuverainen. Wo aber solh ainichait ye nit verfangen mecht werden, fürter darin handlen, wie sich gebürn wirdet. Auch dise Suplication mit dir bringen, überantwurtten und nit ausbleiben wellest. Daran tuest unsern willen und ernstliche maynung.
Geben zu Brichsen ut supra (Mittichen nach Martini 1502).

(Bressanone, Episcopal Archive, Court Registry, VI, 295'. Transcribed by Karl Wolfsgruber; op. cit., pp. 130 ff.)

1507, The Parish Church of S. Lorenzo claims the bequest made by the tailor Maurice in 1462-3 for the construction of the high altar. Notarial protocol by the Judge of Castel S. Michele, Laurens Prugger.

Ich Laurentz Prugker die zeit landtrichter zu sand Michaelspurg bekenn, das für mich kumen ist der erber Peter Tasser obermüllner in dem Phflaurentz, der pat und rueft mich an als richter im als ainem gepaltigen gesatzten kirchenbräbst anstatt und in namen der löblichen sand Laurentzen pfarrkirchen da zu sand Laurentzen kundtschaft zu verhören und stallet für mich am ersten durch geschäft und bevelch des edlen und vesten Georgen Blattenhoffer pfleger auf sand Michaelspurg meines günstigen herren den erbern Sebastian maler zu sand Laurentzen die zeit seiner vestigkait diener als geschworner gerichtsschreiber und darnach durch gerichtsbot die erben Caspar Brüchttinger mesner zu sand Laurentzen und den Lienhart Seeber schneider auch zu sand Laurentzen gesessen, den hab ich als richter von gericht und herschaft wegen auf des vorgenannten kirchenbräbst aufzug jedem insonders zuegesprochen und verschaffen mit allenn notdürftigen worten, die sich dan zu kuntschaften dienen gepüren und recht ist. Darauf haben die vorgedachten Sebastian maler, Caspar Brüchttinger und Lienhart Seeber alle drey ainhellig vor mein und den unden geschriben gezeugen offenlichen bekennt und gesagt, das in allen ainhellig des handels gar woll wäre kunt und guet wissenlichen ist, hab sich begeben zu der zeit als der Mauritz Schneider dieselbe zeit des edlen erenevesten strengen ritter und herren Balthasarn von Welsperg säliger gedächtnus pfleger auf sand Michaelspurg hofschneyder gewesen, den got gnädig sey, in der alten Fridrichin haus hie zu sand Laurentzen in der obern stuben in seinem siechpedl gelegen ist, das nu bey den vier oder fünf und viertzig jaren verschynen ist angevärlichen, da ist bemelter Mauritz Schneyder bewegt worden durch seiner sele hayl willen der löblichen sand Laurentzen pfarrkirchen ain geschäft zu tuen zu ainer tafel die man maister Michel maler von Brawnnegken auf sand Laurentzen altar zu machen angeben hät und bemelter Mauritz Schneyder mit gueter betrachtung mit seinem jüngsten willen der bemelten sand Laurentzen pfarrkirchen und dem lieben heiligen sand Laurentzen ain geschäft getan und von seinem aygenguet, seiner dienst lön und seiner parschaft, so er bey vorgemelten seinem herren herrn Balthasar von Belsperg innerhalben an sold und verschaffen bemelter sand Laurentzen pfarrkirchen zu der tafel zu geben vier und sechtzig hungarische oder ducatengulden, wan zu denselbigen zeiten die reinischen gulden hie umb nit vast geng waren besunder nur die hungrischen und ducatengulden vast geng waren. Aber Sölliche summa gelt vier und sechtzig gulden sand Laurentzen pfarrkirchen nach abgang des bemelten Mauritzen Schneyders und nach seinem geschäft und jüngsten willen nicht gevallen noch nicht geben ist und bey obgemelten herren Balthasarn von Belsperg beliben ist. Inen allen ist auch ainhellig wol wissenlichen, das soliche summa gelt vier und sechtzig gulden geschäft an obgemelten herren Balthasarn von Belsperg nach des Mau-

ritzen tod mer dan einmal in der kirchen raitung ersuecht und ervordert ist worden zu geben, aber albegen antburt geben, er well der kirchen nicht vergessen und auch auf ain zeit als sein strengikait in das pad zu der lerchen reyten wolt, da leget sein strengikait ain testament und geschäft geschriftlichen unter seiner strengikait insygel beschlossen in sand Laurentzen kirchen gelt und sagrer, was got über in auf dem weg gepieten wurde und mit dem tod abgeen wurde, so wirt man in sölichem seinem testament und geschäft der kirchen obgemelte summa gelt und anders mer wol finden auf zu heben, damit sand Laurentzenkirchen kayn nachtayl an im sol haben, er hab der kirchen nicht vergessen zu betrewen. Aber als sein strengikait widerumb anhaym kumen ist, da hat sein strengikait dass selbige sein testament und geschäft also beschlossen wiederumb an sich haym genomen und aber geredt, er well der kirchen nicht vergessen. Aber ob es seyt beschehen ist, das ist inen nicht wissentlichen und das Sebastian maler und Caspar Brüchttinger und Lienhart Seeber söliche ir gegeben kundtschaft sagen also ainhellig gar wol warks kunt und guet wissenlichen ist, darumb so hat ir jeder sein sag mit seinem ayde bestetet jeder gegen got und allen heiligen ainen ayde geschworen wie sich gepüret und recht ist und diser ainhelligen drey kuntschaft sagen begeret obgemelter Peter Müllner als kirchenbräbst im anstatt sand Laurentzen pfarrkirchen von gericht und herschaft wegen under meinem insygel geschriben zu geben und das ich also hiemit als richter getan und mein aygen insygel hie unden fürgedruckt hab, doch dem gericht mir und meinen erben an schaden. Und sein bey mir in verhörung und bestättung dysser kuntschaft sagen zu gezewgen die erbern Hanns peckh, Andre artzt, Veitt schneider, Matheis pinter, alle zu sand Laurentzen und Andre Pader zu Stegen gesessen. Beschehen nach Cristi gepurdt in der jarzall fünfzehenhundert und syben am ertag sand Pangrätzen abendt in dem mayen.

(Bressanone, Archive of the Cathedral Chapter, Box 93. Published by Franz Huter, "Archivalische Funde zur Südtiroler Kunstgeschichte" in *Der Schlern*, XXI, 1946, fasc. 4. p. 98 ff.)

1512, Letter from the Episcopal Judge at Bressanone on the dispute between Anna Pacher and Caspar Neuhauser.

Abschid zwischen Anna weilend Hannsen Pachers Malers zu Brawnneggen gelassne Tochter ains und Caspar Neuhauser anderstails.
Wir, n, unnsers gnädigen Herrn von Brichsen Stathalter und Rete daselbs, thun kundt, als sich zwischen Anna weilennd Hannsen, Malers zu Brawnneggen seligen, gelassene Tochter ains, und Caspar Newhauser zu Gravetsch anderstails, ainer Anfordrung halben wegen zwaien Taffeln und zwaier Ackher auch anders waz darein berürt zu ime haben vermaint, Irrung und Speen halten, deshalben beid Tail auff obgemelts unnsers gnädigen Herrn guetliche Tagsazung

an heut dato vor unns erscheinen, die wir also anstat unnd zu Abwesenheit seiner Fürstlichen Gnaden in der Guete hinzulegen geneigt gegeneinander genuegsamlich verhört. Aber zwischen inen kain Guetlichkait hat wellen verfangen werden. Demnach geben wir baidentailen diesen guetlichen Abschid: Also vermeint die obgenant Fraw gedachten Neuhauser Spruch unnd Fordrung nit zu verlassen, ine darumb an den Ennden da sich solhes gebürt fürneme, wie Recht ist. Dagegen dann bemelter Neuhauser, auf ir fürbracht Instrumennt weilend Michael Pachers, Ires Enen seligen, lesten Willen unnd Testamennts halben, so wir hören lesen, welichs er vor unns nichtig, krafftlos und unteuglich ze sein gehaissen, und darauf nichts, weder wenig noch vill geben auch davon halten, bekennt sich danneben erboten, also wo das Testament zu Krefften gesprochen und ir dasselb etwaz verhilf gebe, welle er ir nicht wider sein, sonnder von wegen seiner Tochter alles gern verfolgen lassen, dessen Vorbehalltung sein Notturft an den Ennden auch Rechten fürzubringen.
Des haben wir auf beider Tail Anruffen zwen gleichlauttend Abschid machen lassen und yedem einen zu geben bevolhen.
Beschehen zu Brichsen an Sand Alexientag im fünffzehenhundertisten und zwelften Jars.

(Bressanone, Episcopal Archive, Court Registry, VII, 274'. Published by Gisela Scheffler, *Hans Klocker*, Innsbruck, 1967, p. 132)

1539, Town register of Brunico.

Spiesshaus, das man auch der Pacherin haus nennt aber Jetzt Hannsen Mairhofer zuegehorig zinss so erstlich durch Liennharden Spiess, zehen Pfund goltz, vmb dreissig Marckh vnd aber für zwo gölten öll auch 5.d. Perner vnd letslich zway Pfund Perner, darzu bringt xxij d. Perner goltz, Verkaufft In vermug dreyer kaufbrief beyeinander ligend.

(Brunico, Archivio comunale)

1545, Notarial protocol of the Innsbruck Government concerning the revenues of Georg Söll of Brunico.

...Item Mesner zu Stegen hat anzeigt, er zinns Im waizen 4 star, Roggen 10 star.
Item das ober guet auf herschwang gibt Im: ...waizen 2 star, Toggen 8 star, Gersten 2 star, habern 10 star, ist zu lehen von pistumb Brichsen.
Dise payde (zehend)... seindt wol seyder dem 1500. isten jar durch Andre Söllen, von Casper Newhauser erkauft; aber der Casper Newhauser, hat sy von seiner hausfrawen, welliche ain tochter des Michel Pachers, der dann ain burger zu Brauneggen ist gewesen. Auch so hat Casper Newhauser nit allein das gehabt, von gedachter seiner hausfrawen, sonder auch das haus so ich (Jörg Söll) yetz innenhabe, auch anders mer, so gedachter Newhauser in ander weg verkumert.

(Innsbruck, Ferdinandeum Museum. Published by K. Fischnaler, "Die Erben Michael Pachers" in *Zeitschrift des Ferdinandeums*, 37, 1893, p. 359)

BIBLIOGRAPHY

1822

PRIMISSER A., "Reise-Nachrichten über Denkmale der Kunst und des Alterhums in österreichischen Abteyen und in einigen anderen Kirchen Österreichs alter Zeit" in *Hormayr's Archiv für Geographie, Historie, Staats- und Kriegskunsts*, 1822, pp. 476 ff. The first mention of the artist with a description of the St. Wolfgang altar and a reading of the inscription.

1834

WEIDMANN F. C., *Führer nach und um Ischl*, Vienna, 1834. He considers only the carvings of the St. Wolfgang altar to be the work of Pacher and attributes the paintings to Wohlgemut.

1838

Bothe für Tirol, 1838, pp. 164 and 168. In contradiction to Weidmann, Pacher is considered the artist responsible for both the paintings and the carving of the St. Wolfgang altar; the Brunico document of 1467 is mentioned and four reliefs from the parish church of Kals in the Ferdinandeum, Innsbruck, are attributed, erroneously, to Pacher.

1844

STAFFLER J. J., *Tirol und Vorarlberg statistisch*, 2 vols., Innsbruck, 1854, p. 174. Information concerning Pacher already published in the *Bothe für Tirol* is given.

1846

KOCH M., *Reise in Tirol in landschaftlicher und staatlicher Beziehung*, Berlin, 1846, p. 27. The author discusses the discovery of the Gries altar and the contract for it and refers to the contract for the altar in the parish church at Bolzano.

1847

LADURNER J., "Kunstnachricht" in *Bothe für Tirol*, 1847, p. 56. Publishes in its entirety the Gries altar contract, the Gries altar having been found neglected in a side chapel of the church.

1851

LADURNER J., *Beiträge zur Geschichte der Pfarrkirche von Bozen*, Bolzano, 1951, pp. 14 ff. Refers for the first time to the documentary evidence on the St. Michael altar made by Michael Pacher for the parish curch.

1853

FÖRSTER E., "Michael Pacher, Maler und Bild-schnitzer von Bruneck" in *Deutsches Kunstblatt*, 1853, pp. 131 ff. Publishes documentary evidence given him by Vintler in Brunico, and attributes to Pacher the paintings of the Monguelfo Tabernacle in addition to other works which were later rejected.
FÖRSTER E., *Geschichte der deutschen Kunst*, II, Leipzig, 1853, pp. 261 ff. Acknowledges Flemish and Venetian or Paduan influences in Pacher's work.

1854

KOCH M., "Michael Pacher" in *Deutsches Kunstblatt*, 1854, p. 427. He corrects Förster, pointing out that the Gries altar contract is of 1471 and not 1481. (Förster, in *Deutsches Kunstblatt*, 1855, p. 79, explains that it was a printer's error).

1857

MESSMER A., "Alte Kunstdenkmale in Bozen und seiner Umgebung" in *Mitt. der k.k. C.C.*, II (1857), pp. 99, 121. Describes the Gries altar after restoration with the addition of alien elements, which he deplores. First reference to the wing reliefs.

1861

WIESS K., "Die kunstarchäologische Ausstellung des Wiener Alterthumsvereins" in *Mitt. der k.k. C.C.*, VI (1861), p. 23. Mentions the centre panels of the St. Wolfgang altar exhibited in Vienna after restoration.
Jahrbuch der k.k.C.C., 1861, p. XV. Report on the restoration of the St. Wolfgang altar.

1862

ATZ K., in *Erste Vereinsgabe* etc., Innsbruck, 1862, p. 37. Description of the Gries altar and criticism of recent restoration. On p. 24 he identifies the Castel Novale altar: "einen mittelalterlichen verwahrlosten Altar, dessen Mittelheil, ein Gemälde, den leidenden Heiland vorstellt von 1465, später aber um 1676 renoviert".
SCHNAASE K., "Zur Geschichte der österreichischen Malerei im XV. Jahrh., in *Mitt. der k.k.C.C.*, VII (1862), pp. 238 ff. Gives a description of the art of Pacher, whom he considers both painter and sculptor, and stresses the Mantegnesque elements.

1863

LÜBKE W., *Geschichte der Plastik*, Leipzig, 1863, pp. 543 ff.

1866

LADURNER J., "Der ehemalige altdeutsche Hochaltar in der alten Pfarrkirche zu Gries b. Bozen, 1471" in *Mitt. f. christliche Kunst*, Innsbruck, 1866, fasc. 6, p. 31. Publishes a correct version of the Gries contract and deplores the recent restoration of the altar.
PEZOLT G., *Vorträge über Geschichte der christlichen Kunst*, Salzburg, 1866, p. 272. Mentions the recent rediscovery of the Virgin of the Salzburg altar and the addition of a new figure of the Child.

1869

SPATZENEGGER L., "Beiträge zur Geschichte der Pfarr- oder Franziskanerkirche in Salzburg" in *Mitt. der Gesellschaft für salzburgische Landeskunde*, IX (1869), pp. 3 ff. Publishes the documents referring to the altar (pp. 23 ff.), and republishes independently of Ladurner the Gries contract, and notes the discovery of the statue of the Virgin on the Baroque altar in May 1864, and its identification by Pezolt.

1881

DAHLKE G., "Michael Pachers Heimat im Mittelalter" in *Vossische Zeitung*, 1881, Beilage 35. Research on Pacher's house at Brunico. The article was republished in the *Tiroler Bote* of 1882 on p. 433.

1882

WOLTMANN-WOERMANN, *Geschichte der Malerei*, II, (1882) p. 127. Gives information about Pacher, referring to the Castel Novale altar.

1885

DAHLKE G., "Michael Pacher" in *Repertorium für Kunstwissenschaft*, VIII, 1885. Attributes to Pacher the fresco in the collegiate church, S. Candido.
ATZ K., *Kunstgeschichten von Tirol*, Bolzano, 1885, p. 334. Gives information on the Castel Novale altar and its recent sale in Vienna.

1886

VISCHER R., *Studien zur Kunstgeschichte*, Stuttgart, 1886, p. 434. Notes on archive material relating to the altar in the parish church, Bolzano.

1887

SEMPER H., "Ein Werk Michael Pachers von Bruneck" in *Zeitschr. d. Ferd.*, 1887, p. 275. First attribution to Pacher of the Fathers of the Church altar now at Munich.

1892

"Michael Pachers Altartafel in der Franziskanerkirche zu Salzburg" in *Der Kunstfreund*, VIII,

1892, p. 15. History of the statue of the Virgin. (ATZ K.), "Zwei merkwürdige Marienstatuen in der Pfarrkirche von St. Lorenzen in P." in *Der Kunstfreund*, VIII (1892), p. 39. The history of the sale and repurchase of Michael Pacher's Virgin in the parish church of S. Lorenzo.

1893

FISCHNALER K., "Die Erben M. Pachers" in *Ztschr. d. Ferd.*, III-37 (1893) pp. 359 ff. Publishes the notarial protocol of 1545 with information on the property of M. Pacher which passed to the Söll family in 1500.

1894

SPORNBERGER A., *Geschicte der Pfarrkirche von Bozen*, Bolzano, 1894, p. 28. Publishes the history of the altar of St. Michael at Bolzano.
SEMPER H., *Wanderungen und Kunststudien in Tirol*, Innsbruck, 1894, pp. 14 ff. (first indication of the frescoes in the Novacella sacristy with attribution to M. Pacher), pp. 86 ff. (the fresco of S. Candido), p. 109 ff. (the Tesido fresco).
MARGUILLER A., "Un maître oublié du XV siècle, Michael Pacher" in *Gazette des Beaux Arts*, 1894, pp. 266 ff.

1895

STROMPEN K., "Der Kirchenväteraltar M. Pachers in der k. Gemäldegalerie in Augsburg und der k. Pinakothek in München" in *Rep. f. Kunstwissenschaft*, XVIII (1895), pp. 114 ff. The writer maintains that the altar comes from the All Saints chapel in Bressanone cathedral and suggests an interpretation of the wing paintings as scenes from the life of St. Wolfgang.
STIASSNY R., "Zwei Werke M. Pachers" in *Zeitschr. f. Bildende Kunst*, N. F. VI (1895), pp. 26 ff. First attribution to Pacher of the two panels at Graz and the statue of St. Michael now in Munich; the latter however he assigns to the master of the carvings of the St. Wolfgang altar, who was only later identified as Pacher himself, as he originally assumed that Pacher was only a painter.

1897

HABERLEITER P., "Pachers Flügelaltar in der Franziskanerkirche zu Salzburg" in *Der Kunstfreund*, N.F. XIII (1897), p. 56. Relates the history of the destruction of the Salzburg altar.

1899

"Urkunden u. Regesten aus dem k.k. Statthalterei-Archiv in Innsbruck, Reg. Nr. 18041" (pp. CLXXIV ff.) in *Jahrb d. kunsth. Sammlungen d. Kaiserhauses*, XX (1899). Publication of the complete Gries contract from a copy in the State Archive, Innsbruck.

1901

RÖTTINGER H., "Das Motiv der vier Kirchenväter bei M. Pacher" in *Rep. f. Kunstwissenschaft*, XXIV (1901). Confirms the derivation of Pacher's compositions at Monguelfo and Munich (Fathers of the Church panel) from the frescoes in the Ovetari chapel, Padua, by Pizzolo.

1902

SEMPER H., *Alttirolische Kunstwerke des 15. u. 16 Jahrh.*, Innsbruck, 1902, Blatt III. Attributes to Michael Pacher the Mystic Marriage of St. Catharine from St. Peter's, Salzburg, now at Castagnola (Lugano).

1903

STIASSNY R., "Die Pacher-Schule" in *Rep. f. Kunstwissenschaft*, XXVI (1903), pp. 23 ff. Confirms the attribution to Pacher of the Marriage of St. Catharine but rejects its origin in the altar of the Franciscan church, Salzburg. Incorrectly attributes to Pacher the panels of St. Primus and St. Ermete by Konrad Laib.
ATZ-SCHATZ, *Der deutsche Anteil des Bistum Trient*, Bolzano, 1903, p. 79. Refers to the Castel Novale altar which disappeared in about 1880, and gives a description of it.

1906

VOLL K., *Vergleichende Gemäldestudien*, I, 1906, p. 106. Denies the influence of Mantegna on the art of Pacher.

1907

FISCHER O., "Marx Reichlich und die Tiroler Malerei in Salzburg" in *Mitt. der Gesellschaft f. Salzb. Landeskunde*, 47 (1907), pp. 121 ff. On p. 123 gives information on the panel by M. Pacher for Aschhof, now lost.

1909

REICHEL A., "Zwei alttirolische Tafelbilder der Landesgalerie Graz" in *Monatshefte für Kunstwissenschaft*, II (1909) pp. 154 ff. Confirms the attribution to Pacher of the two Graz panels.

1910

MANNOWSKY W., *Die Gemälde des Michael Pacher*, Munich, 1910. Publishes all the documents concerning Pacher. On p. 64 (Plate 33) incorrectly attributes to Pacher a fresco in St. Peter's, Vipiteno.
DEHIO G., "Über einige Künstlerinschriften des deutschen 15. Jahrh." in *Rep. f. Kunstwissenschaft*, XXXIII (1910), pp. 55 ff.
SUIDA W., *Österreichische Kunstschätze*, I (1910), pp. 17, 65 ff. Publishes the Graz panels with attribution to Pacher.

1911

SEMPER H., *Michael u. Friedrich Pacher*, Esslingen.
BRAUNE H., *Katalog der k. älteren Pinakothek*, Munich, 1911. First attribution to Pacher of the Coronation of the Virgin panel from Novacella.

1912

ZIBERMAYR J., in *Mitt. d. Institutes f. österr. Geschichtsforschung*, 33 (1912). Publishes the St. Wolfgang altar contract.
LANGHAUS J. E., "Neuentdeckte Werke des alttirolischen Bildhauers M. Pacher" in *Illustrierte Zeitung*, 25.7.1912 (N. 3604). Attributes to Pacher the head of St. John in the Colli Collection, now in the Ferdinandeum, Innsbruck.
HAMMER H., "Der Laurentiusaltar der Werkstätte Michael Pacher's" in *Zeitschr. d. Ferd.*, 56 (1912), pp. 537 ff. Brings together the panels of the St. Lawrence altar now in Vienna and Munich, attributing them to Pacher's workshop.

1913

DOERING O., *Michael Pacher u. die Seinen*, Munich-Gladbach, 1913, pp. 95 ff. Proposes the provenance of the St. Michael altar at Bolzano for the statue of the saint now at Munich.

1915

BRAUNE H., "Verkannte Alttiroler Tafelmalereien" in *Monatshefte f. Kunstwissenschaft*, VIII (1915), pp.

249 ff. Attributes to Pacher the four panels with heads of saints formerly in the Wilten convent and confirms the attribution to Pacher of the Coronation of the Virgin panel now at Munich.

1918

SCHROTT M., "Eine Turmkapelle in Neustift" in *Brixner Chronik*, 3.2.1918. Suggests that the panels of St. Thomas now at Graz, are from the chapel of the saint at Novacella, which he says was "exornata" in 1465.

1919

HABERDITZL F. M., "Zwei Altarbilder von M. Pacher in der Österreichischen Staatsgalerie" in *Die bildenden Künste*, II (1919), pp. 30 ff. On the acquisition of the two panels with the Flagellation and the Betrothal by the antiquarian Otto Fröhlich and their provenance from the St. Michael altar at Bolzano and their attribution to Pacher.
SCHURITZ H., *Die Perspektive in der Kunst A. Dürers*, Frankfurt am Main, 1919, pp. 20 ff. Examines the characteristics of Pacher's use of perspective.
STIASSNY R., *Michael Pachers St. Wolfganger Altar*, Vienna, 1919.

1921

DEHIO G., *Geschichte der deutschen Kunst*, II, Berlin, 1921, pp. 234 ff., 259 ff. A good analysis of Pacher's art and a study of his contact with the work of Donatello in Padua as well as with that of Mantegna.

1922

SUIDA W., in *Belvedere*, I (1922), p. 34. Publishes the Basle fragment attributing it to Pacher and indicating its provenance from Vienna.

1923

WEINGARTNER J., *Die Kunstdenkmäler Südtirols*, I, Vienna, 1923, p. 263. Attributes the S. Lorenzo Virgin to Pacher.

1924

GRITSCH B., "Zur Geschichte des Hochaltars in der Franziskanerkirche zu Salzburg" in *Mitt. d. Ges. f. salzburgische Landeskunde*, 64 (1924), pp. 153 ff.

1926

SUIDA W., *Gotik in Österreich* (Ausstellung), Vienna, 1926, pp. 44 ff. Attributes to Pacher the Graz panels and to his workshop those of S. Lorenzo, with some participation by the master.
WEINGARTNER J., *Die Kunstdenkmäler des Etschlandes*, III, Vienna, 1926, p. 103. Indicates the fresco of the Bolzano Parish church as probably the work of Pacher.

1927

SOMMER C., "Eine Madonnenfigur des M. Pacher in der Stadtpfarrkirche zu Hall i T.", in *Jahrb. d. preuss. Kunstsammlungen*, 1927, pp. 226 ff. The attribution was rejected by Hempel and others.
BOCK E., "Zeichnungen von M. Pacher" in *Festschrift für Max Friedländer*, Leipzig, 1927, pp. 14 ff. Attribution to Pacher of the two Erlangen drawings, which must be rejected.

1928

MORASSI A., "Quattro sculture ignote di M. Pacher" in *Pinacotheca*, I (1928), pp. 93 ff. Unacceptable attribution of four heads in the Museum at Bressanone.

1929

TIETZE H., "Zeichnungen von M. Pacher u. Hans Multscher" in *Wiener Jahrb. f. Kunstgeschichte*, VI (1929), pp. 74 ff. Attribution of a drawing to Pacher, later rejected.

PÄCHT O., *Österreichische Tafelmalerei der Gotik*, Augsburg, 1929, pp. 51 ff., 79 ff. Considers Pacher as deriving from the Uttenheim Master and Friedrich Pacher.

PINDER W., *Die deutsche Plastik der Hochrenaissance*, Postdam, 1929, pp. 382 ff.

BENESCH O., "Bemerkungen zu einigen Bildern des Joanneums" in *Blätter f. Heimatkunde*, VII (1929), p. 67. Indicates the frescoes in St. Paul in Lavant as the work of Friedrick Pacher from designs by Michael.

1930

MAYER A. L., "Die Ausstellung der Sammlung 'Schloss Rohoncz' in der Neuen Pinakothek, München" in *Pantheon*, VI (1930), p. 306. Accepts Buchner's attribution to Pacher of a portrait of a man in the Castagnola-Lugano collection. This suggestion is not tenable.

1931

ALLESCH J., *Michael Pacher*, Liepzig, 1931.

HEMPEL E., *Michael Pacher*, Vienna, 1931.

SCHROTT M., "Die neuaufgedeckten Fresken im Neustifter Kreuzgange" in *Der Schlern*, 1931, p. 424. Attributes the frescoes to Michael and Friedrich Pacher.

VERRES R., "Ein mutmassliches Flügelrelief von Pachers Salzburger Altar" in *Zeitschrift f. bildende Kunst*, 64 (1930-31), pp. 22 ff. A not acceptable proposal.

FISCHER O., "Ein Beitrag zur Pacherforschung" in *Belvedere*, X (1931), fasc. 7-8, pp. 26 ff. Review of Hempel's book with the unacceptable attribution to Pacher of a relief at Salzburg.

PÄCHT O., "Die historische Aufgabe M. Pachers" in *Kunstwissenschaftliche Forschungen*, I (1931), pp. 95 ff.

1932

HEMPEL E., "Michael Pacher" in *Thieme-Becker*, *Allgem. Kstlerlex.*, XXVI (1932), pp. 122 ff.

HEMPEL E., "Die neuesten Ergebnisse der Pacherforschung" in *Belvedere*, XI (1932), pp. 116 ff. Accepts the recent proposal by Schrott for the Novacella fresco.

MÜLLER K. TH., "Neue Forschungen zu Michael Pacher", in *Zeitschrift f. Kunstgeschichte*, I (1932), pp. 56 ff.

1933

SCHWABIK A., *Michael Pachers Grieser Altar*, Munich, 1933. Attributes to Pacher a statue of the Virgin in the church at Gries.

1934

BALDASS L., *Österreichische Tafelmalerei des Spätgotik*, Vienna, 1934, p. 13. Indicates the St. Barbara, formerly in the Colli collection now in the Vienna museum, as a youthful work by Pacher.

1935

KUHN CH. L., "Ein unbekanntes Gemälde des M. Pacher" in *Pantheon*, XV (1935), p. 174. Publishes as a work by Pacher a panel of St. Catharine by Friedrich Pacher.

HEMPEL E., "Michael Pachers Meisterschaft" in *Pantheon*, XVI (1935), pp. 362 ff.

SALVINI R., "La pittura dell'Alto Adige e la formazione artistica di M. Pacher" in *Studi Germanici*, I (1935), p. 631.

1936

DEMUS O., in *Deutsche Kunst u. Denkmalpflege*, 1936, pp. 309 ff. Account of the restoration of the frescoes of St. Paul in Lavant. The writer maintains that some of these should be attributed to Michael and others to Friedrich Pacher.

BENESCH O., *Österreichische Handzeichnungen des 15 u. 16 Jahrh.*, Freiburg i. B., 1936, p. 38. Refers to the Erlangen drawings attributing them to Pacher.

SUIDA W., "Zu Michael Pacher" in *Pantheon*, XVIII (1936), p. 303. Incorrectly attributes to Pacher a panel with St. Florian, assuming it to be the inner part of the St. Barbara panel at Vienna.

HOFNIGER K. TH., "Eine Quittung Michael Pachers" in *Der Schlern*, XVII (1936), pp. 2 ff. Publishes the final deed for the Gries altar and the documents for the St. Michael altar at Bolzano.

1937

HEMPEL E., *Das Werk Michael Pachers*, Vienna, 1937.

SALVINI R., "Sulla posizione storica di M. Pacher" in *Archivio per l'Alto Adige*, XXXII (1937), pp. 5 ff.

1938

BALDASS L., "Albrecht Altdorfers künstlerische Herkunft und Wirkung" in *Jahrb. d. kunsthistorischen Sammlungen in Wien*, N. F. XII (1938), p. 122.

SALVINI R., "Appunti e inediti di scultura atesina" in *Archivio per l'Alto Adige*, XXXIII (1938), p. 318. Incorrectly attributes to Pacher the statue of St. Valentine at Falzes.

1939

HEMPEL E., "Italienische Forschungen über M. Pacher" in *Südostdeutsche Forschungen*, III (1939), pp. 834 ff.

SALVINI R., "Kleine Beiträge zur Pacherforschung" in *Zeitschrift f. Kunstgeschichte*, VIII (1939), pp. 52 ff. Reviews the attribution to Pacher of the Falzes St. Valentine.

FEULNER A., "Eine St. Michaelsfigur von Michael Pacher in Köln" in *Pantheon*, XXIV (1939), pp. 367 ff.

1940

HEMPEL E., "Die Bozner St. Michaelsstatue von Michael Pacher" in *Jahrbuch der preussischen Kunstsammlungen*, LXI (1940), pp. 48 ff.

SCHMIDT H. F., "Voraussetzungen der Kunst Gruenewalds" in *Zeitschr. des deutschen Vereins f. Kunstwissenschaft*, VII (1940), pp. 89 ff. The writer observes the considerable influence of Michael and Friedrich Pacher on the work of Grünewald.

1941

LONGHI R., *Arte italiana e arte tedesca*, Florence, 1941, p. 18. Publishes as a work by Pacher a panel by Friedrich and a portrait which is certainly not by Pacher.

WINKLER F., *Altdeutsche Tafelmalerei*, Munich, 1941, p. 237. The writer assigns to Michael Pacher, under Donatello's influence, the inner sides of the Graz panels with the symbols of the Evangelists, and to the workshop the episodes from the life of St. Thomas Becket on the outer sides.

1942

OETTINGER K., *Altdeutsche Maler der Ostmark*, Vienna, 1942, p. 28 and Pl. 48. Attributes to Pacher the fragment of a panel of St. Anne, showing its provenance from the Salzburg altar.

1944

FRODL W., *Die gotische Wandmalerei in Kärnten*, Klagenfurt, 1944, p. 108. Describes the frescoes of St. Paul in Lavant.

1946

HUTER F., "Neues zur Geschichte der Brunecker Künstlerfamilie Pacher" in *Der Schlern*, XX (1946). pp. 98 ff. Publishes the document concerning the St. Lawrence altar.

THEIL-SALMOIRAGHI E., *Michael Pacher in Neustift*, Milan, 1946.

1947

RASMO N., "Nuovi documenti sulla costruzione dell'altare maggiore della parrocchiale di Bolzano" in *Cultura Atesina*, I (1947). Identifies the remains of the altar which served Pacher as a model for the Gries altar.

1948

WEINGARTNER J., *Gotische Wandmalerei in Südtirol*, Vienna, 1948, p. 58.

MÜLLER K. TH., "Zur Erforschung der spätgotischen Plastik Tirols" in *Veröff. d. Mus. Ferd.*, 20-25 (1948), pp. 79 ff.

RASMO N., "Il maestro dell'Incoronazione di Maria a Sabiona" in *Cultura Atesina*, II (1948), pp. 4 ff. Attributes (note 16) to Michael Pacher the St. Lawrence and St. Thomas altars, dating them to between 1460 and 1465 and identifying Filippo Lippi's and Donatello's influence.

RASMO N., "In margine all'esposizione d'arte dell'Alto Adige a Bolzano" in *Arte Veneta*, II (1948), p. 162 ff. Details on the training of Michael Pacher.

GRITSCH J., "Fresken des Pacherkreises im Kapitelsaal des Stiftes Wilten in Innsbruck" in *Österr. Ztschr. f. Denkmalpflege*, II (1948), pp. 177 ff. Account of the discovery.

RASMO N., "L'altare dei Padri della Chiesa a Novacella" in *Cultura Atesina*, II (1948), p. 51. Demonstrates the origin of the Novacella altar on the basis of a document of 1750.

RASMO N., "L'opera del pittore Claus nella parrocchiale di Bolzano" in *Cultura Atesina*, II (1948), p. 52. Rejects the attribution of the fresco in the parish church at Bolzano to the painter Claus and accepts the attribution to Pacher proposed by Weingartner.

1949

TRAPP O., "Pacherfresken im Stift Wilten aufgedeckt" in *Der Schlern*, XXIII (1949), p. 64. Attributes the frescoes to Pacher.

BAUMEISTER E., "Unbekannte Zeichnungen von Hans Burgkmair" in *Ztschr. f. Kunstwissenschaft*, 1949, p. 73. Attributes to Burgkmair a drawing formerly believed to be by Pacher.

RASMO N., *Arte medioevale nell'Alto Adige*, Bolzano, 1949, pp. 32 ff.

1950

OBERHAMMER V., *Gotik in Tirol*, Innsbruck, 1950, pp. 37 ff. Attribution to Pacher of the panel with St. Andrew and St. Catharine from Salzburg and of the panel with St. Sebastian in the Ferdinandeum, Innsbruck.

LUTTEROTTI O., Review of the Innsbruck Catalogue in *Das Münster*, III (1950, p. 362).

BALDASS L., "Gotik in Tirol", review of the Catalogue of the Innsbruck Exhibition in *Kunstchronik*, III (1950), pp. 215 ff.

RASMO N., "Nuove acquisizioni alla conoscenza dell'arte medioevale nell'Alto Adige" in *Cultura Atesina*, IV (1950).

1951

GOULD C., "A note on a Pacheresque addition in the National Gallery" in *Burlington Magazine*, XCIII (1951), pp. 389 ff. Publishes the London panel.
RINGLER J., "Eine unbekannte Pachertafel?" in *Der Schlern*, XXV (1951), pp. 55 ff. Suggests the authorship of Marx Reichlich for the London panel.
HOCHENEGG H., "Wo befindet sich die Urkunde über den Grieser Altar?" in *Der Schlern*, XXV (1951), p. 232. The document which disappeared after 1865 perhaps came to light again in 1894, according to a mention of it in the *Kunstfreund* of 1895, p. 16.

1952

HEMPEL F., *Das Werk M. Pachers*, 6th ed., Vienna, 1951. The writer accepts much of the chronology and attributions proposed by N. Rasmo (cf. 1948 and 1950).
FREY D., "Michael-Pacher-Studien" in *Wiener Jahrbuch f. Kunstgeschichte*, XV (1952), pp. 23 ff. Distinguishes the personalities of the Master of Moulins from that of the Uttenheim Master and sees Pacher as their follower.

1953

GARZAROLLI-THURNLACKH K., *Museum mittelalterlicher österr. Kunst*, Catalogue, Vienna, 1953, pp. 17 ff.
RINGLER J., "Eine Laurentiusstatue des Ferdinandeums, ein Werk Michael Pachers?" in *Der Schlern*, XXVII (1953), p. 355.

1954

COLLESELLI F., "Der erste Plan zur Errichtung einer Innsbrucker Gemäldegalerie 1807-1813" in *Veröff. d. Mus. Ferd.*, XXXIV (1954), pp. 33,43 ff. List of the works by Michael Pacher taken from Novacella by the Bavarians.
SANTANGELO A., *Catalogo delle sculture*, Rome, 1954, p. 64. Among the carvings exhibited in the Museo di Palazzo Venezia, Rome, is a St. Michael attributed to Pacher by Benesch.
HOPPE TH., "Zur Auffindung eines Tafelbildes Michael Pachers" in *Wiener Jahrbuch f. Kunstgeschichte*, XVI (1954), pp. 82 ff. Reports the discovery of part of a predella wing of the Salzburg altar.
DEMUS O., "Studien zu Michael Pachers Salzburger Hochaltar" in *Wiener Jahrbuch f. Kunstgeschichte*, XVI (1954), pp. 87 ff.

1955

LUCHNER L., "Die Komposition des Altares zu St. Wolfgang von Michael Pacher" in *Schlernschriften 139*, Innsbruck, 1955, p. 85.

1956

HEMPEL E., "Michael Pacher" in *Die grossen Deutschen*, Berlin, 1956, pp. 305 ff. Accepts Frey's theory of the Master of Moulins.
SCHROTT M., "Über Beziehungen der Familie Pache zu Neustift" in *Aus der Chronik des Stiftes Neustift*, Neustift, 1956, pp. 34 ff.
SPARBER A., "Die Aufhebung und Wiederherstellung des Stiftes 1807-1816" in *Aus der Chronik des Stiftes Neustift*, Neustift, 1956, pp. 76 ff.
TRIPP G., "Spätgotische Apostelmedaillons in der Pfarrkirche von St. Wolfgang" in *Österr. Ztschr. f. Denkmalpflege*, 1956, pp. 54 ff. Attributes the frescoes to an assistant of Pacher's.
BENESCH O., "Two unknown works of old German and Austrian art in Italian Museums" in *Scritti di storia dell'arte in onore di Lionello Venturi*, Rome, 1956, pp. 191 ff. Publishes on pp. 196-207 with an attribution to Michael Pacher, the statue of St. Michael in Palazzo Venezia, suggesting its provenance from the St. Michael altar, Bolzano.
MÜNZ L., *Akademie der Bildenden Künste in Wien. Führer und Verzeichnis der sechsten Sonderausstellung*, Vienna, 1956. Publishes three fragments of frescoes from the Alto Adige as youthful works by Pacher.

1957

HALM P., *Der Kirchenväter-Altar*, Stuttgart, 1957.
Führer durch das Tiroler landesmuseum Ferdinandeum Innsbruck, Innsbruck, 1957, p. 9 and Pl. VI. The St. Sebastian panel is published with an attribution to Pacher and dated to *c.* 1480.

1959

SALVINI R., *La pittura tedesca*, Milan, 1959, pp. 74 ff.
REDSLOB E., *Meisterwerke der Malerei aus der Sammlung Thyssen-Bornemisza, 'Sammlung Schloss Rohoncz', in Lugano Castagnola*, Berlin, 1959, p. 11. The panel showing the Mystic Marriage of St. Catharine is published with an attribution to Pacher and dated to *c.* 1480.
ROSCI M., "Una Santa Margherita della cerchia di Michele Pacher" in *Cultura Atesina*, XIII (1959), pp. 128 ff.

RASMO N., "Tavole di predella della cerchia pacheriana" in *Cultura Atesina*, XIII (1959), pp. 130 ff.

1960

STANGE A., *Deutsche Malerei der Gotik*, X, Munich, 1960, pp. 167 ff.

1961

MUSPER H. TH., *Gotische Malerei nördlich der Alpen*, Cologne, 1961, pp. 125 ff.

1962

KOSEGARTEN A., "Restaurierung und Konservierung des hl. Michael von Pacher" in *Kunstchronik*, XV (1962), pp. 63 ff. Corrects information on the provenance of the statue.
PESINA J., *Altdeutsche Meister*, Hannau a.M., 1962, p. 10. Publishes the panel in Rychnov castle with an attribution to the Pacher workshop.

1963

EGG E., "Virgil Hofer, Bergherr zu Rattenberg" in *Tiroler Heimatblätter*, XXXVIII (1963), pp. 1 ff. Biographical note on the principal commissioner of the Salzburg altar.

1966

SCHROTT M., "Michael Pachers Verwandtschaft" in *Cultura Atesina*, XX (1966).

1967

KMENTT I., *Der Meister der Uttenheimer Tafel*, Vienna, 1967. Takes up Pächt's theory that the Uttenheim Master was a forerunner of Michael Pacher.
SCHEFFLER G., *Hans Klocker. Beobachtungen zum Schnitzaltar der Pacherzeit in Südtirol*, Innsbruck, 1967, p. 132. Publishes the document which shows that Hans Pacher was the son of Michael.

1968

RASMO N., "Ein neuentdecktes Tafelbild des Meisters von Uttenheim" in *Der Schlern*, XLII (1968), pp. 223 ff. Confirms the derivation of the Uttenheim Master from Pacher.

1969

WOLFSGRUBER K., "Beiträge zur Pacher-Forschung" in *Der Schlern*, XLII (1969), pp. 128 ff. New biographical documents concerning Pacher, with definite proof of his death in 1498.

INDEX OF NAMES

LIST OF ILLUSTRATIONS

DIAGRAMS IN THE TEXT

Schema for the perspective plan of the Fathers of the Church Altar.
Perspective plan of an architectural composition for the St. Lawrence Altar
Perspective plan of an architectural composition for the St. Wolfgang Altar

Perspective plans of a panel of the Fathers of the Church Altar (the Saint in Ecstasy, Plate 62) and a panel of the St. Augustine Altar at Novacella by the Uttenheim Master (the Mass of St. Augustine, Fig. 146).

SOURCES OF PHOTOGRAPHS

Bolzano, Nicolò Rasmo: 1, 12-14, 16, 24, 26-41, 43-52, 70, 71, 112-114,
116-120, 123, 124, 126, 129-136, 140-146, 150-158, 165, 166, 168, 169, 171-174,
176
Florence, Alinari: 137, 139
London, National Gallery: 55
Munich, Bayerisches Nationalmuseum: 8, 9

Rome, Gabinetto Fotografico Nazionale: 170
St. Wolfgang, Foto Sepp Gastberger: 75
All the colour plates and the following in black and white were made expressly
for this volume by Bruno Balestrini, director of photography at Electa Edi-
trice: 2-7, 10, 11, 15, 25, 42, 53-69, 72-74, 76-111, 115, 121, 122, 125, 138,
147-149, 159-164, 167, 175